T0213971

Communications
in Computer and Information Science   1327

More information about this series at http://www.springer.com/series/7899

Sergio Nesmachnow · Harold Castro ·
Andrei Tchernykh (Eds.)

High Performance Computing

7th Latin American Conference, CARLA 2020
Cuenca, Ecuador, September 2–4, 2020
Revised Selected Papers

 Springer

Editors
Sergio Nesmachnow (iD)
Universidad de la República
Montevideo, Uruguay

Harold Castro (iD)
Universidad de los Andes
Bogotá, Colombia

Andrei Tchernykh (iD)
CICESE Research Center
Ensenada, Mexico

ISSN 1865-0929   ISSN 1865-0937 (electronic)
Communications in Computer and Information Science
ISBN 978-3-030-68034-3   ISBN 978-3-030-68035-0 (eBook)
https://doi.org/10.1007/978-3-030-68035-0

This Springer imprint is published by the registered company Springer Nature Switzerland AG
The registered company address is: Gewerbestrasse 11, 6330 Cham, Switzerland

Preface

This CCIS volume presents selected articles from the 7th edition of the Latin American High Performance Computing Conference (CARLA 2020), which was held on September 2–4, 2020 in Cuenca, Ecuador. Due to the COVID-19 pandemic, CARLA 2020 was held in a virtual format. This event continues the previous conferences held in South America (HPCLATAM) and Mesoamerica (CLCAR), for a total number of 12 conference editions since 2008.

The main goal of the CARLA 2020 Conference was to provide a unified scientific platform for researchers, scientists, teachers, postgraduate students and practitioners from different countries in Latin America and worldwide to share their current findings in various areas of High Performance Computing and Artificial Intelligence. The articles in this volume address these two relevant topics, covering several areas of research and applications.

The main program consisted of seven keynote talks, fourteen oral presentations and four poster presentations from international speakers highlighting recent developments in each of the areas. Over two hundred distinguished participants from 26 countries gathered virtually for this conference. The Program Committee of CARLA 2020 received 35 manuscripts, and 14 submissions were accepted, taking into account the comments by reviewers. All papers included in these CCIS proceedings have undergone careful peer review by three subject-matter experts before being selected for publication.

We would like to express our deep gratitude to all the contributors of CARLA 2020, the Conference Chairs and CEDIA (Ecuadorian Corporation for the Development of Research and Academia) who helped in many ways to organize the conference, and also to the authors and reviewers for their endeavors that made it possible to efficiently review and publish the papers. We also thank the participants of the conference, our industry sponsors and the readers of the proceedings.

October 2020

Harold Castro
Sergio Nesmachnow
Andrei Tchernykh

Organization

General Chairs

Jaime Puente   Lenovo, USA
Juan Pablo Carvallo   CEDIA, Ecuador

Program Committee Chairs

Harold Castro   Universidad de los Andes, Colombia
Dennis Cazar   Universidad San Francisco de Quito, Ecuador

CCIS Publication Chairs

Harold Castro   Universidad de los Andes, Colombia
Sergio Nesmachnow   Universidad de la República, Uruguay
Andrei Tchernykh   CICESE, México

Steering Committee

Mateo Valero   Barcelona Supercomputing Center, Spain
Carla Osthoff   National Laboratory for Scientific Computing, Brazil
Philippe Navaux   Federal University of Rio Grande do Sul, Brazil
Isidoro Gitler   Center for Research and Advanced Studies
                              of the National Polytechnic Institute, Mexico
Esteban Mocskos   University of Buenos Aires, Argentina
Sergio Nesmachnow   Universidad de la República, Uruguay
Alvaro de la Ossa Osegueda   University of Costa Rica, Costa Rica
Esteban Meneses   National High Technology Center, Costa Rica
Carlos Jaime Barrios   Industrial University of Santander, Colombia
  Hernández
Harold Enrique Castro   Universidad de los Andes, Colombia
  Barrera
Ginés Guerrero   Laboratorio Nacional de Computación de Alto
                              Rendimiento, Chile
Rafael Mayo   CIEMAT, Spain
Robinson Díaz   Universidad Central de Venezuela, Venezuela

Program Committee

Mariela Abdalah   Colaboratorio Nacional de Computación Avanzada,
                              Costa Rica
Dennis Cazar   Universidad San Francisco de Quito, Ecuador

Philippe Navaux	U. Federal do Rio Grande do Sul, Brazil
Sergio Nesmachnow	Universidad de la República, Uruguay
Nick Nystrom	Pittsburgh Supercomputing Center, USA
Kary Ocaña	National Laboratory of Scientific Computing, Brazil
Ulises Orozco-Rosas	CETYS Universidad, México
Aline Paes	Universidade Federal Fluminense, Brazil
Maria Pantoja	Cal Poly San Luis Obispo College of Engineering, USA
Guilherme Peretti-Pezzi	Swiss National Supercomputing Centre, Switzerland
Robinson Díaz	Universidad Central de Venezuela, Venezuela
Ricardo Román-Brenes	Universidad de Costa Rica, Costa Rica
Claudia Roncancio	Université Grenoble Alpes, France
Thomas Ropars	Université Grenoble Alpes, France
Isaac Rudomin	U. Nacional Autónoma de México, México
John Sanabria	Universidad del Valle, Colombia
Osman Sarood	University of Illinois at Urbana-Champaign, USA
Bruno Schulze	Laboratório Nacional de Computação Científica, Brazil
Roberto Souto	Laboratório Nacional de Computação Científica, Brazil
Andrei Tchernykh	CICESE, México
Nicolás Wolovick	Universidad Nacional de Córdoba, Argentina
Marcelo Zamith	Universidade Federal Rural do Rio de Janeiro, Brazil

Contents

High Performance Computing
Applications

Dynamically Distributing Tasks from an Unattended Parallel Compiler with Cloudbook

José J. García-Aranda[1], Juan Ramos-Díaz[1], Sergio Molina-Cardín[1],
Xavier Larriva-Novo[2], Andrés Bustos[3], Luis A. Galindo[4],
and Rafael Mayo-García[3(✉)] (iD)

[1] Nokia, María Tubau 9, 28050 Madrid, Spain
[2] ETSIT-UPM, Avda. Complutense s/n, 28040 Madrid, Spain
[3] CIEMAT, Avda. Complutense 40, 28040 Madrid, Spain
rafael.mayo@ciemat.es
[4] Telefónica, Ronda de la Comunicación 2, 28050 Madrid, Spain

Abstract. A dynamic version of Cloudbook is presented in this work, a new tool for automatically and unattendedly parallelizing codes which also lately distributes the tasks dynamically. Cloudbook is designed for Python codes and, above all, makes the parallelization in a way in which the number and main characteristics of the available infrastructure is taken into account for optimizing the execution (performance, bandwidth connection, etc.) in a dynamic way. Cloudbook is designed to allow developers to get the technical benefits of automated distribution and parallelization of programs with a very low learning cost. It only requires labelling the original code with a reduced set of pragmas located at function headers. Results of the tests carried out with Cloudbook with several codes on a real infrastructure are presented as well.

Keywords: Parallel computing · Compiler · Automatization

1 Introduction

In general terms, parallel computing refers to the use in combination of two or more processes (threads, cores, computers…) to solve a single problem. This methodology is carried out by using computing architectures in which several processors execute or process simultaneously an application or computation. Thus, it is possible to perform large computations by dividing the workload between more than one processor, all of which execute their task through the computation at the same time in a predefined scheme.

Compared to serial computing, parallel computing is then much better suited for modelling, simulating, and understanding complex real world phenomena. Thus, the primary objective of parallel computing, also known as parallel processing, is to increase the available computation power for faster application execution or task resolution.

S. Nesmachnow et al. (Eds.): CARLA 2020, CCIS 1327, pp. 3–17, 2021.
https://doi.org/10.1007/978-3-030-68035-0_1

Today's supercomputers employ parallel computing principles to operate and solve complex problems. Some examples of computational science applied to natural sciences are galaxy formation, climate change, weather forecast, energy production, bioinformatics, material science, etc. Although parallel computing was firstly used for scientific computing and the simulation of scientific problems, nowadays it is present in any field, including human and social sciences too. This has led and is still leading to the design of more powerful and efficient parallel hardware and software making a reality the so-called High Performance Computing (HPC).

As a consequence, the use of the HPC infrastructure has become a challenge itself with the advent of many-core systems, i.e. the parallelization of serial programs has become a mainstream and cornerstone programming task.

Additionally, parallel computers based on interconnected networks need to have some kind of routing protocols to enable the transmission of messages between nodes that are not directly connected. The medium used for communication between the processors is likely to be hierarchical in large multiprocessor machines and have a strong influence on the cluster performance when large parallel calculi are executed. The variation of the performance with the number of computer resources is known as scalability and depends on the hardware and architecture of the physical resources as well as on the computational characteristics of the problem to be solved. Scalability must be maximized, but it is usually degraded when the computing resources or the problem size rise.

Summarizing, parallel computing is highly useful, but presents several challenges that become more and more complex to be overcome as the size of the infrastructures increase. Companies must manufacture efficient supercomputers from the energy point of view that, in addition, should be efficiently exploited from the usage point of view. In this sense, the way in which the parallelization is implemented is key as programming to target parallel architectures can be highly difficult and requires human expertise and know-how.

The first aim of this work is to provide a tool that automatically and unattendedly parallelizes a code, releasing the final user of designing such a parallel implantation as well as of debugging processes. Lately, a second goal is achieved by providing dynamic capabilities for distributing the parallel tasks by the tool itself in order to optimize the computational efficiency in terms of performance.

2 Related Work

As aforementioned, multi- and many-core machines are very common nowadays, allowing a number of problems exploiting the tremendous processing power of such machines. Such goal can only be efficiently achieved by parallel compilation. Automatic conversion of serial code into its functionally equivalent parallel version remains as an open challenge for researchers for the last years. These tools are intended to transform legacy serial code into parallel code to execute on parallel architectures.

With respect to parallel compilers, a couple of reviews of the different tools can be found in [1] and [2]. Roughly speaking, these works compare different automatic tools (see references therein) on the basis of technology, language, available platforms and features, and drawbacks. The most important phase within the flowchart for parallelizing the code is the detection of potential blocks, which is also the most time consuming part.

It is also found that most of the tools are either oriented to FORTRAN or C/C++ as they clearly describe the operational flow in the code. Then, it is not strange that even Barve *et al.* developed a serial to parallel C++ code converter for multi-core machines after the publication of their revision [3]. Another posterior work presented a novel architecture based on web services which is able to translate any legacy software application into a parallel code [4]. In a similar way, André *et al.* [5] present an environment for programming distributed memory computers using High Performance Fortran, with emphasis put on compilation techniques and distributed array management. OpenMP should be also highlighted, the well-known application programming interface for shared memory parallel computing [6].

With a focus on data-parallel compiler, the aim has been to equal the performance of carefully hand-optimized parallel codes. For tightly coupled applications based on line sweeps, the Rice dHPF compiler [7] and its extension [8] can be cited. Most closed to Data-analytics, the TOREADOR tool has been recently published [9].

Specific developments for GPU environments such as the thesis by Hsu [10] or for executions carried out by virtual machines with the HPVM framework [11] can be consulted, but those works are less related to the one presented here.

On the other hand, literature about optimizing the execution of codes along runtime taking into account the underlying infrastructure is huge. Just to focus on heterogeneous architectures, the OmpSs framework is able to provide dynamic allocation of jobs among other duties [12], but other solutions for heterogeneous resources are available too [13–15]. For loosely coupled applications, such as Monte Carlos codes, the Montera framework provided good results on real in production distributed heterogeneous platforms [16]. Works like this opened the door to widen this kind of solutions to virtualized environments [17].

Analyzing the existing solutions, it can be deducted that all of them are still far away from their expectations, focused on a specific kind of application/environment, or do not stack a parallel compiler to the available infrastructure along runtime. The aim of this work is then to present a general-purpose tool that will both make codes parallel and will also take into account the infrastructure on which those codes are executed in order to maximize their performance.

3   The Unattended Parallel Compiler

There are two main problems in parallel execution: the generation of pieces of code to be executed on each processor as well as the efficient deployment and coordinated execution of these tasks. This work focuses on both problems by splitting a Python source code into the so-called deployable units (DU) and lately distributing these DUs in a coordinated way allowing communication among them if needed. This solution is called Cloudbook.

In order to achieve an efficient parallel execution, the proposed solution Cloudbook defines several pragmas to be integrated in the source code, which will be interpreted by a "maker" designed to split the code into DUs. The main components of the proposed solution are summarized in the following architecture:

- Maker: comprises the graph analyzer of source code and the splitter, which produces the DUs
- Deployer: assigns the DUs to the available resources and launches the execution
- Agents: execute the DUs.

During execution of Cloudbook programs, there is not need for a central server which attends the requests from agents asking for tasks o providing results, because Cloubook allows agents communicate each other and therefore the figure of a central controller server is not needed.

3.1 Requirements

In order to both optimize parallelism and improve performance, the programmer can include a series of labels in the functions that would indicate the agents how to execute those functions.

Certain Cloudbook Pragmas may reflect the fork-join model spirit [18]. However, in Cloudbook the invokers do not match the concept of "parent" of the fork-join model because (among other details) tasks are executed on different agents, do not share a copy of parent's variables, threads can be either created at invoker or invoked, and parallel functions cannot return values.

Cloudbook supports the following language extensions (pragmas) for functions:

- #__CLOUDBOOK:NONBLOCKING__: functions with this label cannot return anything. When Cloudbook detects a non-blocking function, its code is modified to launch a thread at the invoked agent and returns immediately. These functions cannot return any value. Restriction: function parameters cannot be objects, only basic types.
- #__CLOUDBOOK:PARALLEL__: these functions are deployed in all DUs. These functions are non-blocking by construction and therefore are not allowed to return anything. The difference between non-blocking and parallel consists of the number of DUs in which the function is deployed. Non-blocking functions are deployed in only one DU, whereas parallel functions are deployed in all available DUs. Parallel functions are synchronizable by using #CLOUDBOOK:SYNC__ (see below). Restriction: function parameters cannot be objects, but basic types.
- #__CLOUDBOOK:RECURSIVE__: these functions are deployed in all DUs. The behavior is defined to maximize the level of recursivity. Each recursive invocation from any DU invokes other DU, which means that in a circle with 10 machines you have 10 times more recursive level than in one machine. Restriction: function parameters cannot be objects, only basic types.
- #__CLOUDBOOK:LOCAL__: these functions are deployed in all DUs, in order to be available for local invocations, avoiding communications. This pragma is intended to be considered at "tuning" phase of the program. There is no restriction in the parameters. They can be objects as well as basic types.
- #__CLOUDBOOK:DU0__: these functions are deployed in DU0. This pragma is useful if your program has certain interactive functionality such as GUIs or keyboard input, which can be forced to be executed in Agent 0.

The pragmas at the level of function invocation are:

- #__CLOUDBOOK:NONBLOCKING_INV__: if the function is not defined as NON-BLOCKING but the programmer does not want to wait for its execution, can invoke the function using this label. In this case, a thread is launched at invoker agent, whereas when the label is used at function definition, the thread is created at the invoked agent.
- #__CLOUDBOOK:SYNC[:timeout]__: this will wait until all the non-blocking operations have finished. In order to be able to continue executing in the cases where an agent stops working, the optional parameter timeout (specified in seconds) may be set after the SYNC word and a colon (:). In the case the optional parameter is set, the program will continue running whenever the all non-blocking operations have finished or when the waiting time exceeds the timeout value (whatever happens first). Example: #__CLOUDBOOK:SYNC:3__.

Cloudbook supports global variables, but special treatment is needed:

- global: this Python keyword indicates to Cloudbook that must either load or refresh the value of global var. Since then, a local cache copy of the var is used. The use of a local copy benefits the performance, reducing communications. In this case, "global" is not a Cloudbook pragma, but a Python keyword
- Critical sections: in order to support "safe variables" (which only can be used by one DU at the same time) or any other critical resource, Cloudbook supports the definition of critical sections, which can be defined by the pragmas #__CLOUDBOK:LOCK__ and #__CLOUDBOK:UNLOCK__; this way the modifications of global variables or critical data are only accessed by one agent at a time
- #__CLOUDBOOK:NONSHARED__: the variable is created at any agent but non shared among different agents. This type of variables allows having unique identifiers for each agent, and different data at each agent if it is needed
- #__CLOUDBOOK:CONST__: this pragma allows Cloudbook to manage constant global variables in an efficient way (replicate them among all DUs).

The use of global variables implies the creation of the following strategy:

- Each global variable is translated into one non-idempotent management function. It exists only in a unique DU
- The management function includes the global var as a non-volatile internal attribute Additionally, this management function must be a critical section in order to allow multiple access from DU outside
- Each function using the global var requests its fresh value at the beginning, invoking the management function, and stores it into volatile internal variable, which is used during the function execution time
- If inside the body of a function that use the global variable is required a refresh of its value, it can be possible invoking another local function that get at the beginning a fresh global variable value and returns its value.

In order to be refreshed by Cloudbook conveniently, global variables should be defined explicitly, but there is no need for a specific pragma. On the other side, objects work as a function abstraction, i.e., the maker analyzes the procedural part of the program and generates the different DUs.

Last but not least, the generic configuration parameters for Cloudbook are:

- Circle ID, unique identifier of a circle, being a circle a set of available resources
- Circle definition, which includes features of each machine belonging to the circle
- Distributed file system to be used by all agents, which is part of the circle properties
- Desired deployable units, number of DUs, which normally is greater or equal to the number of machines
- Cloudbook_maxthreads, which allows launching up to CLOUDBOOK_MAXTHREADS functions in parallel and waits to launch the next one until any of the previously launched functions ends. This limit allows keeping under control the number of resources at any invocation of parallel functions.

4 Cloudbook Global Architecture

The Cloudbook global architecture for a dynamic behavior is much simple and is composed of the following components (see Fig. 1 too):

- Agent: This is the component that will be in each machine that is part of the Cloudbook circle. Tasks:

  - Executing code and communicating with other agents
  - Start the application (through invocation to "run" at deployer service)

- Maker: This component receives a link to the code (which is located in the distributed FS). The maker performs two tasks:

  - Graph analysis: parses the code and produces the invocations matrix
  - Split the program: groups functions into code pieces, which are the "Deployable Units" (DU). The number of DU depends on circle definition (number of agents and machines) and possible certain additional criteria.

- Distributed file system: This module stores code and data. It is accessible by all agents; the original code is located on folder the "original" and the maker saves the DUs on the "cloudbook" folder. Agents are agnostic to this component. All machines mount the distributed file system as a local directory and use it in the same way as local
- Deployer service: This module is responsible for the creation of the cloudbook directory, which contains the assignment of the deployable units to the different agents, and starts the execution. Tasks:

  - Create the cloudbook directory
  - When "run" command is invoked, checks if all the required agents are online and then start the execution

 – Stats monitor: this module contains the statistics associated to the DUs' executions in
   order to allow a dynamic behavior of the tool

   Cloudbook relies on distributed file systems to make DUs accessible to all agents
and also as storage for program files, which must be accessed by all agents. Cloudbook
is then agnostic to the file system and the programmer must decide which file system
to use in order to get a scalable communication mechanism avoiding using centralized
servers (for small/medium projects a NFS server may be enough, for big/huge projects
a bit torrent FS may be needed).

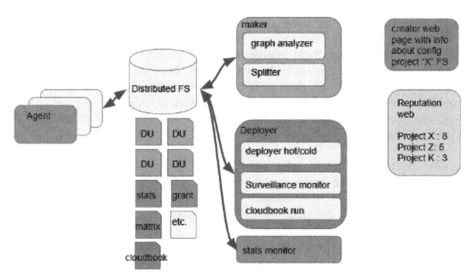

Fig. 1. The Cloudbook architecture

   In order to replace these centralized servers, certain files have been defined for
allowing communication of all platform components:

 – agent_<XXX>_grant.json: written by agent, read by deployer. Includes information
   of agent identification, power granted by the agent, and public/private IP addresses.
   There is one file per agent and the deployer reads and deletes them periodically. The
   agents must re-create the file periodically and the deployer may deduce which agents
   are new and which agents have stopped based on comparison of existing files
 – Alarm files: written by agents, read by the deployer. There are two types of alarm:
   WARNING (if it is possible to continue executing) and CRITICAL (if not possible).
   When the deployer reads this file (only one file for all agents exists), it will perform
   a hot redeployment (WARNING file) or a cold redeployment (CRITICAL file)
 – Redeploy messages: written by the deployer, read by agents. Once the deployer has
   produced a new cloudbook.json dictionary file, it will inform all agents creating a
   COLD_REDEPLOY file or a HOT_REDEPLOY file. This file will be deleted in the
   next deployer monitoring period

- stats_agent_<XX>.json: created by agents, read by the stats monitor. This file contains execution stats which also contains information to tune the matrix at make phase
- matrix_<timestamp>.json: created by the stats monitor, read by the maker: contains a new version of the matrix taking into account execution stats
- du_list.json: created by the maker, read by the deployer, this file contains all DUs, in order to be assigned by the deployer to the alive agents
- function_mapping.json: created by the maker, read by the stats monitor. This file contains the mapping between original name functions and final name functions

5 Dynamic Execution

With the previously described architecture, it is possible to perform dynamic (re)deployment and execution of codes. By profiting from the surveillance monitor, it is possible to periodically check changes in the number of available agents and alarms raised by agents in order to perform both a "hot" (without restarting the program) or "cold" (program must be restarted) redeployment. Redeployments are initiated in the following cases:

- Under critical alarms sent by agents (they cannot continue running), the surveillance monitor must restart the deployment and in some cases the maker
- Under warning alarms sent by agents (they can continue running), the surveillance monitor must make a hot redeployment and inform the agents to load the new Cloudbook
- When new agents have been added or others have stopped, in a way in which the new Cloudbook dictionary must be compatible with the previous one, so orphan DUs, stopped agents, new agents, and critical DUs are properly reassigned by Cloudbook.

In order to keep track of the number of available agents, the surveillance monitor will use the agents_grant.json file. Agents will update this file periodically (period is chosen taking into account both the distributed file system synchronization time and processing time of the monitor) and surveillance monitor will explore this file periodically using a larger interval. With the surveillance monitor component, the deployer will never stop because sleeps and wakes up periodically (this strategy is better than a scheduled OS task and allows easily stopping the deployer and the surveillance monitor mechanism).

The dynamic execution also allows improving performance based on collected statistics. The redeployment for improving performance must take into account stats gathered by agents. These stats provided by the agents feed a stats monitor, which dynamically builds a matrix and compares with existing matrix used at current deployment. Stats generated by agents include the number of times that each function has been invoked by each "invoker" function. In order to make it possible, the name of the "invoker" function will be sent at each invocation.

The existing matrix must be an output from the maker. The latter must invoke the graph analyzer to build and fill the matrix only the first time. Therefore, an optional parameter to use existing filled matrix must be included in the invocation to maker, i.e.

it must be possible to do a "remake" and not only a "make", and for make it possible the matrix parameter is needed. The matrix file used as input is created by the stats monitor and improves the "default" assumptions that maker does when building the matrix. By doing so, the performance can be improved in terms of the way in which the code has been parallelized and distributed, but also in terms of performance based on the underlying infrastructure as additional features can be added for doing an intelligent redeployment. Stats provide real information about invocations among functions and allow taking better decisions when the code of the original program is separated into different DUs, which are executed on different agents. Stats may suggest that certain functions should be deployed together in the same DU.

The way in which the dynamic redeployment is carried out is depicted in Fig. 2.

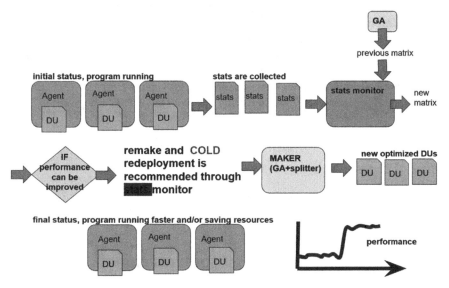

Fig. 2. The Cloudbook dynamic redeployment

6 Results

Experiments have been carried out in two platforms: a group of low-end machines and an HPC cluster.

6.1 Group of Low-End Machines

For proof of concepts tests, platform is composed of four Raspberry Pi2 interconnected with an Ethernet switch and sharing a NFS file system to store the program (DUs) and files published by each agent. The characteristics of this circle of machines are:

- Processor: Broadcom BCM2837B0, Cortex-A53 64-bitSoC@ 1.4 GHz
- RAM: 1 GB LPDDR2 SDRAM
- Wi-Fi+Bluetooth: 2.4 GHz y 5 GHz IEEE 802.11.b/g/n/ac, Bluetooth
- Operating System: Raspbian

In order to test the correctness of Cloudbook, two first examples have been adapted to the tool paradigm in order to include the simple and reduced pragmas that Cloudbook needs to find out within the code in order to successfully make parallel an initial serial code. These two problems are the N-body problem [19] and the tower of Hanoi game [20]. According to the results, they have been used as valid proof of concept for this work.

For the sake of completion, the results related to the N-body problem executed on Cloudbook can be watched in a video [21], where it is demonstrated how the code is run in the four aforementioned raspberries. The time spent in the algorithm by Cloudbook is lower than the sequential version, from a certain number of bodies. The benefit is bigger when the number of bodies processed by one invocation is high, and the communication time becomes non relevant. Regarding the performance and taking into account the test bed, Cloudbook starts performing better than the serial version from ~3,000 bodies on. From this point, the speed up grows linearly, close to a 4x factor as is depicted in Fig. 3.

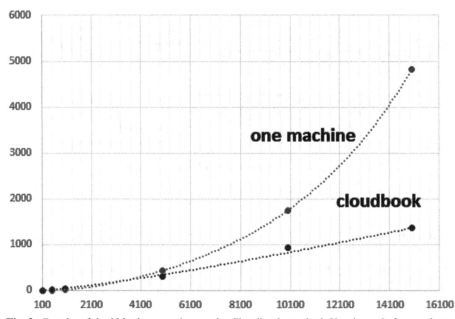

Fig. 3. Results of the N-body execution on the Cloudbook test bed. X-axis reads for number of bodies and Y-Axis for seconds; they are not included in the Figure for readability reasons

With respect to the Hanoi game and in a similar way, it is also found out that Cloudbook provides potentially 4 times bigger stack for recursive invocations in the aforementioned testbed, but what it is most important is to notice how this recursive problem is able not to collapse thanks to Cloudbook. It has been demonstrated that for a ten of pieces a sequential version would crash meanwhile Cloudbook is able to keep on working on finding out the solution. Speed in recursive invocations is not improved but stack size is increased linearly with the number of agents involved.

In order to test the solution proposed with a different approach, some tests have been performed with Cloudbook executing an Intrusion Detection System (IDS). This way, the focus is put most on dataset management and process. The comparison between one machine and Cloudbook execution is shown in Table 1 below.

Table 1. Local and Cloudbook execution times for an IDS.

Data size (lines)	Local execution time (s)	Cloudbook execution time (s)
100,000	5.67	4.25
1,000,000	51.82	25.52
5,000,000	257.06	139.70
10,000,000	529.09	300.96
50,000,000	2,737.52	1,363.32
157,602,189	13,846.43	6,451.53

6.2 HPC Cluster

Two more computationally demanding tests have been carried out on a HPC environment. We run with CloudBook a genetic algorithm in the XULA cluster, located at the CIEMAT data center. We use the new partition of the cluster (upgraded in March 2020, named Xula2), which is composed of 56 computing nodes and connected through IB HDR100. Each node contains 2 processors Intel® Xeon® Gold 6254 (18C, 36T) @3.10 GHz and 192 GB of RAM memory. The common folder for Cloudbook is mounted on a Lustre filesystem.

The genetic algorithm adapted to Cloudbook is DiVoS [22]. DiVoS is a simulation code that finds the minimum energy of a superconducting layer by finding the optimal position of its magnetic vortices. In the genetic algorithm, the chromosomes are the position of the vortices and the fitness function is precisely the (negative) energy of the system. By means of heritage, crossovers, and natural selection rules, the algorithm finds the best individual of the population, i.e. the one with lowest energy and thus the most likely state of the system.

The DiVoS adaptation to CloudBook is rather straightforward: we have parallelized a parameters scan in the input configuration file. In this way, we can easily perform physical parameters sweeps and numerical convergence studies in a fast and easy way from the user point of view. We must point out that this parallelization does not require any communication between the agents. The two tests carried out are intended to show the scaling of the computing time with the number of agents for a fixed problem size and to compare the performance with the Multiprocessing Python built-in library. For Cloudbook, the time measure is the execution time of the cloudbook_run.py program, not taking into account the time needed to make, deploy, or activate the agents.

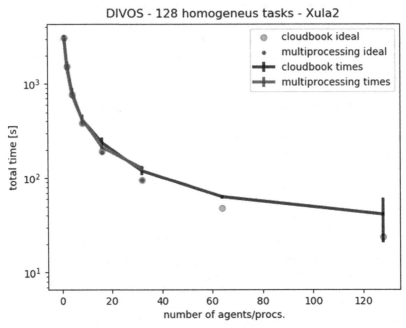

Fig. 4. Results of the DiVoS execution profiting from the Cloudbook solution and the Multiprocessing Python built-in library (homogenous tasks)

In the first test we consider a problem that consists of 128 identical tasks, and measure the execution time in terms of the number of agents (or CPUs) used for the computation both with Cloudbook and the Multiprocessing library. A number of tasks equal to the number of available agents is run simultaneously, with a #__CLOUDBOOK:SYNC__ pragma at the end of each batch of tasks. Each case is executed 5-10 times, using the average value and assuming an error equal to twice the standard deviation. We also calculate the execution time corresponding to ideal scaling in the two cases. The results are plotted in Fig. 4.

In the second test the problem is formed by 80 inhomogeneous tasks. Due to the synchronization step, the scaling here is a bit worse, as can be seen in Fig. 5:

We can extract two conclusions from these tests:

- Cloudbook presents very similar performance as the Multiprocessing library within the error bars.

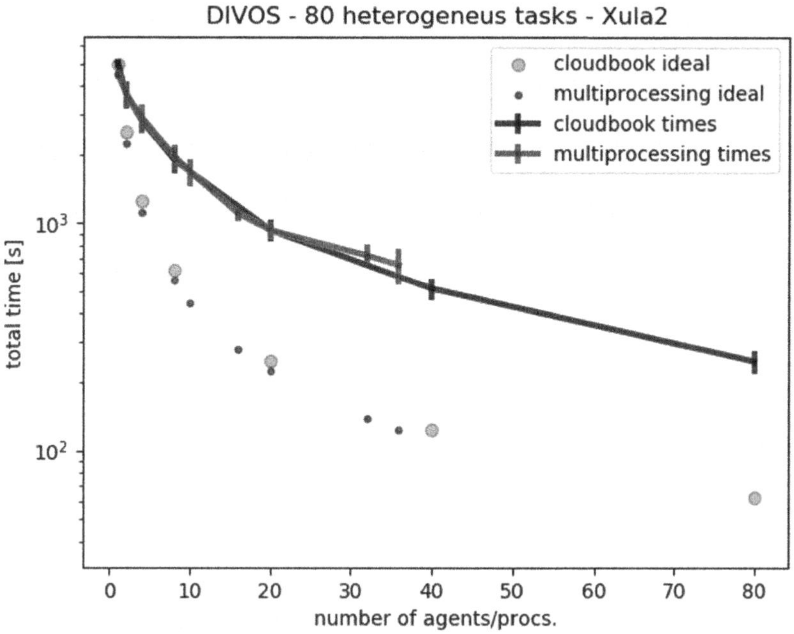

DIVOS - 80 heterogeneus tasks - Xula2

Fig. 5. Results of the DiVoS execution profiting from the Cloudbook solution and the Multiprocessing Python built-in library (heterogeneous tasks)

– Cloudbook can scale up much more than the Multiprocessing library, because the latter is limited to the number of available processors in each node (36 in Xula2) and Cloudbook allows the deployment between any number of nodes.

7 Conclusions

In this work, a new tool called Cloudbook that automatically and unattendedly parallelizes serial codes is presented. Unlike previous similar solutions, it is focused on Python codes and has produced tangible results on production infrastructures at scale, which are also reported via digital content. Cloudbook does not only make the parallelization, but also is aware of the number and main characteristics (performance, bandwidth connection, etc.) that the available resources provide in order to decide a smart distribution of the parallel tasks (DUs) in order to optimize the performance.

The limits of the efficiency of parallel programming with Cloudbook are given by the size of the problem and the cost of communication. Performance results can be improved by taking advantage of the multi-processing in the agents, using their available cores.

Cloudbook follows the model of HPC and HTC computing in a versatile way and can be adapted to a large set of problems, without forcing the programmer to make a distributed design of the problem. The main contributions of Cludbook are:

– Provision of automatic splitting
– Generic, not simply bounded to master-slave based programs, for example

- Valid for both distributed and parallel environments
- Dynamic redeployment based on performance
- Low required level of knowledge

Having demonstrated its correctness, the methodology that Cloudbook applies for making parallel a serial code is also extended to dynamic environments in which resources are continuously integrated and decommissioned into/from the available infrastructure, while the tool successfully responds to that on-the-fly.

References

1. Barve, A., Khandelwal, S., Khan, N., Keshatiwar, S., Botre, S.: Serial to parallel code converter tools: a review. Int. J. Res. Advent Tech. Special Issue National Conference "NCPCI-2016" (2016)
2. Varsha, K.R.: Automatic parallelization tools: a review. IJESC **7**(3), 5780–5784 (2017)
3. Barve, A., Khomane, S., Kulkarni, B., Katare, S., Ghadage, S.: A serial to parallel C++ code converter for multi-core machines. In: Proceedings of the International Conference on ICT in Business Industry & Government (2016)
4. Alsubhi, K.: An architecture for translating sequential code to parallel. In: Proceedings of the 2nd International Conference on Information System and Data Mining, pp. 88–92, April 2018
5. André, F., Le Fur, M., Mahéo, Y., Pazat, J.-L.: The Pandore data-parallel compiler and its portable runtime. In: Hertzberger, B., Serazzi, G. (eds.) HPCN-Europe 1995. LNCS, vol. 919, pp. 176–183. Springer, Heidelberg (1995). https://doi.org/10.1007/BFb0046627
6. Chapman, B., Jost, G., van der Pas, R.: Using OpenMP. The MIT Press, Cambridge (2008)
7. Chavarria-Miranda, D., Mellor-Crummey, J.: An evaluation of data-parallel compiler support for line-sweep applications. In: Proceedings of the International Conference on Parallel Architectures and Compilation Techniques, pp. 7–17. IEEE, New York (2002)
8. Chavarría-Miranda, D., Mellor-Crummey, J., Sarang, T.: Data-parallel compiler support for multipartitioning. In: Sakellariou, R., Gurd, J., Freeman, L., Keane, J. (eds.) Euro-Par 2001. LNCS, vol. 2150, pp. 241–253. Springer, Heidelberg (2001). https://doi.org/10.1007/3-540-44681-8_36
9. Di Martino, B., Esposito, A., D'Angelo, S., Maisto, S.A., Nacchia, S.: A compiler for agnostic programming and deployment of big data analytics on multiple platforms. IEEE Trans. Parallel Distrib. Syst. **30**(9), 1920–1931 (2019). https://doi.org/10.1109/TPDS.2019.2901488
10. Hsu, A.W.: A Data Parallel Compiler Hosted on the GPU. Indiana University, Bloomington (2019)
11. Kotsifakou, M.: HPVM: heterogeneous parallel virtual machine. In: Proceedings of the 23rd ACM SIGPLAN Symposium on Principles and Practice of Parallel Programming, pp. 68–80. ACM Digital Library (2018)
12. Iserte, S., et al.: Dynamic management of resource allocation for OmpSs jobs. In: Proceedings of the First Ph.D. Symposium on Sustainable Ultrascale Computing Systems, NESUS COST Action, Timisoara (2016)
13. Becker, T., Karl, W., Schüle, T.: Evaluating dynamic task scheduling in a task-based runtime system for heterogeneous architectures. In: Schoeberl, M., Hochberger, C., Uhrig, S., Brehm, J., Pionteck, T. (eds.) ARCS 2019. LNCS, vol. 11479, pp. 142–155. Springer, Cham (2019). https://doi.org/10.1007/978-3-030-18656-2_11

14. Ramírez-Velarde, R., Tchernykh, A., Barba-Jimenez, C., Hirales-Carbajal, A., Nolazco-Flores, J.: Adaptive resource allocation with job runtime uncertainty. J. Grid Comput. **15**(4), 415–434 (2017). https://doi.org/10.1007/s10723-017-9410-6

15. Becker, T., Busse, P., Schuele, T.: Evaluation of dynamic task scheduling algorithms in a runtime system for heterogeneous architectures. In: 31st International Conference on Architecture of Computing Systems, Braunschweig, pp. 1–8 (2018)

16. Rodriguez-Pascual, M., Mayo-García, R.M., Llorente, I.M.: Montera: a framework for efficient execution of Monte Carlo codes on grid infrastructure. Comput. Inform. **32**, 113–144 (2013)

17. Rubio-Montero, A.J., Rodríguez-Pascual, M.A., Mayo-García, R.: A simple model to exploit reliable algorithms in cloud federations. Soft. Comput. **21**, 4543–4555 (2017). https://doi.org/10.1007/s00500-016-2143-9

18. Kumar, A., Shorey, R.: Performance analysis and scheduling of stochastic fork-join jobs in a multicomputer system. IEEE Trans. Parallel Distrib. Syst. **4**, 1147–1164 (1993). https://doi.org/10.1109/71.246075

19. Heggie, D.C.: The Classical Gravitational N-Body Problem. Encyclopaedia of Mathematical Physics, Elsevier (2006)

20. Romik, D.: Shortest paths in the Tower of Hanoi graph and finite automata. SIAM J. Discret. Math. **20**, 610–622 (2006)

21. Demo of the N-Body proof of concept and how it performs. https://drive.google.com/open?id=193f30luFq22cy8QUjzzWHgMA8zKfUAv4

22. Rodríguez-Pascual, M.A., et al.: Superconducting vortex lattice configurations on periodic potentials: simulation and experiment. J. Supercond. Nov. Magn. **25**, 2127–2130 (2012). https://doi.org/10.1007/s10948-012-1636-8

Fostering Remote Visualization: Experiences in Two Different HPC Sites

Sergio Augusto Gélvez Cortés[1]([✉]) [ID], César A. Bernal[1] [ID], Carlos J. Barrios[1] [ID], and Benjamín Hernández[2] [ID]

[1] Supercomputación y Cálculo Científico, Universidad Industrial de Santander, Bucaramanga, Colombia
`sergio.gelvez@correo.uis.edu.co`
[2] Oak Ridge National Laboratory, Oak Ridge, TN, USA

Abstract. Visualization of scientific data is crucial for scientific discovery to gain insight into the results of simulations and experiments. Remote visualization is of crucial importance to access infrastructure, data and computational resources and, to avoid data movement from where data is produced and to where data will be analyzed. Remote visualization enables geographically diverse collaboration and enhances user experience through graphical user interfaces. This paper presents two approaches deployed by two different HPC centers: The SC3 - Supercomputación y Cálculo Científico Center in Colombia and the Oak Ridge Leadership Computing Facility in USA. We overview our remote visualization experiences, adopted technologies, use cases, and challenges encountered. Our contribution is to signal the commonality between approaches in terms of the end goal, showing their fitness for their contexts, while not focusing only on attempting to provide a general picture of remote visualization, given the differences between centers in terms of purposes, needs, resources, and national impact.

Keywords: Remote visualization · Scientific visualization · HPC

1 Introduction

SC3 - Supercomputación y Cálculo Científico is a high performance computing center at Universidad Industrial de Santander (UIS), a government sponsored university in Bucaramanga, Colombia. It supports research initiatives derived from the creation of the technology park at Guatiguará[1]. The mission of the center is to provide computational resources to projects in research areas critical to the region and boost research in fields such as Materials Sciences, Oil and Gas, Biotechnology and Agroindustry, among others. The UIS acts as a research hub of Santander region and shares research partnerships with Ecopetrol, Colombia's Oil & Gas company.

---

[1] A research complex aimed to increase R&D+i in the region.

© Springer Nature Switzerland AG 2021
S. Nesmachnow et al. (Eds.): CARLA 2020, CCIS 1327, pp. 18–33, 2021.
https://doi.org/10.1007/978-3-030-68035-0_2

The Oak Ridge Leadership Computing Facility (OLCF) at Oak Ridge National Laboratory (ORNL) is funded by the U.S. Department of Energy with the main objective of providing the computational and data resources required to solve the most challenging problems in areas such as Materials Sciences, Biology, Chemistry, Engineering, Computer Sciences, among others. Through user programs such as the Innovative and Novel Computational Impact on Theory and Experiment (INCITE) [19] and the ASCR Leadership Computing Challenge (ALCC) [18], the OLCF offers researchers computing and data analysis resources many times more powerful than they could access elsewhere [11].

The SC3 and the OLCF are user based facilities available for international use, in addition to computational resources, both offer data analysis and visualization expertise and infrastructure. Both sites collaborate with users that have a diversity of skills and geographic location. These collaborations extend through the life cycle of data, from computation to analysis and visualization.

Through interactions with our users, we noted an increased need for remote visualization services. In particular, SC3's users need to shift from a workstation centered workflow to a HPC centric one. This shift implies SC3's users get to know HPC centric skills to do their work. On the other hand, the scale of data produced at OLCF goes from a few terabytes to several petabytes. It is unfeasible for our data intensive users perform data analysis and visualization on their local systems. In particular, moving data from OLCF to researchers' facility is a time and energy consuming process that demands high network bandwidth and significant storage resources to house their data. In addition, data analysis and visualization of big scientific data requires HPC hardware, scalable software and expertise that may not be available at the users' premises.

This paper presents experiences to support SC3 and OLCF users' remote visualization needs. Specifically, YAJE, the SC3's solution, is aimed at improving user experience and reduce the learning curve of HPC centric workflows. YAJE offers a containerized remote desktop solution based on virtual network computing (VNC) with integration with the SC3's job scheduler. Whereas, SIGHT, the OLCF solution, is aimed at eliminating data transfers and enabling scalable interactive exploration of large datasets. These two solutions tackle different aspects of visualization, owing to the differences in the challenges and resources of the centers in which they were conceived.

The remainder of this paper is organized as follows: in Sect. 2 we will introduce a technical background of remote visualization processes. In Sect. 3 we will introduce SC3, the user challenges they face, along with an specific use case and a proposed solution. The results of this solution will also be discussed. Section 4 will present OLCF in the same manner and finally in Sect. 5, we will present some discussions and future plans.

2   Technical Background

Scientific visualization allows the understanding and/or validation of simulation and experiment results. It enables collaborative interaction and decision making, during and after simulation. High resolution, interactivity and the possibility of processing ever increasingly large scale datasets are desirable features in the visualization process, no matter the scale size of the simulation campaign.

SC3 and OLCF's users perform different modalities of scientific visualization, i.e. batch based visualization, in-situ visualization and exploratory visualization. For the purposes of this paper, we define each as follows:

– *Batch based visualization.* Visualization is usually performed after simulation and executed in batch jobs, intensive data movement is required between simulation and visualization tasks.
– *In-situ visualization.* Visualization and analysis tasks are performed while the simulation is running, sharing the same HPC resources.
– *Exploratory visualization.* Visualization represents complex scientific data interactively and fully as possible for model preparation, iterative hypothesis verification, feature extraction and quantitative analysis.

Sustaining a good performance level and continuous improvements of each visualization modality, poses interesting challenges for SC3 and OLCF users, due to costs in data transfers, storage, and specialized or custom software. As a result, an alternative solution to reduce this burden is the adoption of remote visualization.

Remote visualization allows access to resources that cannot be afforded by our scientists in their institutions. It enhances collaborative work, strengthening community bounds. However, remote visualization also presents its own set of challenges, for example, inter-site data transfer costs in terms of latency and channel quality-of-service (QoS), user interaction (e.g adoption of new kind of workflows), data compression [3], among others.

Infrastructure for remote visualization requires a distributed computing system comprising software and data resources, HPC systems and independent computers connected through a communication network. The HPC system stores and transforms data into visualizations artifacts and, compresses and delivers results. Independent computers connect to the HPC system, receives, decompresses and displays visualizations. A software stack establishes and maintains secure communications, and coordinates the execution of applications. In the next subsections we provide a general overview of technologies for remote visualization.

2.1   Remote Desktops and GPU Based Alternatives

The X Window System provides support for OpenGL based rasterization commonly used in visualization packages. The X Window Server encapsulates GUI and OpenGL's commands in a X Window protocol stream coming from the running application. Then, this stream is sent to the client machine where the client's X Window Server passes the OpenGL commands to the client's rendering system.

X Forwarding has been historically supported by both sites. It performs well in applications with simple user interfaces, low refresh rate and low rendering complexity (e.g. Ncview, gnuplot). For complex visualization and analysis tools, X Forwarding has some disadvantages. First, X protocol has high latency, i.e. it requires the client or server to wait for an acknowledgement before it can transmit a new stream. Second, encapsulating OpenGL's and GUI commands in X Window protocol streams easily produces large sized packets that are not compressed by the X Window System, this make X Forwarding unfeasible in low network bandwidth environments. Finally, all OpenGL commands are produced in the remote server but executed in the client machine, this imposes limitations for large visualization workloads and advanced graphics features.

The Virtual Network Computing. The Virtual Network Computing (VNC) extends X Window System remote capabilities and offers a totally functional remote desktop experience [13]. VNC provides a viewer which the user interact with, and a server that shares the desktop of the remote system. Client and server communicates with each other via the OS agnostic VNC's protocol a.k.a. RFB protocol. VNC has been extended to support advanced features such as SIMD compression (TurboJPEG library), GPU based OpenGL (VirtualGL) and web based viewers.

NiceDCV. NiceDCV enables full GPU acceleration for streaming encoding and OpenGL applications. This approach interpose the DCV library between application and the system's OpenGL libraries, then the 3D rendered images are streamed to remote client using the DCV protocol and 2D images are streamed over the RFB protocol. NiceDCV is a proprietary tool.

2.2 Containers on HPC Visualizations

Containers (formally known as OS-level virtualization technology) are an important tool in HPC environments because they provide isolation for applications to run safely, and low overhead in terms of computing resources. Portability and reproducibility are other advantages of container technology as well. Deploying visualization tools in complex systems can be facilitated by this technology, given its portability: an application environment set up can be replicated without cumbersome procedures; containers also ensure that the application has all dependencies met.

But OS-level virtualization can be problematic in terms of flexibility, i.e. some implementations require superuser level permission for operation. Technologies that can deploy container images without the use of superuser level permission are desirable, specially in shared infrastructure situations. Singularity has this flexibility ingrained in its design [17].

The main advantages of containers in HPC and visualization systems is that they ensure that each application will run the same way and will produce the same result in any supported environment. Singularity is designed with the capabilities to simplify the process of moving containers across a single infrastructure or across hybrid environments, while preserving privilege separation to satisfy the security, privacy, and auditing requirements found in HPC environments.

3   Site 1: SC3 at UIS

GUANE-1 (GpUs AdvaNced Environment) is the flagship computing infrastructure at SC3. It was conceived to support highly parallel, GPU based, high
performance computing. The first version of GUANE-1 was built in 2012, and
an improved version (named GUANE-1 Reload) was finished in 2014. Today,
GUANE-1 Reload offers 128 GPUs NVIDIA Fermi M2050/M2075 (8 by node)
in 16 nodes with three different models of Intel Xeon Processors (in the E56XX
family at 2.1 Ghz, 2.4 Ghz and 2.6 Ghz). Each node has 104 GB of installed RAM.
GUANE-1 Reload has an interconnect comprised of three different networks: An
Infiniband Network (40 Gbps for application data transfer) and two Ethernet
networks (one of 1 Gbps for administration and other of 10 Gbps for user special
requirements in software environments). This platform was initially conceived
for computing, not visualization (Fig. 1).

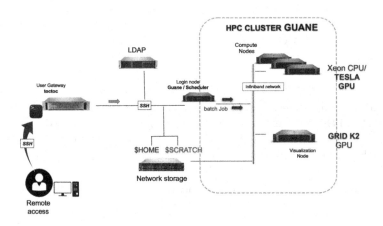

Fig. 1. Guane-1

3.1   SC3 User Challenges

The number of users and usage of the resources at the site have grown in the last
eight years, bringing simulation workloads from diverse areas of knowledge such
as computer fluid dynamics, materials science, seismics, astrophysics, catalysis,
digital humanities, etc; and with this growth also came the demand for visualization tools within the computing environment. Also, researchers at our University
ask for tools that simplify simulation workloads; some of those researchers come
from non-technical or non-computing backgrounds, and find the prospect of having to learn new tools to do their work appalling, specially command line tools.
Presenting our users with experiences similar to the ones they are familiar with
when working in their workstations is of great value to them. The implementation of remote visualization in the site can be a way to offer this experience to
the users.

3.2   YAJE 2.0 a Solution for Remote Visualization Using Linux Containers

YAJE, the solution for remote visualization developed at SC3, uses a VNC implementation with the VirtualGL library for hardware acceleration, very similar to TurboVNC. For the client, YAJE uses noVNC which is a web based VNC client. In addition, a proxy is configured to map websockets based noVNC messages to TCP based VNC messages. The services are isolated using Singularity containers. The interaction is started by the user using a script via the GUANE-1's SLURM scheduler, which starts the services in the containers. Then, the user can access the remote visualization using a browser with a zero-install approach (Fig. 2).

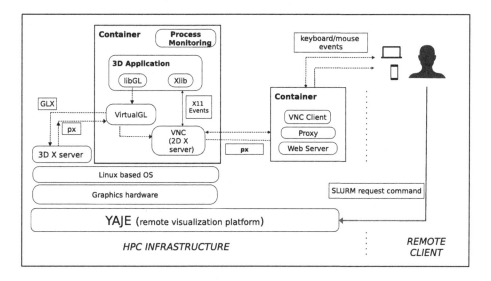

Fig. 2. YAJE 2.0 implementation

This configuration allows for remote visualization of applications without a client/server model, since the streaming is independent of the application code, as is handled by the Remote Frame Buffer Protocol (RFB) via a web browser. The isolation of the processes in the machine using containers maintains security and enables deployment as Software as a service (SaaS). This configuration works in this fashion thanks to the on-demand control over the platform, allowing 3D X server installation and proxy configuration on GUANE-1's nodes.

In this implementation we do not deliver a complete desktop environment to the user. Instead, to minimize the required bandwidth and the computational resources, only a lightweight desktop manager (Openbox) and the application requested by the user are displayed inside the container. Likewise, a series of monitoring scripts are deployed to keep the session alive without additional user interaction. It is of importance to note that the main components of the implementation are open source tools, and that the integration is low cost in terms of deployment, since it was carried out mainly using scripts, with no internal modification to the tools and APIs used.

3.3   Use Case

The specific problem that kickstarted the development of YAJE was a computational fluid dynamics simulation code based on OpenFOAM, provided by the Department of Mechanical Engineering of our University. These researchers desired a quick and easy way to visually check the results of their simulations, to fine tune different OpenFOAM scenarios. They wanted to avoid the cycle of downloading results (over a slow local channel), inspect them in their local machines, and then rerun the simulation. For the first iteration of the deployment, an uncoupled simulation was used: They ran the simulation, visually inspected the results using YAJE, and then reran the simulations with the modifications they required. Further refinements to this implementation are in the YAJE's development roadmap.

3.4   Results

For the first test on YAJE, frame rate was selected as the main metric for the performance evaluation of the system using the `glxspheres64` benchmark. A series of tests were carried out on two network connections, one with low latency (5 ms) and another with high latency (150 ms) at different screen resolutions. In addition, several virtual desktop resolutions were used for the measurement and the number of spheres on screen was varied, acting as the independent variables in the performance model. The machine used for the testing has a NVIDIA Grid K2 GPU. Table 1 present the frame rate results at different latencies and different resolutions.

Table 1. Comparison FPS to different resolutions with low and high latencies

	YAJE		NiceDCV	
	5 (ms) .	150 (ms) .	5 (ms) .	150 (ms) .
720p	18.1	5.1	29.3	19.3
1080p	7	3.0	25	14.6

This first metric, user side FPS for the `glxspheres64` benchmark executed on the visualization node has been measured directly on the web browser, which is the interaction point for the user. The performance offered by NiceDCV using the same benchmark in its web client version acted as a control value.

The purpose of this comparison is to show the capabilities of an open source implementation against one using proprietary tools, providing a similar service.

Of note is the limitations of the YAJE implementation which uses CPU based streaming encoding in contrast to NiceDCV that implements GPU based streaming encoding.

On the other hand, two specific use cases of relevance to SC3 were selected: an openFOAM visualization on Paraview (no Catalyst, single node visualization) [6], and a simple VMD visualization using molecular dynamics results from a catalyst design experiment using MOFs [2]. Also, network performance metrics were taken from a machine inside the organization's network, and from outside, trying to represent the conditions in which a researcher would connect to the service from their home machine. The metrics to evaluate were latency, bandwidth, and browser framerate. For the first set of tests only the OpenFOAM visualization was used. The connection parameters for both test set are presented in Table 2. Note that in the second test set both visualization cases were used.

Table 2. Connection parameters for network performance testing

Parameter	Value
First test set	
Broadband nominal speed	10 Mbits/s
Last segment of connection	Ethernet. 1 Gbit/s
Browser	Chrome
Machine screen resolution	1920 × 1080 p
Streaming resolution	1920 × 1080 p (downscaled at browser)
Second test set	
Broadband nominal speed	200 Mbits/s
Last segment of connection	Wi-fi (n)
Browser	Firefox
Machine screen resolution	1920 × 1080 p
Streaming resolution	1920 × 1080 p (downscaled at browser)

The results of the first set of tests showed an ample disparity between average frames rendered in the server vs frames received in the client (615.4 fps in the server 4.7 fps in the client); the latency was estimated at 55 ms. Deeper discussion of the results are presented in [4]. It is important to note that during the development of the project and the execution of the testing procedures the university upgraded its network infrastructure, improving the performance of the network; this led to a second test set, with significantly better results. Also, the latency and bandwidth measurements were conducted independently from the frame rate tests, using similar time slots; this test was designed in this manner in order not to have the bandwidth test impact the frame rate test, since a large amount of data is transmitted for the former clearly diminishing the performance of the latter.

The results of the latency and bandwidth tests can be summarized in the top half of Table 3 in page 9, whereas the results of the frame rate tests are presented in Table 4 in page 9.

Table 3. Bandwidth and latency tests results

Parameter	min	max	avg	std
Second test set				
Bandwidth [Mbits/s]	0.176	170.0	66.2	63.3
Latency [ms]	30.9	235.9	40.0	26.8
Second test set using RENATA				
Bandwidth [Mbits/s]	3.770	212.000	167.877	46.491
Latency [ms]	30.275	61.275	31.958	2.966

Table 4. Frame rate test results, second test set

	Second test set					
	VMD			OpenFOAM		
Parameter	min	max	avg	min	max	avg
FPS	10.2	60	51.8	25.5	60	59.0

Furthermore, there is also the possibility of using RENATA, an academic high-speed interconnection network[2], although not all of SC3 HPC services are available using that channel yet. At the moment we cannot test the frame rate on the browser, but we have the bandwidth and latency data, and the results are promising. The results are presented in the bottom half of Table 3 in page 9.

It is important to note that the bandwidth maximum value is near the maximum in the channel: Taking into account the variability of the connection speed in a residential channel, with RENATA we can have a much faster connection to the server. Also, the latency maximum is significantly lower, the average is much closer to the minimum value, and the standard deviation is lower; this data shows more stability in terms of latency, which can be very beneficial to this type of application [5].

Another important aspect of the results is the reception from the users. The users from the mechanical engineering department reported satisfaction with the

---

[2] RENATA, Red Nacional Académica de Tecnología Avanzada (Academic National Advanced Technology Network): the computer network is named after the organization. https://www.renata.edu.co/.

usability of Yaje; although the experience is not perfect, and the frame rate is not locked at 60 fps, it is sufficient for an adequate interaction with the visualization tools they requested. This effectively creates a new form of interaction with their results, in a manner similar to their local desktop experience, saving them time and effort in learning new tools for their workflow.

This results, although modest, are promising for the first iteration of the project, and they provide the stakeholders at the site with the reassurance to continue this path forward.

4 Site 2: Oak Ridge Leadership Computing Facility

OLCF provides scientific expertise in the area of data analysis and visualization as part of the INCITE program. We engage and collaborate with users through the life cycle of their data. Examples of collaborations includes consultation in all data analysis and visualization aspects of using OLCF resources, maintain relationships with INCITE teams to ensure OLCF is meeting their data analysis and visualizations needs and, when standard solutions does not fit the user's needs, we develop custom software solutions. In addition, OLCF provides access to compute systems and, data and visualization infrastructure. Compute systems includes Summit, a 4,608 node IBM AC922 system, Rhea a 512 node Intel Xeon E5-2650 cluster, Andes a 704 node AMD EPYC 7302 and 9 fat GPU node cluster, and the Exploratory Visualization Environment for Research in Science and Technology (EVEREST) facility for collaborative analysis and visualization of simulation data. EVEREST comprises a power wall of 32 megapixeles and a large format panel of a resolution of 1080p (Fig. 3 left).

4.1 OLCF's User Challenges

We engage with INCITE teams electronically and by face-to-face conversations. Electronic engagement includes follow-up email conversations after they have submitted a technical support ticket and video-calls to get familiar with their issues, challenges and needs. Face-to-face engagement usually occurs in events such as the Annual OLCF User Meeting, OLCF's training events, workshops or conferences. Face-to-face engagement is important for us because it creates a personal connection and builds trust between our team and the INCITE teams.

A recurrent finding after user engagement is that OLCF users have three requirements in common. First, the scale of data they are producing or plan to produce calls for solutions for remote visualization infrastructure; users are interested in having ad hoc solutions to support their exploratory visualization tasks (interactive model preparation or inspection). Second, users require remote visualization solutions capable of handling large datasets or solutions to enhance their current tools. Third, users are interested in easy-to-use tools and interactive performance.

4.2   SIGHT, a Custom Solution for Remote Visualization

Following user requirements, we developed and deployed SIGHT, a custom solution for interactive data analysis and remote visualization of atomistic simulations [16]. SIGHT (Fig. 3 left) uses a client-server architecture [1] where SIGHT's server manages remote visualization resources (data loading, analysis, rendering, communications and visualizations streaming and delivery) and SIGHT's client receives visualization streams, provides a simplified user interface (UI) and presents results to the users. Components depicted in Fig. 3 left are detailed next:

- A multi-threaded parser that take advantage of CPU cores to load datasets in parallel. It loads the dataset into main memory and makes it available for the Ray tracing and Data parallel Analysis components.
- A ray tracing backend that supports both Nvidia Optix [12] and Intel OSPray [20] libraries to enable interactive and scalable ray tracing.
- The data parallel analysis component includes algorithms to generate transversal views of atomistic models, atom selection and filtering and, calculation of Euler distance between atoms [10]. Analysis is implemented using data parallel primitives exposed in NVIDIA Thrust to support parallel computations on CPUs and GPUs.
- The frame server enables SIGHT's remote visualization capabilities and is in charge of compressing and delivering the visualization frames produced by the ray tracing backend and analysis component. The frame server also dispatches the user commands from the client to other SIGHT's components accordingly.
- SIGHT's client is a web based UI that receives and decompress the visualization streams and presents the results to the user. The client supports regular displays and powerwalls (Fig. 3 right).

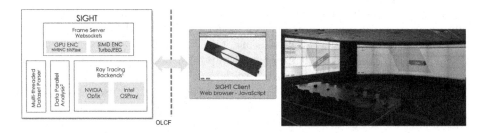

Fig. 3. Left, SIGHT's system architecture. Right, the Exploratory Visualization Environment for Research in Science and Technology (EVEREST) facility.

4.3   Use Case

During their INCITE allocation, a team from University of Virginia, lead by Dr. Leonid Zhigilei, ran billion scale atomistic simulations of laser ablation on metals [21]. Each simulation campaign produced several time steps of around 500 GB each and their analysis and visualization workflow consisted on moving a time step from OLCF to the team's facility, then it involved cutting the time step into several pieces and reassembling the images produced for different pieces. Their workflow was restricted to the generation of static images and was time consuming. After user engagement, we found traditional visualization tools (e.g. Paraview and VisIt) were cumbersome and provided a steep learning curve for the team's analysis (generate transversal views of the atomistic model, atom selection and filtering, calculation of Euler distance between atoms) and visualization tasks.

SIGHT was under development from 2016 to 2019 to support Dr. Zhigilei's team. After each simulation campaign, the team used SIGHT's remote visualization capabilities to reduce and/or eliminate data transfers between OLCF and Dr. Zhigilei's facilities. SIGHT's parallel features enabled the team to perform exploratory analysis and visualization on systems of size of up to a few billions atoms. SIGHT's design allowed the team to take advantage transparently of Rhea's and Summit heterogeneous node architecture.

4.4   Results

We present some SIGHT's qualitative and quantitative results in this section. In particular, the qualitative results are based on Dr. Zhigilei's team publications where SIGHT was used successfully, i.e. [14–16] and two videos[3] demonstrating SIGHT's capabilities. On the other hand, the quantitative results focus on SIGHT's remote visualization streaming performance, which is under the scope of this paper; the interested reader is referred to [7, 8, 10] for details about SIGHT's ray tracing and data analysis performance.

Encoding and decoding speed in visualization streaming is of crucial importance to maintain latency low which results in a smooth interaction between the user and the system. SIGHT's frame server provides CPU and GPU based image encoders. We used TurboJPEG library for JPEG compression using Intel's SIMD instructions and NVIDIA NVENC for GPU based H.264 encoding. Selected encoders are conceptually different by design, in particular, we opted for TurboJPEG because of its availability in VNC based solutions and ease of use. On the other hand, to decode JPEG visualization frames, SIGHT's client uses web browser's built-in JPEG image decoding and to decode H.264 frames, it uses the Media Source Extensions (MSE) and the Broadway.js library.

We designed an experiment to evaluate the performance of SIGHT's frame server. The objective of the experiment was to analyze CPU and GPU based encoding and decoding performance under different image resolutions. The

---

[3] https://youtu.be/0nremmyPyG0, https://youtu.be/q6vmgYbVhe0.

Table 5. SIGHT's streaming visualization performance results.

	NVENC	NVENC+MP4	TJPEG
Encoding Full HD (ms)	4.65	6.05	16.71
Encoding 4K (ms)	12.13	17.89	51.89
Frame size Full HD (KB)	116.00	139.61	409.76
Frame size 4K (KB)	106.32	150.65	569.04

experiment included different encoding/decoding scenarios. The first scenario consisted on using NIVIDA NVENC for H.264 encoding and Broadway.js for "direct" decoding in the web browser. In the second scenario, we used NVIDIA NVENC and on-the-fly MP4 wrapping for encoding and MSE for decoding. The last scenario, consisted on using TurboJPEG for encoding and web browser's built-in JPEG for decoding.

The experiment was run in a NVIDIA DGX-1 Volta system with network bandwidth of 800 Mbps between SIGHT's server and its client. H.264 quality settings were set at 32 MBPS, 30 FPS, PROFILE BASELINE and JPEG quality settings to 50. We performed simple calibration of both encoders based on visual observation to set their quality settings at the same equivalent levels. We used FireFox 65 with Broadway.js for "direct" H.264 decoding, and Chrome 72 for MSE and built-in JPEG decoders. During the experiment, we tracked the behavior of the encoders and decoders in a session of one minute. The session consisted on navigating through a model, zooming in, zooming out, rotation and translation.

Table 5 reports average encoding/decoding latency in milliseconds and the size, in kilobytes, of the stream after encoding Full HD (1920 × 1080 pixels) and 4K (3840×2160 pixels) resolutions. We conclude encoding using NVENC for Full HD resolution was 3.6× faster than TurboJPEG whereas NVENC 4K resolution was 4.3× faster. On the other hand, the media source extensions (MSE) provided the best decoding performance, i.e. MSE for Full HD resolution was 1.1× faster than Broadway.js and 1.95× faster than web browser's built-in JPEG decoder. F4K resolution, MSE was 1.65× faster than Broadway.js and 3.72× faster than built-in JPEG decoder.

5   Discussion and Future Plans

The significant increase in computing power, demonstrated by the deployment of Summit supercomputer, provides an opportunity to solve larger and more comprehensive problems in different scientific domains. This also raises opportunities to efficiently handling data-intensive applications through deployment of remote visualization solutions as demonstrated by SIGHT. On the other hand, HPC infrastructure, traditionally configured and deployed for compute workloads, comprises manycore and multicore processors that should be used for visualization. Intel's Software Defined Visualization [9] initiative or NVIDIA's continuous graphics support in their Tesla based products, exposes the visualization capabilities of these processors. We have been in touch with both vendors to design SIGHT's infrastructure and to enable (remote) visualization capabilities on OLCF's x86 and POWER9 clusters. In addition, we use Summit for in-situ visualization and, Rhea and Andes cluster for pre- and post-processing including analysis, visualization and remote desktops based on TurboVNC and NiceDCV solutions.

Along with the increase in computing power comes growth in the number of users and types of usage, as evidenced by the situation at SC3. These new users bring along expectations about usability. From the users' perspective, integrating HPC resources in their workflow can be very daunting. Users normally prefer to carry on using the tools (and modes of interaction) they know best: this is understandable given the costs associated with learning new tools and methodologies, specially when highly specialized tools are considered. This work presented an approach to facilitate the interaction of users with HPC resources at SC3, using remote visualization for specific applications without a desktop client; bypassing the console as much as possible is of utmost importance. The main objective was to present the users an experience as close as the one presented in their desktops as possible. YAJE 2.0 was the implementation resulting from this attempt. From the results of the tests carried out on the implementation we can conclude that a mechanism of interaction for the users at SC3 similar to a local desktop, using remote visualization over the web, was developed. The resulting solution has low overhead in resources, low cost of implementation, and gentle learning curve. The main limitation of the solution is its dependence upon the domestic internet connection of the users and the stability of our University network, specially in terms of latency. We consider this results satisfactory, given the fact that latency is the main limitation in similar applications in different areas of remote visualization, both scientific and commercial. It is important to note that the service is being rolled out to users, and their experience has been positive; this feedback will ensure the continuity of the project.

As next steps in the YAJE roadmap, we are working on a better work flow for the OpenFOAM and VMD based use cases, including the possibility of a an In-transit coupled simulation. YAJE is in its early stages of development, and we are considering several other angles to improve it: including more use cases from other domains to obtain insight on a possible general set of requirements, measuring the impact on the users using Human Computer Interaction metrics, expanding the use of the tool, and working on improving the efficiency, exploring options both in the containers and the data transfers; for this last part, the expertise of the team at OLCF is of paramount importance.

An important lesson we learned at SC3 with the implementation of YAJE was the preponderance of the user experience in HPC adoption processes: what started as, in its very first conception, a project to develop and showcase technical capabilities using existing hardware, quickly became a endeavour much more grounded in the necessities of the users. It is now geared toward improving the acceptance of the infrastructures by the researchers, traditionally skeptics on the matter, thus aiding in the solution of a very real problem in newer high performance computing sites: low usage rate of the platforms.

While the SC3 and OLCF are different in terms of users, applications, and resources they share the same end goal: to provide support for scientists for increasingly difficult problems. Both centers worked on an aspect related to this end goal, i.e. remote visualization, which serves directly the scientists. Each center tackled a different part of the visualization, according to their strengths and limitations, and generated novel solutions according to their road maps; even though these solutions are not comparable, and are not tackling the same exact need, they show commonality in their conception.

Acknowledgments. This research partially used resources of the Oak Ridge Leadership Computing Facility, which is a DOE Office of Science User Facility supported under Contract DE-AC05-00OR22725. SIGHT's datasets provided by OLCF INCITE 2017–2019 "Petascale Simulations of Short Pulse Laser Interaction with Metals" PI Leonid Zhigilei, University of Virginia. This research also used resources from Supercomputación y Cálculo Científico (SC3), a High Performance Computing Centre at Universidad Industrial de Santander (UIS), Colombia. The funding came from Vicerrectoría de Investigación y Extensión (VIE), the Research unit of UIS.

References

1. Adler, R.M.: Distributed coordination models for client/server computing. Computer **28**(4), 14–22 (1995). https://doi.org/10.1109/2.375173
2. Ardila-Suárez, C., Perez-Beltran, S., Ramírez-Caballero, G.E., Balbuena, P.B.: Enhanced acidity of defective mof-808: effects of the activation process and missing linker defects. Catal. Sci. Technol. **8**, 847–857 (2018). https://doi.org/10.1039/C7CY02462B
3. Bennett, J.C., Childs, H., Garth, C., Hentschel, B.: In situ visualization for computational science (Dagstuhl Seminar 18271). Dagstuhl Rep. **8**(7), 1–43 (2019). https://doi.org/10.4230/DagRep.8.7.1, http://drops.dagstuhl.de/opus/volltexte/2019/10171
4. Bernal Diaz, C.A.: Visualizacion de fluidos mediante tecnicas en dinamica de fluidos computacionales sobre maquinas masivamente paralelas basadas en gpus (2018)
5. Choi, J., Ko, J.: RemoteGL - towards low-latency interactive cloud graphics experience for mobile devices (demo). In: Proceedings of the 17th Annual International Conference on Mobile Systems, Applications, and Services, MobiSys 2019, Seoul, Republic of Korea, pp. 693–694. Association for Computing Machinery. https://doi.org/10.1145/3307334.3328587
6. Gonzalez Esteban, F.E.: Evaluación de un convertidor de energia undimotriz en colombia. Master Thesis
7. Hernández, B.: Exploratory visualization of petascale particle data in nvidia dgx-1. In: NVIDIA GPU Technology Conference 2017, Silicon Valley CA, USA (2017)
8. Hernández, B.: Heterogeneous selection algorithms for interactive analysis of billion scale atomistic datasets. In: NVIDIA GPU Technology Conference 2017, Silicon Valley CA, USA (2017)
9. Intel: Software Defined Visualization. http://sdvis.org/. Accessed 10 June 2020

10. Kawakami, Y., Hernández, B.: Early experiences on OpenPOWER architecture: analysis of billion-scale atomistic datasets. In: The International Conference for High Performance Computing, Networking, Storage, and Analysis (SC 2019), Denver, CO, USA (2019)
11. OLCF: Overview the Oak Ridge Leadership Computing Facility. https://www.olcf.ornl.gov/about-olcf/overview/. Accessed 31 May 2020
12. Parker, S.G., et al.: Optix: a general purpose ray tracing engine. ACM Trans. Graph. 29(4), 66:1–66:13 (2010). https://doi.org/10.1145/1778765.1778803
13. Richardson, T., Stafford-Fraser, Q., Wood, K.R., Hopper, A.: Virtual network computing. IEEE Internet Comput. 2(1), 33–38 (1998). https://doi.org/10.1109/4236.656066
14. Shih, C.Y., Shugaev, M.V., Wu, C., Zhigilei, L.V.: Generation of subsurface voids, incubation effect, and formation of nanoparticles in short pulse laser interactions with bulk metal targets in liquid: molecular dynamics study. J. Phys. Chem. C Nanomater. Interfaces 121(30), 16549–16567 (2017). https://doi.org/10.1021/acs.jpcc.7b02301
15. Shih, C.Y., et al.: Two mechanisms of nanoparticle generation in picosecond laser ablation in liquids: the origin of the bimodal size distribution. Nanoscale 10(15), 6900–6910 (2018). https://doi.org/10.1039/C7NR08614H. Publisher: The Royal Society of Chemistry
16. Shugaev, M.V., et al.: Fundamentals of ultrafast laser–material interaction. MRS Bull. 41(12), 960–968 (2016). https://doi.org/10.1557/mrs.2016.274
17. Syslabs.io: Singularity Community and SingularityPRO on high-performance servers. https://www.sylabs.io/singularity/#1543372082288-68c2f2d1-031d. Accessed 10 June 2020
18. US Department of Energy Office of Science: ALCC. https://science.energy.gov/ascr/facilities/accessing-ascr-facilities/alcc/. Accessed 14 May 2020
19. US Department of Energy Office of Science: INCITE. http://www.doeleadershipcomputing.org/. Accessed 14 May 2020
20. Wald, I., et al.: Ospray - a CPU ray tracing framework for scientific visualization. IEEE Trans. Visual. Comput. Graph. 23(1), 931–940 (2017). https://doi.org/10.1109/TVCG.2016.2599041
21. Zhigilei, L.: Petascale simulations of short pulse laser interaction with metals. https://www.olcf.ornl.gov/web-project/petascale-simulations-of-short-pulse-laser-interaction-with-metals/. Accessed 6 June 2020

High Performance Computing Simulations of Granular Media in Silos

Miguel Da Silva, Sergio Nesmachnow, Santiago Iturriaga$^{(\boxtimes)}$, and Gabriel Usera

Universidad de la República, Montevideo, Uruguay
{mdasilva,sergion,siturria,gusera}@fing.edu.uy

Abstract. This article presents the application of high performance computing for efficient simulations of granular media in silos. Granular media are extensively used in industry, where storage and proper treatment pose several challenges to the scientific community. A relevant problem concerns the study of granular media stored in a silo. Determining the behavior of the media during load and discharge stages is critical. Knowing how the stored particles interact with each other and how they interact with the storage structure can lead to understanding and preventing undesirable effects (e.g., the collapse of the structure) during the silo operation. Charge and discharge processes of granular media in silos are frequently studied using computer simulations. High performance computing comes to help researchers to perform granular media simulations for systems with a large number of particles, in order to model realistic situations in reasonable computing times. This article describes the application of a parallel/distributed high performance computing approach for studying the mechanisms that control the charging and discharging process of silos, in which grains pass through a bottleneck. Simulations are performed applying the Discrete Element Method, and the experimental evaluation is performed over the high performance computing infrastructure of the National Supercomputing Center in Uruguay. The analysis includes large realistic scenarios considering the physical properties of different grains, involving up to 450,000 particles. The proposed implementation allowed to reduce the execution time of simulations up to 42%, demonstrating the capabilities of the proposed parallel/distributed computing approach to scale to solve large problem instances properly.

Keywords: HPC · Granular media simulations · Silos · LIGGGHTS-PUBLIC

1 Introduction

Granular media (or granular materials) are conglomerates of discrete solid, macroscopic particles, that conform bodies of different shapes, dimensions, and composition. Some examples of granular media are rock agglomerates, plant grains, sand, minerals, and also astronomical bodies (e.g., asteroids and the

© Springer Nature Switzerland AG 2021
S. Nesmachnow et al. (Eds.): CARLA 2020, CCIS 1327, pp. 34–48, 2021.
https://doi.org/10.1007/978-3-030-68035-0_3

rings of Saturn). Beyond their great diversity, granular media share some common physical characteristics, and they are often considered the fourth state of matter [11].

Granular media have a broad application in the industry: granular is the second most used type of material in industrial processes, after water [20]. Some examples of industrial equipment that operate with granular media are fluid chemical reactors, conveyor belts, and storage silos. The industrial use of specialized equipment to handle granular media requires knowing the material's behavior during the operation. In 1979, Cundall and Strack [5] proposed the Discrete Elements Method (DEM), which enables performing computer simulations for studying the dynamics of granular media.

DEM simulates the behavior over time of each particle of a granular media system by applying Newton's second law. This feature implies that simulations of systems that contain a high number of particles are modeled using intensive computing tasks. Many works have addressed the efficient execution of DEM algorithms in multiprocessor or multicore computers [1,2,9,23].

Simulation of systems involving many particles usually demands significant execution time. Numerical simulation systems for DEM usually include several functionalities for using multiple processing units to improve the performance of numerical simulations using different strategies and algorithms. One of the main strategies to improve performance is the ability to redistribute the workload among multiple processing units throughout a simulation, i.e., dynamic workload distribution [15,19]. The consolidation of DEM as a valid method for simulation of granular media systems led to the development of software packages that offer a broad set of tools for research on granular media dynamics, including EDEM [6], MFIX [16], and LIGGGHTS [14].

LIGGGHTS-PUBLIC is a popular and well-known open-source version of the LIGGGHTS package for DEM simulations. However, it does not include a dynamic workload distribution mechanism. Its workload distribution is static, with workloads being assigned to processes at the beginning of each simulation. The lack of a dynamic workload distribution mechanism means the overall performance of simulations of granular media using LIGGGHTS-PUBLIC is sub-optimal, especially when simulating large systems. This is because some processes may be assigned far larger workloads than others, slowing down the simulation's execution time.

This article proposes to study the simulation of discharge flows of granular media stored in silos using LIGGGHTS-PUBLIC. These simulations allow studying the distribution of pressures exerted on the walls of a silo during the discharge process. Furthermore, this article proposes to apply high performance techniques for improving simulation efficiency by implementing a new domain decomposition algorithm for dynamic workload distribution on LIGGGHTS-PUBLIC. This domain decomposition algorithm is implemented using MPI and is based on the mobile planes strategy proposed by Markauskas et al. [15].

The efficiency results obtained in the experimental analysis show that the proposed solution is able to reduce the execution times of granular dynamics simulations when compared with the static strategy for workload distribution. The proposed domain decomposition algorithm is robust, as it was able to properly handle granular media systems with particles of equal radius and particles with different radios. Furthermore, the proposed method shows good scalability properties, since the efficiency results improved as the number of processes in the simulation increased.

The main contributions of the research reported in this article are: i) studying the mechanisms that control the charging and discharging process of granular media stored in silos, ii) high performance implementation for dynamic domain decomposition for granular media simulations, iii) experimental evaluation on a high performance computing infrastructure over large realistic scenarios involving up to 450,000 particles. The main results of the experimental evaluation indicate that the proposed approach allows reducing up to 42% the execution time of simulations over traditional LIGGGHTS-PUBLIC simulations and has appropriate scaling capabilities.

The article is organized as follows. Section 2 describes the problem of simulating flows in granular media stored in silos and reviews related works. Section 3 describes the proposed dynamic domain decomposition strategy and its integration to LIGGGHTS-PUBLIC. The experimental evaluation and results are reported and discussed in Sect. 4. Finally, the conclusions and the main lines for future work are presented in Sect. 5.

2   Simulation of Flows in Granular Media Stored in Silos

This section describes the simulation of flows in granular media stored in silos and reviews related works on the application of DEM to study the dynamics of such granular media.

2.1   Computational Simulation of Granular Media on Silos

Granular media are extensively used in industry, where storage and proper treatment pose several challenges to the scientific community. A relevant problem concerns to the study of granular media stored in a silo. Determining the behavior of the media during load and discharge stages is critical. Knowing how the stored particles interact with each other and how they interact with the storage structure can lead to understanding and preventing undesirable effects (e.g., the collapse of the structure) during the operation of the silo.

A line of research with direct applicability in the construction and operation of silos is the study of granular media flows in the discharge stage. Researchers have determined that the flow pattern within the silo is related to the pressure distribution in the discharge stage when a concentric outlet orifice is used (i.e., the exit orifice is in the center of the of the circumference determined by the structure of the silo). Likewise, it has been verified that the results obtained in small-scale models do not offer good approximations of the expected results in real scale models [18]. Due to the aforementioned issues, the scientific community has applied computer simulations to carry out experiments for large-scale silo models [5,13,22]

Two flow patterns are observed in a silo with a concentric discharge orifice: (a) *mass flow*, where all the particles stored in the silo have a simultaneous movement, and (b) *funnel flow*, where a region with particles that do not move (stagnant zone) is observed, and the remaining particles move forming a flow channel. Detailed studies of granular media dynamics have been presented for both mass flow and funnel flow patterns [12]. However, when discharging a silo through an eccentric orifice, a flow-through pattern contiguous to the wall closest to the exit orifice (*eccentric funnel flow*) is observed.

Experiments for studying granular media flow patterns in the discharge of silos at real-scale are scarce in the literature, and the instrumentation to perform an experiment on that scale is very complex [3]. Furthermore, reported measurements in real-scale experiments do not include the values for the distribution of pressures and their correlation with the flow pattern [4,21].

Computational Fluid Dynamics and DEM are applied to study the dynamics of granular media, primarily to determine the flow patterns during the discharge stage, since the behavior of the particles directly influences the physical integrity of the silo. Accidents that occur during the operation of a storage silo can be fatal; for instance, in Uruguay in 2015, two workers died [7].

2.2   Related Work

Markauskas et al. [15] introduced the theoretical basis of a dynamic domain decomposition algorithm based on moving planes. The goal of the mobile planes algorithm is to distribute the total workload among several processes in an equitable manner. Two ways were considered for defining the workload of a process p: i) the total number of particles assigned to p divided by the time necessary to execute an iteration of the DEM method, and ii) the total number of particles assigned to p. The authors used the first workload definition to prevent relatively slower processes from being overloaded with a high number of particles. A tolerance level is used to determine when the workload distribution algorithm must be executed. At the end of a DEM cycle, the workloads of each processor are evaluated and if some of them are overloaded (i.e., the relative workload is higher than the predefined tolerance level), the mobile planes algorithm is invoked. The algorithm allows setting the volume of each subdomain so that the workload of each processor is not higher than the predefined tolerance level. The domain decomposition model used by the authors assigned each subdomain to a processor and the volume adjustment was done iteratively. An implementation of the mobile planes method was incorporated into a DEM simulator developed by the authors and used in an experimental analysis for two problems of discharge of silos. The proposed method was able to balance the workload properly, starting from an unbalanced scenario to an equilibrium in which all processors shared approximately the same load.

Berger et al. [2] presented a parallel hybrid implementation for LIGGGHTS combining distributed memory, implemented with the MPI library, and shared memory, implemented with OpenMP. The main goals of including the second level of parallelism using OpenMP were increasing the parallelism level of LIGGGHTS and providing a dynamic domain decomposition strategy. The proposed hybrid model has two main components: (1) a component using MPI that is responsible for the domain decomposition into subdomains and (2) a component using MPI and OpenMP directives, which is responsible for the execution threads created for the parallel processing of particles contained in a subdomain. The authors described the strategy for dynamic domain decomposition in the full version of LIGGGHTS and how they adapted the calculation algorithms using OpenMP. Regardless of the domain decomposition strategy used, LIGGGHTS bi-univocally assigns one MPI process to each generated subdomain. The modified version generates n partitions from the corresponding subdomain, creates n OpenMP threads to process the movement and interaction of the particles within each subdomain, and assign them bi-univocally to each partition. The Recursive Coordinate Bisection algorithm was applied for generating the partitions. The strategies used by LIGGGHTS for allocating MPI processes to subdomains and dynamic domain decomposition were not modified.

Other articles have applied simple static domain decomposition approaches. Kacianauskas et al. [13] proposed a parallel algorithm for DEM simulations of polydisperse granular media using MPI. The proposed algorithm applied a homogeneous domain division in subdomains of equal volume, used the linked-cell lists for efficient contact detection, and applied the Gear predictor-corrector scheme for solving high-order differential equations. No explicit load balance method was included, and the experiments were limited to 10 processors, to minimize the impact of data communications and "maintain appropriate load balancing." Shigeto and Sakai [22] proposed a parallel algorithm using OpenMP for DEM simulations using the linked-cell method and providing support for execution on Graphics Processing Units (GPU). Different implementations were developed, accounting for the execution platform (CPU or GPU) and single or double precision for floating-point numbers. Mixed efficiency results were obtained in the experimental evaluation: the GPU version using single precision floats was 3 times faster than its CPU counterpart for small scenarios, but simulations using double precision and a large number of particles were up to 13% faster when executed in CPU. No load balancing analysis was performed or reported.

Overall, the analysis of related works allowed to conclude that high performance computing techniques have been applied to successfully improve the efficiency and reduce the execution time of DEM simulations for granular media. Those researches that have also applied load balancing techniques were able to further benefit from the capabilities of the parallel models when using a proper workload distribution. In this line of work, this article proposes a dynamic domain decomposition strategy applying mobile planes integrated to LIGGGHTS-PUBLIC. The main details of the proposed algorithm are presented in the next section.

3 Dynamic Domain Decomposition Strategy

This section describes the proposed dynamic domain decomposition strategy and its integration to the LIGGGHTS-PUBLIC software package.

3.1 Overall Description

The proposed dynamic domain decomposition strategy applies the mobile planes strategy by Markauskas et al. [15]. The first step for applying the proposed algorithm is to determine the load of a given computing resource (processor or core). This work defines the processor load metric as its number of assigned particles.

A workload reorganization/domain redefinition, using the mobile planes algorithm, is applied when any given processor's workload p_i is larger than a given threshold (fixed in 20%, but configurable) with respect to the workload of other processor p_j. Following the MPI notation (i.e., using *ranks* to identify processes in execution), the algorithm is executed when the expression in Eq. 1 holds (n is the number of processes and $l(p_i)$ is the load of process p_i).

$$\{p_i \mid \exists p_j, i, j \in \{0, \ldots, n-1\}, i \neq j, |(l(p_i) - l(p_j)| > 0.2 \times l(p_j)\} \tag{1}$$

The execution cycle of LIGGGHTS-PUBLIC was modified to include the dynamic domain decomposition of the flow. Figure 1 presents the original cycle in LIGGGHTS-PUBLIC and the modified cycle including the dynamic domain decomposition.

3.2 Process Grouping and Workload Calculation

Process grouping follows a 1D decomposition strategy where a group of processes shares the coordinates on a given axis e of the boundary points that define the subdomains, according to the user-defined partitions for axis e. For a given axis e, P_e partitions are defined and processes p_i and p_j belong to the same group if $e_i^{min} = e_j^{min}$ and $e_i^{max} = e_j^{max}$, being e_i^{min} and e_i^{max} the minimum and maximum values of the coordinates in axis e of the points that define the subdomain to which p_i was assigned. Figure 2 shows sample groups respect to axis y and z for $P_x = 4$, and $P_y = P_z = 2$.

Process grouping is performed before starting the integration loop. The boundaries defined by the new cutting points in axis e remain parallel to the axis and subdomains remain orthoedric. Thus, processes in a group do not change during the simulation and there is no need to generate process grouping many times.

The method for generating the groups for a given axis (e.g., axis x) iterates over subdomains and changes the coordinates for the remaining axis. The method creates a 3D matrix of ranks that stores $PARTS_1 \times PARTS_2 \times PARTS_3$ integers representing an attribute of the Comm class that stores in position (i, j, k) the rank of the process assigned to the subdomain identified by coordinates (i, j, k).

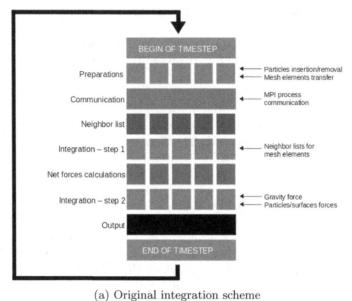

(a) Original integration scheme

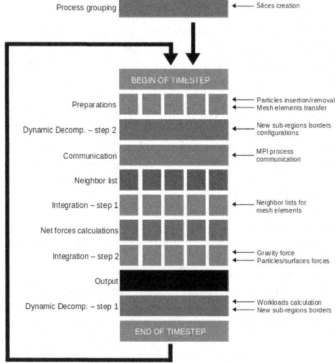

(b) Modified integration scheme

Fig. 1. Execution cycles in LIGGGHTS-PUBLIC

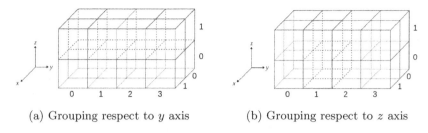

(a) Grouping respect to y axis   (b) Grouping respect to z axis

Fig. 2. Two samples of 1D decomposition process grouping

The workload of process p is the proportion of the simulated particles contained in the subdomain where p was assigned [15]. Specific modifications were performed in LIGGGHTS-PUBLIC to include data structures to store the workload information. Attributes of the Atom class were extended to (the total number of particles, natoms, the number of particles in a subdomain nlocal, and the number of ghost particles, nghost). An iterative two-stages algorithm was implemented in MPI to compute the workload of a process grouping. The algorithm is included in the new version of LIGGGHTS-PUBLIC as Verlet::compute_load(). The workload of each process grouping respect to each coordinate are stored in the sliceLoadArray matrix.

3.3 Dynamic Subdomain Boundaries

Using the information about the workload of each process grouping, the mobile planes strategy is applied to compute the new boundaries of subdomains. The computation is performed twice in the integration cycle. The details of each computation are described in this section.

New Subdomain Boundaries. The method applied to compute the workload of each process grouping is also applied to compute the new subdomain boundaries, just before ending each step of the integration cycle. The new method Verlet::generate_split() was implemented to perform this action. New boundaries computed at the end of a given step are available to be used by LIGGGHTS-PUBLIC at the beginning of the next step, where some actions that depend on the domain decomposition are performed (e.g., inserting new particles).

A Map-Reduce approach is applied, based on *Dynamic strip decomposition* (DSD) from Hanxleden and Scott [10]. A new method Verlet::coord2SubSlice() was developed to return the index of the fraction W_r^i to whom particle x(part) belongs to. Vector x (in class Atom) stores the coordinates of particles in subdomain r. All results are computed for each process and one MPI communicator (subWorldSlices) is created per each group. MPI_Reduce is used to consolidate all results in vector totalPartInSubslice. After the computations and the reduction phase, a master process centrally defines the boundaries. The proposed implementation iterates over the discretization defined for subintervals for each coordinate. A new method Verlet::newSplitPointBoxCoord() was implemented to determine the cutting point that defines the new boundary according to the index for each fraction W_r^i. When all cutting points have been computed, a flag is set to indicate that the new boundaries must be applied in the next timestep.

Application of New Boundaries. Specific code was developed and included into the `Verlet::run()` method of LIGGGHTS-PUBLIC to check if a new domain decomposition must be considered and to implement that decomposition if needed, by modifying the new boundaries between subdomains. The adjustments are performed iteratively by following the integration cycle of LIGGGHTS-PUBLIC. A specific feature of this method is that the Irregular pattern for communications is applied, in order to properly adjust the dimension of the subdomains and move particles to processes for which the associated subdomains are not contiguous to the subdomain of the origin process.

The new domain decomposition is applied by updating all the data structures that store the cutting points for each coordinate and reconfiguring the subdomains' dimensions. The `Comm` class stores in attributes `xsplit`, `ysplit`, and `zsplit` the cutting points for each axis. The new method `Verlet::applyDomain()` stores the new cutting points in the corresponding attributes and calls the methods to reconfigure the subdomains. The assignment of processes to subdomains does not change. The method `Verlet::generate_split()` is executed regularly, in intervals defined by the user, just before ending an iteration of the integration cycle. LIGGGHTS-PUBLIC regenerates the list of neighbouring particles every ten timesteps and checks if a new domain decomposition must be applied, only if the list of neighbours changed. In case the time of application of a new domain decomposition does not coincide with the timestep of LIGGGHTS-PUBLIC, the new decomposition is delayed until both timesteps are synchronized.

Two methods were implemented to define the properties of the domain decomposition: `Input::cload()` to configure parameters and `Input::dddecomp()` to define the frequency of application of the dynamic domain decomposition.

4   Experimental Evaluation

This section describes the experimental evaluation of the proposed approach using LIGGGHTS-PUBLIC.

4.1   Validation Problem and Instances

The *Binflow* problem is used for validation of the proposed domain decomposition strategy. Binflow simulates the loading and unloading of a silo, and it is part of the benchmark problems included in LIGGGHTS-PUBLIC. Figure 3 shows the silo considered in the experiments: it has two sections and a concentric exit orifice. The first (upper) section has a cylindrical shape and the second (lower) section has a funneled shape.

Particles are inserted at the top of the silo with initial velocity $\vec{v_0} = (0, 0, -1)$ and move towards the bottom of the silo in a free fall motion. The configuration of particles insertion with an initial velocity towards the bottom of the silo

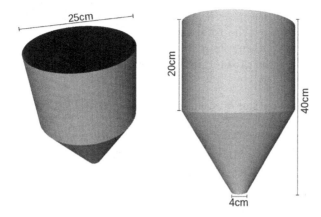

Fig. 3. Silo of the Binflow problem

simulates a charging procedure usually found in the industry, where the particles reach the top of the silo through a conveyor belt and are introduced through a hole. The discharge stage begins once the loading stage has finished and the particles leave the silo through the hole in the bottom of the structure.

The physical-chemical properties of the materials considered in the simulations are not especially relevant for the performance evaluation, so standard values were used: Young's modulus = 25 MPa, friction coefficient between particles = 0.175, friction coefficient between particle and surface = 0.2, particles density = 1,000 kg/m^3. Different instances of the problem were generated by varying two parameters in the simulations, in order to generate different workloads: (1) particle diameter and (2) number of particles in the system. The variation of these parameters allows studying the robustness of the implemented dynamic domain decomposition strategy with respect to changes in the material.

4.2 Numerical Results

Two configurations of the Binflow problem were defined: using 150,000 particles with a radius of 1.5 mm, and 450,000 particles with a radius of 1.5 mm. Two types of scenarios were defined for each configuration, in order to evaluate the two versions of the proposed algorithms: static scenarios (bf_*) and dynamic scenarios (bf_dyn_*), taking into account the strategy for domain decomposition used.

Four instances of the problem were defined for each scenario: three for the configuration with 150,000 particles, using 8 (bf_8 and bf_dyn_8), 16 (bf_16 and bf_dyn_16), and 24 (bf_24 and bf_dyn_24) processes, and one for the configuration with 450,000 particles (bf_450K and bf_dyn_450K). A version of the problem with 150,000 particles executed sequentially (bf_serial) was defined to be used as a baseline for the comparison in the computational efficiency analysis, as used in the related work by Berger et al. [2].

The detail of the instances is presented in Table 1. The table reports the instance of the problem, the total number of particles in the simulation, the number and duration of timesteps, the process configuration, and the values of frequency defined by the `cload()` and `dddecomp()` methods.

Table 1. Configurations of scenarios and instances of the Binflow problem

Instance	#particles	Timesteps		#process		Frequency	
		Total	Duration(s)	#	Config	cload	dddecomp
bf_serial	1.5×10^5	3.5×10^5	5.0×10^{-6}	1	–	–	–
Static scenario							
bf_8	1.5×10^5	3.5×10^5	5.0×10^{-6}	8	$2 \times 2 \times 2$	20000	–
bf_16	1.5×10^5	3.5×10^5	5.0×10^{-6}	16	$2 \times 2 \times 4$	25000	–
bf_24	1.5×10^5	3.5×10^5	5.0×10^{-6}	24	$2 \times 2 \times 8$	25000	–
bf_450K	4.5×10^5	1.3×10^7	5.0×10^{-6}	16	$2 \times 2 \times 4$	25000	–
Dynamic scenario							
bf_dyn_8	1.5×10^5	3.5×10^5	5.0×10^{-6}	8	$2 \times 2 \times 2$	20000	100000
bf_dyn_16	1.5×10^5	3.5×10^5	5.0×10^{-6}	16	$2 \times 2 \times 4$	25000	50000
bf_dyn_24	1.5×10^5	3.5×10^5	5.0×10^{-6}	24	$2 \times 2 \times 8$	25000	50000
bf_dyn_450K	4.5×10^5	1.3×10^7	5.0×10^{-6}	16	$2 \times 2 \times 4$	25000	100000

For each problem instance and version of the algorithm, 30 independent executions were performed to reduce the impact of non-expected deviations on the execution time due to asynchronism. Experiments with up to 8 processes were performed on a server with Intel Xeon E5430 processors, with 8 cores 2.66 GHz and 8 GB RAM. Experiments with more than 8 processes were executed on a server with AMD Opteron 6172 processor, 24 cores 2.10 GHz and 24 GB RAM. Both servers are from Cluster FING, the High Performance Computing facility at Universidad de la República, Uruguay [17]. Servers were selected according to the availability of computing resources and to consider the two most important architectures for high performance simulations nowadays.

Table 2 reports the minimum, maximum, average, and standard deviation of the execution time for the sequential, static, and dynamic versions of the simulations. The average improvement on the execution time and the speedup of the versions using 8, 16, and 24 processes and the proposed load-balancing dynamic domain decomposition are also reported.

The average improvement is computed from the results reported in Table 2, for the same configuration of processes over the different executions. For example, considering executions with 16 processes and 150,000 particles the improvement is $1 - 4{:}54/8{:}20 = 0.42$. The standard methodology to compute the relative speedup is applied, dividing the execution time of the average execution time of the sequential algorithm (bf_serial) using a single computing resource and the

Table 2. Execution time and efficiency metrics for sequential, static, and dynamic versions of the proposed algorithm for the Binflow problem

Instance	Execution time (mm:ss)				Improvement	Speedup
	Min.	Max.	Avg.	Std. dev.		
bf_serial	37:39	45:52	41:02	1:56	–	–
bf_8	9:12	9:41	9:23	0:07	–	–
bf_dyn_8	6:04	6:23	6:10	0:06	34%	6.65
bf_16	7:27	10:06	8:20	0:47	–	–
bf_dyn_16	3:50	7:36	4:54	0:44	42%	8.37
bf_24	5:55	6:23	6:04	0:07	–	–
bf_dyn_24	3:23	3:57	3:30	0:06	42%	11.72
bf_450K	80:28	88:30	84:32	2:46	–	–
bf_dyn_450K	50:02	58:17	53:30	2:22	37%	–

average execution time of the parallel algorithm using p computing resources. For example, for version bf_dyn_8 the speedup is $41:02/6:10 = 6.65$.

Figure 4 reports the performance improvement when using different number of processes and the speedup analysis for a representative instance of the Binflow problem with 150,000 particles. Results in Fig. 4 indicate that the pro-

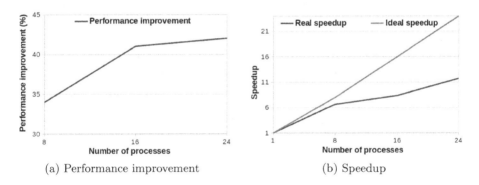

(a) Performance improvement	(b) Speedup

Fig. 4. Efficiency analysis for a representative instance of the Binflow problem with 150,000 particles

posed domain decomposition method achieved the best efficiency results when the number of processes increases. The mobile planes strategy benefits from the geometrical properties of the scenario to create more subdomains and adjust the dimension of the subdomains precisely, in order to distribute the workload evenly.

Figure 5 reports the average workload distribution among processes for version bf_mp_8 of Binflow, which is a representative case of the behavior observed

for other versions. Each column in the graphic represents the workload assigned
to each process in a given timestep of the simulation.

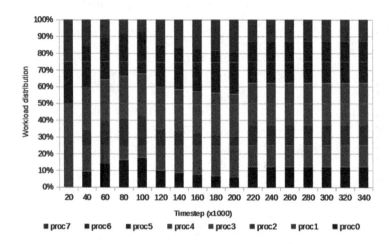

Fig. 5. Workload distribution for instance bf_mp_8 of the Binflow problem

Results in Fig. 5 summarize how the workload distribution evolves in a representative execution of the simulations. For example, the graphic shows that
for timestep 20×10^3, processes 2, 4, 6, and 8 are idle and particles in the simulation distribute to processes 1, 3, 5 and 7 (nearly 25% of the particles to each
process). This not-evenly distribution is because the dynamic load balancing
algorithm has not been called in timestep 20×10^3 and particles have not moved
to subdomains to which processes 2, 4, 6 y 8 have been assigned. When times
advances, more particles are loaded into the simulation and existing particles
move to other subdomains.

When the dynamic load balancing algorithm is applied, the workload starts to
distribute evenly, as observed for timesteps 220×10^3 to 340×10^3 in the graphic.
These results imply a better use of the available computing resources and a
correct distribution of the workload that results in a lower overall execution
time of the simulation.

5   Conclusions and Future Work

This article studied the charging and discharging process of granular media
stored in silos, and proposed and evaluated a dynamic domain decomposition method based on the mobile planes strategy to be applied for granular
media simulations. The proposed method was designed to be implemented into
the LIGGGHTS-PUBLIC open-source simulation software. It was developed to
properly balance the workload between processes in a simulation, in order to
improve the computational efficiency and reduce the overall execution time.

The experimental methodology evaluated the efficiency and the correct workload distribution of simulation using the proposed method. Several versions and instances of the Binflow problem were studied, accounting for 150,000 and 450,000 particles. The main results indicate that the proposed dynamic domain decomposition method is able to evenly distribute the workload and achieve a proper load balancing, allowing to improve the execution time of simulations up to 42%. An additional analysis over a large realistic scenario involving 450,000 particles shows that the proposed dynamic domain decomposition method has appropriate scaling capabilities.

The main lines for future work are related to extending the performance evaluation of the proposed methods by including realistic scenarios with more particles and different computing environments. In addition, the proposed method can be applied to the study of other granular media with application on science (e.g., astronomical bodies [8]) and industry (e.g., different materials).

References

1. Amritkar, A., Deb, S., Tafti, D.: Efficient parallel CFD-DEM simulations using OpenMP. J. Comput. Phys. **256**, 501–519 (2014)
2. Berger, R., Kloss, C., Kohlmeyer, A., Pirkera, S.: Hybrid parallelization of the LIGGGHTS open-source DEM code. Powder Technol. **278**, 234–247 (2015)
3. Chen, J., Rotter, J., Ooi, J., Zhong, Z.: Flow pattern measurement in a full scale silo containing iron ore. Chem. Eng. Sci. **60**, 3029–3041 (2005)
4. Chen, J., Rotter, J., Ooi, J., Zhong, Z.: Correlation between the flow pattern and wall pressures in a full scale experimental silo. Eng. Struct. **29**(9), 2308–2320 (2007)
5. Cundall, P., Strack, O.: A discrete numerical model for granular assemblies. Géotechnique **29**(1), 47–65 (1979)
6. DEM Solutions: EDEM-The leading Discrete Element Method (DEM) software. https://www.edemsimulation.com/. Accessed 6 July 2020
7. El Observador: Hallan muertos a los dos operarios de Fadisol. https://www.elobservador.com.uy/hallan-muertos-los-dos-operarios-fadisol-n297567. Accessed 6 July 2020
8. Frascarelli, D., Nesmachnow, S., Tancredi, G.: High-performance computing of self-gravity for small solar system bodies. IEEE Comput. **47**(9), 34–39 (2014)
9. Gopalakrishnan, P., Tafti, D.: Development of parallel DEM for the open source code MFIX. Powder Technol. **235**, 33–41 (2013)
10. Hanxleden, R., Scott, L.: Load balancing on message passing architectures. J. Parallel Distrib. Comput. **13**(3), 312–324 (1991)
11. Jaeger, H., Nagel, S., Behringer, R.: Granular solids, liquids, and gases. Rev. Mod. Phys. **68**(4), 1259 (1996)
12. Jenike, A., Johanson, J., Carson, J.: Bin loads–parts 2, 3 and 4: concepts, mass-flow bins, funnel-flow bins. J. Eng. Ind. **95**(1), 1–16 (1973)
13. Kačianuskas, R., Maknickas, A., Kačeniauskas, A., Markauskas, D., Balevičius, R.: Parallel discrete element simulation of poly-dispersed granular material. Adv. Eng. Softw. **41**, 52–63 (2010)
14. Kloss, C., Goniva, C., Hager, A., Amberger, S., Pirker, S.: Models, algorithms and validation for opensource DEM and CFD-DEM. Powder Technol. **12**(2/3), 140–152 (2012)

15. Markauskas, D., Kačeniauskas, A., Maknickas, A.: Dynamic domain decomposition applied to hopper discharge simulation by discrete element method. Inf. Technol. Control **40**(4), 286–292 (2011)
16. National Energy Technology Laboratory: MFIX - Multiphase Flow with Interphase eXchanges. https://mfix.netl.doe.gov/. Accessed 06 June 2020
17. Nesmachnow, S.: Computación científica de alto desempeño en la Facultad de Ingeniería. Universidad de la República. Revista de la Asociación de Ingenieros del Uruguay **61**(1), 12–15 (2010). Text in Spanish
18. Nielsen, J.: Pressures from flowing granular solids in silos. Philos. Trans.: Math. Phys. Eng. Sci. **1747**, 2667 (1998)
19. Plimpton, S.: Fast parallel algorithms for short-range molecular dynamics. J. Comput. Phys. **117**, 1–19 (1995)
20. Richard, P., Nicodemi, M., Delannay, R., Ribiere, P., Bideau, D.: Slow relaxation and compaction of granular systems. Nature Mater. **4**(2), 121–128 (2005)
21. Schuricht, T., Fürll, C., Enstad, G.: Full scale silo tests and numerical simulations of the "cone in cone" concept for mass flow. In: Levy, A., Kalman, H. (eds.) Handbook of Conveying and Handling of Particulate Solids, Handbooks of Powder Technology, vol. 10, pp. 175–180. Elsevier Science B.V. (2001)
22. Shigeto, Y., Sakai, M.: Parallel computing of discrete element method on multi-core processors. Particuology **9**, 398–405 (2011)
23. Tancredi, G., Maciel, A., Heredia, L., Richeri, P., Nesmachnow, S.: Granular physics in low-gravity environments using discrete element method. Monthly Notices Roy. Astron. Soc. **420**(4), 3368–3380 (2012)

Performance Analysis of Main Public Cloud Big Data Services Processing Brazilian Government Data

Leonardo Rebouças de Carvalho⊙, Marcelo Augusto da Cruz Motta$^{(\boxtimes)}$⊙, and Aleteia Patricia Favacho de Araújo⊙

Department of Computer Science, University of Brasilia, Brasilia, Brazil
leouesb@gmail.com, motta_marcelo@hotmail.com, aleteia@unb.br

Abstract. The growing amount of information generated by big data systems has driven the use of tools that facilitate their processing, such as Hadoop and its entire ecosystem. These tools can run on computational clouds whose benefits include payment on-demand, self-service, and elasticity. This article evaluates three cloud services that delivers fully-configured Hadoop ecosystems: AWS Elastic Map Reduce (EMR), Google Dataproc, and Microsoft HDInsight. This evaluation was made by measuring their performance and computational resource consumption by performing workloads using data from the Bolsa Família, a social welfare program of the Brazilian Government. The results showed that HDInsight had better runtime performance. Variations in the consumption of resources related to memory, disk activity, cost, and processing were found, providing an insight into the strategy of each provider that can be useful in the decision-making processes.

Keywords: Big data · Cloud computing · Hadoop · Bolsa família Program · Google cloud platform · Amazon web services · Microsoft AZURE

1 Introduction

The growing volume of data generated by society has produced an overwhelming flow of data [1]. The volume of digital data is expected to jump from 33 zettabytes in 2018 to 175 zettabytes in 2025 [25]. The amount of data generated by China alone by 2020 is expected to exceed 10 times the amount of grains of sand on the entire planet Earth [27]. This is not just an increase in business data volume, but an increase of several orders of magnitude, commonly generated outside of traditional enterprise applications and generally composed of unstructured or semi-structured information types in huge amounts and continuous flow. This reality has generated a demand for alternatives that can exploit these masses of information and new data types, since traditional means have become insufficient to meet the demand [9]. This paradigm was popularly called Big Data [26].

© Springer Nature Switzerland AG 2021
S. Nesmachnow et al. (Eds.): CARLA 2020, CCIS 1327, pp. 49–61, 2021.
https://doi.org/10.1007/978-3-030-68035-0_4

A Big Data environment faces challenges related to data processing and management [27], as well as data characteristics (whether by volume, speed, variety, etc.). These challenges could be solved by investing in large data processing centers. Given the high cost of installing and maintaining data centers, cloud computing is an alternative to enabling big data scenarios. This makes companies able to extract from the mass of data the information they need to make strategic decisions without the need for high investments.

As such, cloud providers may be made available exclusively by an organization, such as private clouds [7], or may be contracted from public clouds, such as Amazon, Google, and Microsoft. However, the process of choosing can be complex due to the wide variety of companies offering this service.

This paper aims to comparatively analyze the performance (considering the execution time and the consumption of computational resources) of the three public cloud services that are designed to process large volumes of data using Hadoop, whose providers are considered leaders of Gartner consults [8] in its magic quadrant of 2019. The services reviewed were Google's Dataproc [5], Amazon's Elastic Map Reduce (EMR) [20], and Microsoft's HDInsight. These providers were chosen because they are considered market leaders [8], in addition to their popularity and low cost. Among Big Data solutions (BigPanda [17], StreamSets [18], WebAction [19], among others), the choice of Hadoop for this study is justified because it is an open-source tool, having greater popularity and a large number of contributors that contribute the growth and improvement of the tool [11].

2   Big Data and Cloud Computing

Using Big Data presents many opportunities, whether it is supporting real-time decisions, enabling risk management, or achieving organizational goals [12], among other possibilities. Challenges such as volume, variety, velocity, veracity, collection, storage, scalability, security, and privacy are common in this context [10]. One area that has helped address these challenges is Cloud Computing.

Today, the concept of cloud computing is a well-established reality, with on-demand access to many configured computing resources [3], such as infrastructure as a service (IaaS), platform as a service (PaaS), and software as a service (SaaS). Cloud services have become a robust and affordable tool for performing complex large-scale computing tasks, spanning many IT functions like storage, processing, database services, e-mail, websites, and more.

The focus of this paper is to comparatively investigate the performance of public cloud services in Big Data processing, providing information that can support eventual decision making [7]. The providers for this analysis were chosen by consulting the Gartner Magic Quadrant [8], which indicates that the leaders in the public cloud segment, are Google Cloud Platform (GCP), Amazon Web Services (AWS), and Microsoft Windows AZURE [21].

As a public cloud, AWS [6] provides database processing, storage, and power, among other services. It also offers big data options such as Amazon Elastic

MapReduce (EMR). This service is considered one of the most prominent examples of programming structures for distributed computing in large data sets [9].

EMR provides a managed Apache Hadoop framework, promising to make it easy, fast, and cost-effective to process large volumes of data on dynamically scalable Amazon EC2 instances. EMR lets you run other components of the Hadoop ecosystem, such as Apache Spark, HBase, Presto, and more. EMR operates seamlessly with other AWS services, such as S3 and AWS DynamoDB.

GCP offers a collection of services, including already hosted applications, enabling the storage and development of applications running on Google hardware. The range of services that Google Cloud Platform offers range from IaaS with virtual machines; PaaS, with access to a scalable way of hosting where developers can use kits like JDK[1] through App Engine. Other types of services are also available, such as Dataproc, which provides Hadoop ecosystem applications for big data processing.

In Dataproc, the client assembles the environment by setting-up the quantity and configuration of each server. This service is intended to be fully manageable, fast, and simple to operate. It runs the Apache Spark and Apache Hadoop clusters, charging for the use of virtual instances.

In October 2008 Microsoft announced the launch of its cloud service platform, Azure [21]. However, only in February 2010 did the provider effectively start its operation [29]. AZURE delivers cloud services from three traditional models: SaaS, PaaS, and IaaS. These include HDInsight [30], whose delivery includes the ecosystem that makes up the Hadoop Big Data solution with a Dataproc and EMR equivalent stack. HDInsight also includes the following solutions: Apache Spark [31], Apache Kafka [34], Apache HBase [35], Apache Hive [32] and Apache Storm [33].

Both Dataproc, EMR, and HDInsight are the best of their respective providers for the massive cloud data processing offering. All follow the same operational approach to service delivery. From a parameter setting, the environment is provisioned with the requested settings within minutes. Access to the machines is through security keys created during the environment request process, or even previously existing in the cloud. Google's service offers greater flexibility compared to the others. While AWS and Microsoft offer predefined options, Google allows direct configuration of parameters such as: Hadoop version, CPU and RAM amount, disk, cluster architecture, and number of nodes. Other cluster types are also offered in these services, such as Apache Spark [31] and HBase [35], but this article will explore only Hadoop.

3   Hadoop

Big Data is changing the landscape of analytics. Analysis, using tools and techniques that work on structured data, is giving way to the chaotic universe of unstructured data, very common in today's internet blogging context. Unstructured data analysis has grown rapidly in importance because of its ability to

---

[1] JDK - *Java Development Kit.*

exploit information from diverse sources such as social networks and virtual traffic, for example [28].

To meet the new challenges brought by unstructured data, a number of tools and technologies have grown in number and relevance. One platform that stands out in this context is Hadoop. The combination of a powerful Hadoop Distributed File System (HDFS) and a divide and conquer (MapReduce) processing strategy has made Hadoop a popular choice for big data projects.

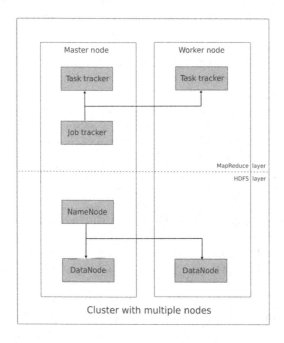

Fig. 1. Hadoop architecture [16].

Hadoop's processing system is quite different from traditional systems. In a web system, for example, data is sent for processing on a centralized server that does all the work and then returns the result to the client. Assuming there is a need to process a large data mass, using the traditional approach would need to transfer them to the server, and this can be time consuming and requires the server to support the volume of data. On the other hand, Hadoop's strategy is the opposite: once the data is loaded into your distributed file system, the application is sent to each node that holds a fraction of the data and that node performs the processing. With a portion of the result, the node sends it for consolidation. Figure 1 illustrates Hadoop architecture, showing the relationship between the main node and the working nodes.

Hadoop's strategy takes advantage of parallelism to leverage the reduction in processing time [14]. However, its implementation is more complex than the traditional one, and for this reason several other tools have emerged to increase its potential and reduce complexity. These tools range from those for working with the application like Pig [22] to even database systems like HBase [35]. This whole set of tools, each with its own specific functions, has been referred to as the Hadoop ecosystem [15].

4 The Bolsa Família Program

The Brazilian government has been providing data on various governmental actions and programs. This information results in masses of data from various analyses, either for content interpretation or performance testing. Considering the large volume of data as well as the social importance, in this work we chose to use the Bolsa Familia Program (BFP) database. The BFP data were obtained from the Transparency Portal, a project of the Federal Controllership of Union, which provides various public data, with the aim of improving the transparency of public management [4].

The Bolsa Família Program assists in tackling extreme poverty and combating inequality throughout the Brazilian territory. Families receive a card and a Social Identification Number (NIS) through which it is possible, for example, to identify how many benefits have been directed to a particular family, as well as the state in which the reside. Despite its broad potential, this work took advantage of only the volume of data to simulate actual workloads on the evaluated cloud services.

5 Methodology

In order to exploit the potential of massive data processing services, two workloads were developed on the Bolsa Família Program data. Each workload has a processing characteristic and will be further detailed in Sect. 5.1.

To perform the tests, a service cluster was provisioned in each of the providers according to the configurations shown in Fig. 2. Once the cluster was delivered by the provider, the Node Exporter service was configured on all its instances to enable communication with the monitoring stack. In each case, an additional instance was created outside the cluster and within the same geographic region to perform dedicated monitoring of CPU, RAM, network traffic, and disk activity without geographic location interference. The architecture of this stack is made up of the Prometheus [36], NodeExporter [37] and Grafana [38] tools, that can be better understood in Fig. 3, which shows that NodeExporter collects the metrics directly on the machines and passes them to Prometheus, which keeps periodic records of this information. Grafana, on the other hand, obtains Prometheus historical series and displays analytical panels. In more elaborate configurations Grafana can trigger alerts in certain situations. These tools were chosen because

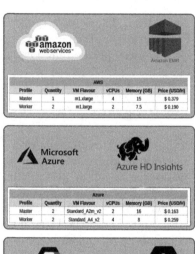

Fig. 2. Clusters parameters.

they are open source alternatives, widely used by the community and simple to configure.

Algorithm 1: Workload 1

Result: Identifies how many payments were made per federation unit
while *year in 2014 to 2019* **do**
    while *month in jan to dec* **do**
        | Result[year][month][federationUnit] = sum(count(hdfs[A-Z][a-z]))
    end
end

Algorithm 2: Workload 2

Result: Identifies how many payments were made for each identification
        number (NIS)
while *year in 2014 to 2019* **do**
    while *month in jan to dec* **do**
        | result[NIS] = sum(hdfs[NIS])
    end
end

Fig. 3. Interactions between NodeExporter, Prometheus and Grafana.

Ten tests were performed for each workload in each cluster, enabling averages for each monitored metric, preventing any single event from interfering with the overall test result. The tests were performed between December, 27, 2019 and January, 01, 2020 and lasted approximately 12 hours. In each provider, the cluster configurations were selected in order to guarantee the greatest possible similarity in their architectures.

The EMR and Dataproc clusters are equivalent in number of nodes, processors and memory configuration, with one master node (4Vcpu, 16 GB) and two workers nodes (2Vcpu, 8 GB). In HDInsigth, the minimum allowed architecture was two masters nodes (2Vcpu, 16 GB) and two workers nodes(4Vcpu, 8 GB). The standard storage services for each product were selected, in the case of EMR, EBS (gp2) [39], for Dataproc the Standard Permanent Disks (pd-standard) [40], and for Hdinsigth, Storage - General use V1. [41].

The physical location of data centers was not considered to be a relevant factor for testing because measurements occurred exclusively within the internal virtual network created by the providers. The process of obtaining data was not considered for the calculation of metrics.

The mass of data was composed of information on family allowance receipts from January 2014 to November 2019 and totaled approximately 90 GB of data. This was used by both workloads and was downloaded only once from each provider.

5.1   Test Scenarios

In order to obtain a behavior analysis of the selected providers, two calculation processes were created under a mass of data. The Algorithm 1 identifies how many payments were made per state. The processing result has two columns, the first being the number of scholarships paid to beneficiaries in the period comprised by the mass of data and the second the state.

The Algorithm 2 identifies how many payments were paid for each identification number (NIS), that is, the frequency of receipts grouped by the number of times the NIS appears. Based on the result of the first processing, another calculation is made to measure how many times each receipt appears. Thereby, the workload can quantify how many families received payments from 1 to "n" times in the period. The result has 2 columns, the first being the amount of payments a family has received, and the second the number of beneficiaries who have received that amount of times. The workload 2 uses the features of the Hadoop cluster differently from workload 1 as it does two successive MapReduce runs, giving providers the opportunity to demonstrate different strategies for different issues.

5.2   Metrics

In order to evaluate different aspects of provider performance, the following metrics were observed while performing workloads:

– runtime;
– CPU consumption;
– memory consumption;
– disk activity;
– network traffic.

6   Related Works

In the paper [2] the authors make an analysis of energy efficiency and performance of Hadoop in physical and virtual clusters, but the workload used is the benchmark of Hadoop itself using TeraSort [23] and TeraGen [24] as workload tools. A comparison is made between the different data allocation and processing configurations, but it does not refer to the performance of different public cloud providers, the objective of this work. On the other hand, this study proposes a comparison between providers and uses a different data mass, composed by Bolsa Família data. In addition, it performs workloads directly on the main server from the provider-supplied Hadoop installation, eliminating interference from intermediate tools.

The article [13] compares the performance of the AWS EC2 public cloud service with a private cloud managed by OpenNebula cloud controller for the creation/destruction, suspension/recovery, and restart of virtual machines tasks. The results demonstrate that elasticity can be provided by the evaluated platforms at reasonable times, and that the choice of either cloud depends on the applications and the user's technical and financial conditions. This article is not intended to compare public and private clouds, but different public cloud providers. Nor does it focus on elasticity, but on another fundamental requirement of cloud services: performance.

7   Results

The graphical analysis of the data allows us to observe the behavior of each provider in the face of the challenges proposed by the two workloads of this work. The horizontal axis (x) shows the result obtained in each execution of the same workflow. The vertical axis (y) was reserved for the parameter values under analysis. The AWS EMR service curve is in blue, the Dataproc, Google Cloud curve is yellow, and AZURE HDInsight is red.

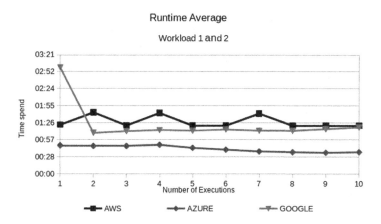

Fig. 4. Runtime average of Workloads 1 and 2.

Figure 4 shows that the execution time of the 10 tests, for workloads 1 and 2, has a better result in AZURE when compared to the others, with an average of 42 min per execution. It was also observed that Dataproc, even with an average of approximately 84 min per execution, suffered time degradation only in the first round, better than the EMR, which obtained the highest average of 88 min. This performance divergence from AZURE to the others suggests the interference of the second master in the architecture, which could not be equalized for testing because the provider did not allow HDInsight cluster configuration like the other providers did.

7.1   Resource Consumption Analysis

The methodology used to consolidate the data obtained by monitoring the instances of each cluster, considers the average maximum CPU utilization of each node, obtaining the average consumption per cluster. Figure 5 shows graphs of cluster-consolidated CPU and RAM Memory consumption during the ten runs of workloads 1 and 2.

It can be seen that CPU usage from the 5th execution onwards remains fairly close across all three providers, however, while AZURE has remained close to 100% in the first three runs, it is clear that Google has remained below 40%

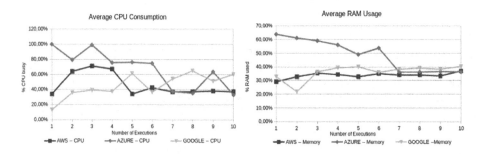

Fig. 5. CPU and RAM Memory usage.

and AWS, between the two, near 60% usage. Thus, it can be noted that AZURE used more than twice the computational processing power employed by Google and AWS to accomplish the same task.

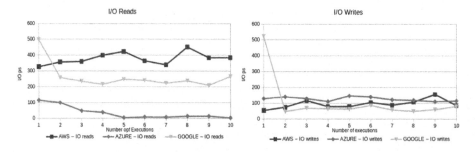

Fig. 6. Disk activity per cluster (reads and writes).

It is also possible to see that during the first six runs, AZURE servers promote large sinusoidal oscillations in the memory consumption curves. This demonstrates intense management of this feature, preventing continued growth. From the 7th run on, AZURE's memory consumption curve follows the Google and AWS threshold, but demonstrates lower manageability as it maintains long periods of high consumption. As of the 7th run, the memory consumption of the three providers is equivalent to close to 40%, regardless of the performance of the additional master node in AZURE.

Figure 6 shows the cluster disks utilization. It considers the maximum write and read I/O values of all nodes in the cluster, allowing the analysis of the writing and reading dynamics on the disks in the three providers. It is possible to notice that only AZURE had a higher writing rate than reading rate. It is also noticeable that Google, both in reading and writing had, in its first execution a much higher average than the other executions. In relation to writing, the three providers remain very close after the first execution, varying around 100 I/O per second, while in relation to reading, AZURE obtained the lowest rate, followed by Google with records close to 300 I/O per second and finally AWS with registers close to 400 I/O per second.

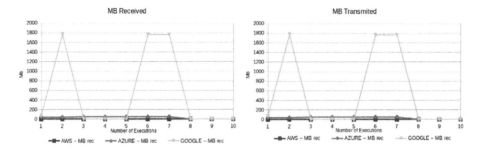

Fig. 7. Network traffic per cluster (received and transmited).

Figure 7 shows the average of the maximum network traffic records, considering both the transmission and reception of data through the interfaces present in the cluster instances.

Their analysis shows that Google's servers demonstrated higher network resource consumption than AZURE and AWS, particularly in the 2nd, 6th, and 5th runs of workloads. In all other runs, the three providers do not show much network activity, although in AWS there are more variations than in Google, though small.

8   Conclusion

Given the tests performed, Microsoft AZURE provider, through the HDInsight service, performed better then Google's Dataproc competitors and AWS EMR. Although the parameters obtained in the tests were calculated to compensate for the difference between cluster component configurations, the graph interpretation shows that despite the linearity of workload execution times, Microsoft AZURE has a higher resource consumption, suggesting concern with resource pricing at the provider.

Google's Dataproc, while consuming more time on its first run, remained ahead and more constant than Amazon's EMR on other workload runs, demonstrating superior efficiency by keeping disk writes down while apparently generating more network traffic in three of the ten runs.

Amazon's EMR, which demonstrated higher memory consumption efficiency compared to other providers, also proved to be more efficient in CPU utilization from the 5th run of workloads, however it required considerably more disk reads to complete the task.

Considering the cost per hour and the average time of workload executions in each provider, Microsoft AZURE even suggesting a higher consumption of resources, proves to be the most viable provider in relation to cost, with an average of approximately USD 0.30 per execution. Followed by Google with USD 0.59 and Amazon USD 0.83.

For future work, it is suggested to use a data source with a more significant size allowing better comparisons to be made with different workloads, including studies that explore other criteria (such as resilience, elasticity, among others) using clusters with different configurations than those used in this work, in order to increasingly support the decision process in choosing the cloud service for big data processing.

In addition, it is suggested that work be carried out to interpret data from analyses of the Bolsa Família Program database, exploring causes and consequences of discrepancies, either in the geographical distribution of payments or in the amount of benefits paid to some beneficiaries of the program.

Considering academic research as a response to the real demands of society, this comparative study can be an important tool in fostering decision making, whether for users looking for better cloud service performance alternatives in Big Data processing, or for providers to identify and correct weaknesses, and enhance the most robust aspects of services.

References

1. Hashem, I., Yaqoob, I., Anua, N., Mokhtar, S., Gani, A., Khan, S.: The rise of "big data" on cloud computing, review and open research issues. Inf. Syst. **47**, 98–115 (2015)
2. Feller, E., Ramakrishnan, L., Morin, C.: Performance and energy efficiency of big data applications in cloud environments. J. Parallel Distrib. Comput. **79–80**, 80–89 (2015)
3. Huane, L.: Big data drives cloud adoption in enterprise. IEEE Internet Comput. **17**, 68–71 (2013)
4. Brasil, Cidadãos e Justiça. http://www.brasil.gov.br/cidadania-e-justica/2017/05/cidadaos-tem-acesso-a-dados-do-cadastro-unico-na-internet. Accessed 23 June 2019
5. DataProc, Google. https://cloud.google.com/dataproc. Accessed 23 Dec 2019
6. Amazon Web Services, Amazon. https://docs.aws.amazon.com. Accessed 23 June 2019
7. Mell, P., Grance, T.: The NIST definition of cloud computing. National Institute of Standards and Technology (2011)
8. Gartner, magic quadrant for cloud infrastructure as a service, worldwide. https://www.gartner.com/doc/reprints?id=1-1CMAPXNO&ct=190709&st=sb. Accessed 22 Dec 2019
9. Correia, R.C.M., et al.: Hadoop cluster deployment: a methodological approach. Information (2019). http://www.mdpi.com/2078-2489/9/6/131
10. Zicari, R.V., Akerkar, R. (eds.): Big Data Computing. CRC Press, Boco Raton (2014)
11. Franco, A.L., Bessa, G.M.A.: Aplicabilidade, utilidade e ganhos do Big Data utilizando a ferramenta Hadoop, Caderno de Estudos em Sistemas de Informação (2016)
12. Kaur, P.D., Kaur, A., Kaur, S.: Performance Analysis in Bigdata, Int. J. Inf. Technol. Comput. Sci. (2015)
13. Azevêdo, E.M., et al.: Nuvem Pública vesrus Privada. In: Anais X Workshop em Clouds e Aplicações (WCGA, Variações de desempenho de Infraestrutura para Elasticidade, p. 2012 (2012)

14. Assunção, M.D., Calheiros, R.N., Neto, M.A.S., Bianchi, S., Buyya, R.: Big Data computing and clouds, trends and future directions. J. Parallel Distrib. Comput. **79**, 3–15 (2015)
15. Haikal, L.: Prevenção da Dengue utilizando o sistema especialista para Big Data Hadoop. Revista Academus - Gestão e Tecnologia (2017)
16. Scolati, R., Fronza, I., El Ioini, N., Samir, A., Pahl, C.: A containerized big data streaming architecture for edge cloud computing on clustered single-board devices (2019)
17. BigPanda, Big Panda: Autonomous Operations, Intelligent Automation for IT Incident Management. https://www.bigpanda.io/. Accessed 18 Apr 2019
18. StreamSets, StreamSets: Where DevOps Meets Data Integration, Efficiency. Agility. Reliability. Confidence. https://streamsets.com/. Accessed 18 Apr 2019
19. LuxCer, WebAction. http://webaction.luxcer.com/platform/. Accessed 18 Apr 2019
20. Amazon, EMR. https://aws.amazon.com/emr/. Accessed 18 Apr 2019
21. Microsoft, Azure. https://azure.microsoft.com. Accessed 18 Oct 2019
22. Apache, Pig. https://pig.apache.org/. Accessed 18 Apr 2019
23. MAPR, TeraSort Benchmark Comparison for YARN. https://mapr.com/whitepapers/terasort-benchmark-comparison-yarn/assets/terasort-comparison-yarn.pdf. Accessed 18 Apr 2019
24. Nghiem, P., Figueira, S.: Towards efficient resource provisioning in MapReduce. J. Parallel Distrib. Comput. **95**, 29–41 (2016)
25. Reinsel, D., Gantz, J., Rydning, J.: The digitization of the world: from edge to core, IDC (2018)
26. Uthayasankar, S., Kamal, M.M., Irani, Z., Weerakkody, V.: Critical analysis of Big Data challenges and analytical methods. J. Bus. Res. **70**, 263–286 (2017)
27. Xuewei, L., Xue Yan, L.: Big data and its key technology in the future. Comput. Sci. Eng. **20**, 75–88 (2018)
28. Matrizes, E., Schroeder, R.: Big data: shaping knowledge, shaping everyday life, vol. 12, pp. 135–163 (2018). https://www.revistas.usp.br/matrizes/article/view/149604
29. Hauger, D.: Windows Azure General Availability. https://blogs.microsoft.com/blog/2010/02/01/windows-azure-general-availability/. Accessed 18 May 2019
30. Microsoft, HDInsight. https://azure.microsoft.com/pt-br/services/hdinsight. Accessed 18 Dec 2019
31. Apache, Spark. https://spark.apache.org/. Accessed 18 Dec 2019
32. Apache, Hive. https://hive.apache.org/. Accessed 18 Dec 2019
33. Apache, Storm. https://storm.apache.org/. Accessed 18 Dec 2019
34. Apache, Kafta. https://kafka.apache.org/. Accessed 18 Dec 2019
35. Apache, Hbase. https://hbase.apache.org/. Accessed 18 Dec 2019
36. The Linux Foundation, Prometheus. https://prometheus.io/. Accessed 18 Dec 2019
37. The Linux Foundation, Node Exporter. https://prometheus.io/docs/guides/node-exporter/. Accessed 18 Dec 2019
38. Grafana Labs, Grafana. https://grafana.com/. Accessed 18 Dec 2019
39. Amazon Web Services, EBS Volume Types. https://docs.aws.amazon.com/pt-br/AWSEC2/latest/UserGuide/ebs-volume-types.html. Accessed 18 Aug 2020
40. Google, Google Cloud Platform. https://cloud.google.com/compute/docs/disks/performance. Accessed 18 Aug 2020
41. Microsoft Azure, HDInsight. https://docs.microsoft.com/pt-br/azure/hdinsight/hdinsight-hadoop-use-blob-storage. Accessed 18 Aug 2020

Accelerating Machine Learning Algorithms with TensorFlow Using Thread Mapping Policies

Matheus W. Camargo$^{(\boxtimes)}$, Matheus S. Serpa, Danilo Carastan-Santos, Alexandre Carissimi, and Philippe O. A. Navaux

Informatics Institute, Federal University of Rio Grande do Sul – UFRGS, Porto Alegre, Brazil
{mwcamargo,msserpa,danilo.csantos,asc,navaux}@inf.ufrgs.br

Abstract. Machine Learning (ML) algorithms are increasingly being used in various scientific and industrial problems, with the time of execution of these algorithms as an important concern. In this work, we explore mappings of threads in multi-core architectures and their impact on new ML algorithms running with Python and TensorFlow. Using smart thread mapping, we were able to reduce the execution time of both training and inference phases for up to 46% and 29%, respectively.

Keywords: Machine learning · Thread mapping · Multi-core · TensorFlow

1 Introduction

Due to the growth of data and processing power availability nowadays, machine learning (ML) is an area of research that is in constant progress. Such progress is fueled by the increasing use of ML in various scientific and industrial applications, such as fraud detection systems, recommendation mechanisms, autonomous cars, demand forecasting, and even automated medical diagnosis services [5,17,20].

However, the emergence of more complex ML algorithms, combined with the increase in the amount of data available, leads to increasing demand for computational power. Studying ways to improve the performance of these algorithms, therefore, becomes an essential task. One of the most common strategies to increase ML algorithms' performance is using the Graphics Processing Unit (GPU) computing [16]. However, using GPUs requires knowledge about the GPU specificities, and often leads to either code refactorization or partial/full dependence on specific ML libraries or GPU manufacturers.

In this context, running ML algorithms on multi-core architectures is still a significant matter, since CPUs (Central Processing Units) are more common (and thus more broadly available) processing devices. In regards to CPU computing, thread mapping presents itself as a useful resource to increase performance

S. Nesmachnow et al. (Eds.): CARLA 2020, CCIS 1327, pp. 62–70, 2021.
https://doi.org/10.1007/978-3-030-68035-0_5

on multi-core architectures, since such techniques can provide performance gains with low implementation cost [2,8,18].

By aiming at keeping threads that share data near each other in terms of memory hierarchy for thread mapping policies, several applications can benefit from performance improvement by reducing the latency associated with remote memory access [4,7,14,19]. Therefore, this work aims to answer the following question: *Can smart thread mapping policies accelerate the performance of recent ML algorithms on multi-core architectures?*

To shed light on this question, in this work, we analyze how new machine learning algorithms react when using different thread mapping policies. We utilized an ML benchmark, namely AI-Benchmark [11,12], which relies on Python and TensorFlow. Experimental results have shown that numerous ML algorithms benefited from using smart thread mappings.

We organized the remainder of this paper in the following manner. Section 2 shows the related work. Section 3 presents a brief discussion of the ML algorithms present in the benchmark used. Section 4 describes the experimental methodology used in the research, presenting how the experiments were organized as well as an explanation of the thread mappings used. Section 5 discusses the results, and lastly, Sect. 6 presents conclusions and future work.

We follow a reproducible and open methodology in our investigation. This work's companion material is publicly available at https://github.com/MatheusWoeffel/thread-data-mapping, containing the application code, the data analysis code, and all data collected during experiments that culminated in this manuscript.

2   Related Work

Thread mapping of applications is studied mainly in the context of High-Performance Computing (HPC). For instance, Mazouz *et al.* [15] analyze the thread mapping effects on the SPEC OMP benchmark, which is a well known HPC benchmark. They show that specific thread mappings can significantly improve the performance of SPEC OMP.

In light of these findings, many works [3,6,9] also propose algorithms to automatically perform active thread mapping of applications. However, in one of our previous works [18] we show that in most cases, the execution time largely depends on the patterns of memory access and data sharing between the threads that constitute the algorithms, hence being challenging to determine which type of algorithms may benefit from thread mapping without a previous execution. This highlights the importance of experimental studies with a broad set of applications.

Similarly, in [1], broquedis et al. demonstrated that thread mapping could outperform the first-touch default mapping used in Linux kernels, employing a dynamic thread mapping from an OpenMP runtime perspective. You et al. [21] refactor machine learning algorithms in order to improve communication.

Although the performance of thread mapping optimizations may be hardware architecture-dependent and hence not portable, [22] showed that when those optimizations are not static, a certain degree of portability can be achieved. Using data locality, the authors proposed a mapping algorithm that presented not only better performance but as well as lower energy consumption.

3   Machine Learning Algorithms Optimized

The AI-Benchmark has 21 machine learning algorithms, implemented using Python and Tensorflow [12]. The applications include different fields such as computer vision, digital image processing and natural language processing. Each algorithm has two phases: (i) training, where ML models are optimized by the respective training algorithms and (ii) inference, where the trained model is used for its final purpose (predictions, image processing). Although a more significant part of the computational cost of ML algorithms comes from training, we analyzed both phases of execution, aiming to further insight into how the mappings and different types of applications behave.

The applications are separated as follows:

- **Object Recognition/Classification:** Automatic recognition of an object present in the input. The applications are MobileNet-V2 Large, MobileNet-V2 and Inception-V3.
- **Face Recognition:** Automatic detection of a person based on a face photo. The application is MobileNet-V3.
- **Optical Character Recognition:** Prediction of text based on images (e.g logos). The applications are CRNN and Bi-LSTMs.
- **Image Deblurring:** Reduce the blur effect on images, making them sharper. The application is Pynet.
- **Image Super-Resolution:** Upgrade the image resolution from a downgraded version. The applications are VGG-19 and SRGAN;
- **Bokeh Simulation:** Insert blur effect only on the background of pictures, maintaining the actual focus of the picture. The application is Unet.
- **Semantic Segmentation:** Automatic detection of categories of objects (e.g: pedestrians, cars, roads) in a traffic picture. The application is Deeplab-V3+.
- **Photo Enhancement:**Transformation of pictures of low-end devices to approximations of DSLR cameras pictures. The application is DPED-Resnet.
- **Text Completion:** Automatic fill of word gaps present in a text. Similar to word suggestions in new smartphone keyboards. The applications are Static RNN and LSTM;
- **Memory Limits:** Image processing of high-resolution images on memory constraints. The applications are SRCNN 9-5-5.

All applications listed above use 50 epochs for training iterations and MSE for loss function, Adam for optimizer and a learning rate of 10^{-14}. Table 1 list each application with its input size and batch size.

The benchmark uses the TensorFlow library, which we used the Intel TensorFlow [13] implementation to select between the mappings described in the Experimental Methodology section. It is important to notice that by using this implementation, the algorithms run entirely on the CPU. More details of the benchmark can be accessed in the benchmark paper [12] or the actual Python package that we used in the research [10].

Table 1. Input and batch size of different applications.

Application	Input size	Batch size
Deeplab	224 × 224	50
ICNet	1024 × 1563	10
Inception-Resnet-V2	346 × 346	8
Inception-V3	346 × 346	20
Inception-V4	346 × 346	10
LSTM-Sentiment	1024 × 300	10
MobileNet-V2	224 × 224	50
Nvidia-SPADE	128 × 128	1
Pixel-RNN	64 × 64	10
PSPNet	512 × 512	1
ResNet-DPED	128 × 128	15
Resnet-SRGAN	512 × 512	5
Resnet-V2-152	256 × 256	10
Resnet-V2-50	346 × 346	10
SRCNN-9-5-5	512 × 512	10
U-Net	256 × 256	4
VGG-16	224 × 224	2
VGG-19-Super-Res	224 × 224	10

4   Experimental Methodology

In this section, we present how we assess the impact of the different mappings on AI-Benchmark algorithms. First, we present a description of the different mappings used. Lastly, we discuss the architecture, the execution environment, and how they are essential in thread mapping.

The following thread mappings were utilized:

- **Baseline:** Default mapping employed by Linux focuses on load balancing on the nodes available for execution.
- **Round Robin:** Mapping in which the threads are mapped cyclically between the nodes available for execution.
- **Compact:** Mapping in which threads with nearby ids are mapped to nearby nodes, trying to minimize the distance between neighboring threads.

– **Scatter:** Mapping where the threads are arranged in the most evenly way possible between the nodes available for execution, in this way, is the opposite of compact.

The distance between the threads mentioned before is related to the distance between two cores executing these threads concerning how far these cores are in terms of the memory hierarchy. In that way, two threads running on the same processor are closer than two threads running on different NUMA nodes. As the first threads may share data by subsequent read/writes on L1 caches and the latter could only be shared by remote read/writes, the latter's latency is higher, thus hazarding an application's performance.

The experiments were partitioned into several steps. Each step consists of several executions of the benchmark applications, considering all possible combinations of thread mappings and the applications themselves. The order of combinations was randomized, and in total, each combination was executed ten times intertwined with other applications. At the end of each step, the execution times of all AI-Benchmark algorithms were collected.

The experiments were performed on a computational node, containing two Haswell Intel Xeon E5-2650 v3 (Q3'14) processors, 2.3 GHz, totaling 20 cores and 40 threads for each node.

5 AI Benchmark Performance Results

In this section, we show the usage of thread mapping policies in the algorithms of AI Benchmark implemented with Python and TensorFlow. Inference and training modes are presented in their proper subsection.

5.1 Improving Performance of Training Algorithms

The algorithm's performance improvements in training mode when thread mapping policies were used is presented in Fig. 1. We present the normalized execution time where the baseline is the Linux Default mapping. In the X-axis, the algorithms are presented, and finally, on the Y-axis, the performance improvements for each algorithm.

The highest performance improvement with thread mapping was obtained by the Resnet-V2-152 (46.8%) when the scatter mapping was used. We can further note that there were other applications on which the highest performance improvement was obtained with scatter mapping as well: Deeplab, Inception-Resnet-V2, Inception V4, Resnet-V2-152.

Another group of applications presented a different behavior, with the highest and very similar performance improvements achieved by compact and scatter mappings: MobileNet-V2, PSPNet, U-net, VGG-16, VGG-19 Super Res. As scatter and compact employ different strategies for the placement of threads, a question can be raised on the origin of such gains in the above applications. A hypothesis is that, as the threads are placed differently relative to each other,

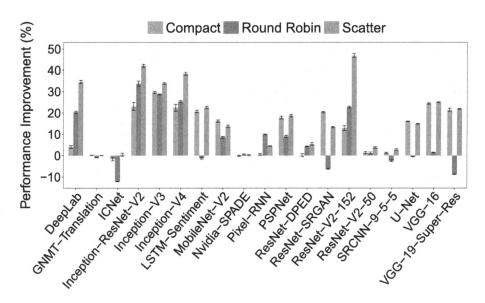

Fig. 1. Performance improvement using thread mapping policies in training algorithms

those gains were not provided by reduced latency when the threads shared data, but rather because of improved data locality. A strategy to verify such a hypothesis is discussed further in Sect. 6.

Besides, we can remark that although all thread mapping policies provided some performance improvement in general, round-robin mapping presented a performance loss in several applications such as ICNet, ResNet-SRGAN, SRCNN-955 and VGG-19-Super-Res. It happens because round-robin does not take the memory hierarchy for its decisions, resulting in lousy mapping decisions.

5.2   Performance Improvements for Inference Algorithms

The algorithm's performance improvements in inference mode when thread mapping policies were used are presented in Fig. 2. The axis is the same as in Fig. 1, the difference being that now the results are from the inference algorithms.

In the inference algorithms, the highest performance gain was 29.5%, obtained by the Inception-V4 when compact was used. Similar to what happened to the training applications scatter also presented similar results with other applications such as Inception-V3, Inception-V4, PSPNet, Resnet-V2-152, Resnet-V2-50 and SRC-955. As an exception, the LSTM-Sentient presented similar performance improvement when RR or Scatter was used.

Comparably to the training algorithms results, some applications presented a loss of performance when Round Robin mapping is used. The reason for this behavior was already discussed in the previous section. It is important to remark that when the inference and training algorithms are compared, all training algorithms presented a more significant reduction of execution time.

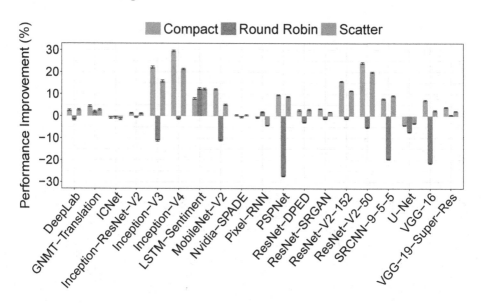

Fig. 2. Performance improvement using thread mapping policies in inference algorithms

6   Conclusion and Future Work

Machine Learning (ML) algorithms and models are becoming common in many scientific and industrial applications. The performance of ML algorithms has become, therefore, one of the main concerns. Researchers and practitioners endlessly pursue for faster processing times, which can be rather challenging.

In this work, we exploit smart policies to assign threads to cores (the so-called thread mapping policies). The objective is to attest if we can obtain better performances from several ML algorithms and models present in the AI Benchmark built on top of TensorFlow and Python. We performed an extensive and publicly available[1] experimental campaign, and the results showed significant performance improvements by applying such smart mappings, up to 46%, and 29% for the algorithms' training and inference phases.

It is important to highlight here that these performance improvements were obtained by only changing the application environment variable that set the thread mapping policy. These included compacting the threads into the cores or scattering them among the cores. Using these smart policies, the ML algorithms and models can process faster than using the default system's policy. There was no change to the ML algorithms and models to achieve such performances, which reinforces the advantage and importance of choosing an appropriate thread mapping.

---

[1] Full companion material at https://github.com/MatheusWoeffel/thread-data-mapping.

An appropriate thread mapping can be even more critical for processors with low processing power, such as those present on mobile devices. Many of the ML algorithms and models considered in this work run on mobile devices, where the processing time on the inference phase of the algorithms is critical. In this regard, we foresee that similar performance improvements can be achieved on mobile devices if the underlying systems implement the smart thread mapping policies adopted in this work.

Besides asserting if thread mapping can accelerate the processing of ML algorithms on mobile devices, we can devise several future works. Arguably the most engaging future work is to find the origin of the observed performance improvements. We can achieve this task by looking at the data present in the hardware counters during the algorithms' execution. With this further investigation, we hope to define the thread mapping policy beforehand (i.e., before executing the algorithms).

Acknowledgments. This work has been partially supported by Petrobras (2016/00133-9, 2018/00263-5) and Green Cloud project (2016/2551-0000 488-9), from FAPERGS and CNPq Brazil, program PRONEX 12/2014. We also thank *RICAP*, partially funded by the Ibero-American Program of Science and Technology for Development (*CYTED*), Ref. 517RT0529.

References

1. Broquedis, F., Furmento, N., Goglin, B., Namyst, R., Wacrenier, P.-A.: Dynamic task and data placement over NUMA architectures: an OpenMP runtime perspective. In: Müller, M.S., de Supinski, B.R., Chapman, B.M. (eds.) IWOMP 2009. LNCS, vol. 5568, pp. 79–92. Springer, Heidelberg (2009). https://doi.org/10.1007/978-3-642-02303-3_7
2. Castro, M., Góes, L.F.W., Méhaut, J.F.: Adaptive thread mapping strategies for transactional memory applications. J. Parallel Distrib. Comput. **74**(9), 2845–2859 (2014)
3. Cruz, E.H., Diener, M., Alves, M.A., Pilla, L.L., Navaux, P.O.: LAPT: a locality-aware page table for thread and data mapping. Parallel Comput. **54**, 59–71 (2016)
4. Cruz, E.H., Diener, M., Serpa, M.S., Navaux, P.O.A., Pilla, L., Koren, I.: Improving communication and load balancing with thread mapping in manycore systems. In: 2018 26th Euromicro International Conference on Parallel, Distributed and Network-Based Processing (PDP), pp. 93–100. IEEE (2018)
5. Culkin, R., Das, S.R.: Machine learning in finance: the case of deep learning for option pricing. J. Invest. Manag. **15**(4), 92–100 (2017)
6. Diener, M., Cruz, E.H., Alves, M.A., Navaux, P.O., Busse, A., Heiss, H.U.: Kernel-based thread and data mapping for improved memory affinity. IEEE Trans. Parallel Distrib. Syst. **27**(9), 2653–2666 (2015)
7. Diener, M., Cruz, E.H., Pilla, L.L., Dupros, F., Navaux, P.O.: Characterizing communication and page usage of parallel applications for thread and data mapping. Perform. Eval. **88**, 18–36 (2015)
8. Eastep, J., Wingate, D., Agarwal, A.: Smart data structures: an online machine learning approach to multicore data structures. In: Proceedings of the 8th ACM International Conference on Autonomic Computing, pp. 11–20 (2011)

9. He, J., Chen, W., Tang, Z.: NestedMP: enabling cache-aware thread mapping for nested parallel shared memory applications. Parallel Comput. **51**, 56–66 (2016)
10. Ignatov, A.: AI Benchmark. https://pypi.org/project/ai-benchmark/ (2020). Accessed 29 March 2020
11. Ignatov, A., et al.: AI benchmark: running deep neural networks on android smartphones. In: Proceedings of the European Conference on Computer Vision (ECCV) (2018)
12. Ignatov, A., et al.: AI benchmark: all about deep learning on smartphones in 2019. In: 2019 IEEE/CVF International Conference on Computer Vision Workshop (ICCVW), pp. 3617–3635. IEEE (2019)
13. Intel: Intel TensorFlow. https://pypi.org/project/intel-tensorflow/ (2020). Accessed. In: 29 May 2020
14. Kandemir, M., Ozturk, O., Muralidhara, S.P.: Dynamic thread and data mapping for NoC based CMPS. In: 2009 46th ACM/IEEE Design Automation Conference, pp. 852–857. IEEE (2009)
15. Mazouz, A., Barthou, D., et al.: Performance evaluation and analysis of thread pinning strategies on multi-core platforms: case study of SPEC OMP applications on intel architectures. In: 2011 International Conference on High Performance Computing & Simulation, pp. 273–279. IEEE (2011)
16. Owens, J.D., Houston, M., Luebke, D., Green, S., Stone, J.E., Phillips, J.C.: GPU computing. Proc. IEEE **96**(5), 879–899 (2008)
17. Perols, J.: Financial statement fraud detection: an analysis of statistical and machine learning algorithms. Auditing J. Pract. Theory **30**(2), 19–50 (2011)
18. Serpa, M.S., Krause, A.M., Cruz, E.H., Navaux, P.O.A., Pasin, M., Felber, P.: Optimizing machine learning algorithms on multi-core and many-core architectures using thread and data mapping. In: 2018 26th Euromicro International Conference on Parallel, Distributed and Network-based Processing (PDP), pp. 329–333. IEEE (2018)
19. Serpa, M.S., et al.: Memory performance and bottlenecks in multicore and GPU architectures. In: 2019 27th Euromicro International Conference on Parallel, Distributed and Network-Based Processing (PDP), pp. 233–236. IEEE (2019)
20. Stavens, D.M., et al.: Learning to drive: perception for autonomous cars. Ph.D. Thesis, Citeseer (2011)
21. You, Y., Buluç, A., Demmel, J.: Scaling deep learning on GPU and knights landing clusters. In: Proceedings of the International Conference for High Performance Computing, Networking, Storage and Analysis, pp. 1–12 (2017)
22. Ştirb, I.: NUMA-BTDM: a thread mapping algorithm for balanced data locality on NUMA systems. In: 2016 17th International Conference on Parallel and Distributed Computing, Applications and Technologies (PDCAT), pp. 317–320 (2016)

Methodology for Design and Implementation an Efficient HPC Cluster

L. A. Torres[1,2](✉) ⓘ and Carlos J. Barrios[1,2](✉) ⓘ

[1] Supercomputación y Cálculo Científico (SC3), Universidad Industrial de Santander, Bucaramanga 680002, Colombia
luis.torres@correo.uis.edu.co, cbarrios@uis.edu.co
[2] Grupo de Investigación Computo Avanzado y a Gran Escala (CAGE), Universidad Industrial de Santander, Bucaramanga 680002, Colombia

Abstract. For years, clusters for HPC have been implemented through the typical process of obtaining the source code, configuring and compiling each of the tools that make up the infrastructure services. Each administrator based on their experience and knowledge assumes a series of considerations to design and implement a cluster that is considered efficient by installing base tools such as NTP, NFS, a task manager (that is, SLURM), LDAP, among others. In order to reduce these times, several open-source initiatives have emerged, such as Rocks, that allow the rapid implementation of an HPC cluster despite its low configuration flexibility. OpenHPC emerges as an alternative that provides the necessary tools in a software repository and that once installed allows the same flexibility of customization and adaptation as if they had been installed in a typical way. It's worth mentioning that OpenHPC provides all of those standardized tools in order to spread best practices in building and managing HPC data centers, but unlike Rocks, OpenHPC requires pre-design of the platform, including network infrastructure, storage services, and the different tools to implement, requiring prior knowledge by the administrator about each of them. The objective of this paper is to present the fundamental basis for implementing an efficient cluster by using OpenHPC without becoming a technical installation guide, but rather a series of steps in a methodology used by the Supercomputación y Cálculo Cienfífico Laboratory SC3.

Keywords: Cluster computing · OpenHPC implementation · HPL metrics and evaluation

1 Introduction

HPC has reached a level where it has become indispensable in the different fields of scientific research. Areas such as artificial intelligence, bioinformatics, climate prediction, among others, are some of these fields that depend on supercomputing centers to carry out their research. However, the design and implementation

S. Nesmachnow et al. (Eds.): CARLA 2020, CCIS 1327, pp. 71–85, 2021.
https://doi.org/10.1007/978-3-030-68035-0_6

of these have always been a task that depends on the experience of the administrators and that despite this can lead to long implementation and commissioning times. To remedy this problem, tools such as Rocks have emerged that have facilitated implementation but their cost-benefit in relation to the administration of the HPC platform makes them little-used [1]. Consequently, OpenHPC appears as an alternative to facilitate administrators with quick implementation and start-up by providing a software repository with different alternatives for administrators [1].

The use of OpenHPC is presented as a set of tools rather than as a definitive solution in the implementation of a cluster. Therefore, this paper presents the methodology used for the implementation of the GUANE[1] cluster of the Supercomputing Center and Scientific Calculation SC3 [13] showing the basic components necessary to take into account in the design and implementation in a supercomputing platform. The first section introduces the basic concepts and tools needed. The second describes the proposed methodology and the different tools implemented in such a way that the order in which they are presented is the order in which they must be installed and configured. The third shows a description of the Linpack benchmark, its configuration, and the results obtained. Finally, the conclusions of the methodology used are presented together with a comparison made at the efficiency level with the first five machines that appear in the Top500 [14].

2   Background

In our experience, the HPC system administrator must know a lot of concepts raging from Linux to the main hardware deployed in any cluster. With this background, we offer an overview of OpenHPC and the main tools implemented in this methodology.

2.1   High Performance Computing

HPC is a field of computing that seeks to improve performance in solving major problems in science, engineering, and business. Generally speaking, these computationally complex problems are mathematically modeled and, through parallel computing techniques, they become code instructions that are executed on machines known as supercomputers. These machines run these intensive programs on specialized CPU or GPU, significantly reducing the time to run on regular hardware [15].

The supercomputers were introduced in the 1960s by Seymour Cray of CDC (Control Data Corporation) [2], and for many years associated companies bearing this surname controlled this market. The vector processor with the ability to operate on large data sets was introduced in the 1970s, and it was not until the 1990s that massively parallel supercomputers began to be used with standard

---

[1] GpUs Advanced computiNg Environment.

processors, which to date are the norm. It should be noted that the performance of these machines is measured in floating point operations per second (FLOPS) and not in millions of operations per second (MIPS), because the latter is more a measure of the performance of a task in comparison to a reference and not a measure of execution speed. In recent years, higher performance speeds than petaFLOP have been achieved and it is hoped to achieve exaFLOPS in the near future [3].

This evolution of supercomputers and high performance computing is due to the increasing demand for computing speeds to solve problems in areas such as quantum mechanics, weather forecasting, oil and gas exploration, among others. In the last decade, this demand has reached very high levels due to the use of different artificial intelligence algorithms, particularly machine learning and deep learning algorithms.

Lastly, the HPC hardware falls into three main categories: Symmetric multi-processor (SMP), vector processors, and clusters [15] and with the latter being the subject of study in this methodology.

Cluster. It is the most widely used supercomputer and is a collection of many servers (nodes) which are connected through a high speed and high bandwidth network. These clustered servers can behave as a single server and a combination of the following services must be provided: high performance, high availability, load balancing, and scalable. Clusters can be classified according to their characteristics into:

- Fail-over clusters
- Load-balancing clusters
- High-performance clusters

These differ depending on the type of applications and their purpose. The Fail-over clusters and the Load-balancing clusters are used in mission-critical applications where consistent, throughput availability of services is required through many instances of one or more applications on different nodes. Finally, the High-performance clusters are designed to increase performance and decrease computing times when running work on multiple nodes at the same time [15].

2.2 OpenHPC

OpenHPC was launched in 2015 and formalized as a collaborative project of the Linux Foundation in 2016 [1]. This project is comprised of 25 organizations with representation in academia, research laboratories and industry. It has a large number of software components that include provisioning tools, resource management and scientific libraries. The main objective of this project is to make best practices available to administrators and to provide a software repository for HPC clusters.

For administrators, manually installing and configuring an HPC cluster can be tedious and complicated. For this reason, several open-source solutions emerged, among which Rocks and OSCAR stand out. Rocks [4] is a CentOS-based Linux distribution that contains additional software components for cluster deployment and administration without the need for other external packages. On the other hand, OSCAR (Open Source Cluster Application Resources) [5] is a fully integrated software package that, unlike Rocks, you must first install the frontend and then download and install the cluster configuration and administration tools. The project is no longer maintained and the latest version was released in 2011.

A common issue with these tools is the lack of balance between customization and ease of use [6], which is why OpenHPC takes a more basic approach when providing a software repository. This approach requires the administrator to be experienced but offers a variety of software components to promote flexibility in different environments and scales. OpenHPC includes two end-user projects that seek to reduce the complexity of installing and configuring scientific and HPC software: Easybuild [7] and Spack [8].

2.3 Lightweight Directory Access Protocol

LDAP is a set of open protocols that are used to access information that is centralized through the network. It is based on the X.500 standard but is less complex and uses fewer resources. The information is organized in a hierarchical and categorized model through the use of directories that can contain a large amount of information. LDAP is a client/server system where the server uses a database to store directories and is optimized for fast, high-volume readings. When connecting to the server, the LDAP client can make queries or modify a directory. In the latter case, the server verifies that the user has the permissions to carry out this operation before making the change and updating the information [16].

OpenLDAP is the free and open-source implementation of LDAP, supports LDIFv1 and LDAP versions 2 and 3. In relation to supercomputing clusters, OpenLDAP provides HPC infrastructures with a way to manage platform users. One of the great advantages of using LDAP v3 is the possibility of using dynamic groups, which allow the system administrator to create a tree with different access privileges to the directories of the HPC system storage.

2.4 Simple Linux Utility for Resource Management

Linux clusters require a resource management system that performs tasks such as scheduling user jobs, monitoring machine and job status, and managing machine settings as such. This system should be simple to use, fault-tolerant, efficient, scalable, and portable. With this in mind, Lawrence Livermore National Laboratory, SchedMD, Linux NetworX, Hewlett-Packard, and Groupe Bull produced the first slurm design [9].

Slurm enables efficient management of clusters regardless of size or architecture, is highly scalable, requires no kernel modification, and is relatively self-contained. The basic components are shown in Fig. 1.

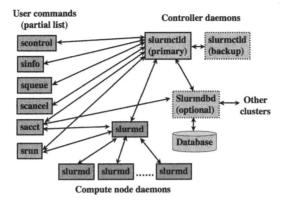

Fig. 1. Slurm components [17]

In essence, slurm works using two daemons, one on the frontend called slurmctld and the other on nodes called slurmd. The slurmd daemon provides fault-tolerant hierarchical communications and is responsible for initiating and managing user jobs. On the other hand, the slurmctld daemon sometimes referred to as the "controller", is in charge of orchestrating slurm activities, including job queuing, monitoring the status of jobs, and allocating resources to jobs. As shown in the Fig. 1, a backup to this daemon can be included which will automatically take over in case of failure of the primary controller, which will regain control when service is restored [9]. There is another optional daemon in slurm called slurmdbd, which allows storing the accounting records of the jobs in a database, allowing to generate reports about the platform.

Lastly, we find the user commands that allow them to run and monitor each of the jobs that are sent to the HPC platform. The sbatch and srun commands are used to run jobs, scancel command to cancel them, scontrol is used to view or modify Slurm configuration and state and, sacct command displays accounting data for all jobs and job steps in the Slurm job accounting log or Slurm database [9].

2.5   System Security Services Daemon (SSSD)

This daemon has the primary function of providing remote access to different authentication mechanisms through a common framework. These mechanisms are known as identity providers and SSSD allows them to connect to it as backends [18].

SSSD provides caching and offline support for applications that require authentication using standard PAM and NSS interfaces. With this feature, applications do not need to connect directly to identity providers (e.g. LDAP, NIS, Samba, etc.) and even if they are not available, the SSSD cache allows the applications to authenticate. Another important feature of SSSD is its ability to use multiple providers of the same type, such as two different LDAP servers [18].

2.6 High-Performance Linpack (HPL)

HPL is an implementation of the Linpack benchmark [11] for computers with distributed memory. This benchmark solves a dense linear random system in double-precision arithmetic. Basically it only requires a configuration file where the main parameters for creating the problem to be solved are specified.

The main parameters are:

- N: Order of the coefficient matrix A
- NB: Block size
- P: Number of processes - row
- Q: Number of processes - column

In general, the product of PxQ should be the number of MPI processes and the value of Q should be greater than or equal to P. The value of N should be chosen as close as possible to the total physical memory. For choosing N, the following formula is usually used:

$$N \approx \sqrt{\frac{Total\_Memory\_Size\_in\_bytes}{sizeof(double)}} \tag{1}$$

Where N must be an integer and must be a multiple of the selected NB block size. The size in bytes for the double-precision floating-point is 8.

The results obtained by HPL are the effective performance measures Rmax finds for each of the configurations. Another important value to calculate is the theoretical peak of Rpeak performance using the following equation:

$$R_{peak} = Num_{CPU} * Num_{Core} * Frequency * Num_{FLOPs/cycle} \tag{2}$$

Finally, the efficiency of the cluster is obtained by [10]:

$$Efficiency = R_{max}/R_{peak} \tag{3}$$

These topics cover the main components in the HPC cluster and in our implementation but exist others that didn't name in this section because we consider tools that any Linux administrator knows. The integration of these topics and other tools will be shown in the next section where will be described our methodology.

3   Methodology

By referring to the word "efficiency", the aim is to adequately fulfill a certain function. There are several ways to design and implement an HPC cluster but the knowledge and experience of the administrators is what leads to what can be considered to be really efficient. Many variables can be evaluated to determine the real efficiency of the cluster such as: user experience, performance, security, among others. However, the performance obtained from the HPL test will only be evaluated in order to show that it is possible to deploy an HPC cluster using this methodology, obtaining acceptable performance values. Finally, the objective of this methodology is to provide a guide that allows rapid deployment, both to experienced administrators and those new to the HPC world, and that is adaptable to the knowledge and experience of administrators.

3.1 Buildind a Efficient Cluster

Basic Architecture. In this first part, a general proposal of the organization of the elements that are considered basic in the deployment of an HPC cluster is presented. Two main points have been taken into account: ease of administration and speed of communication. The design scheme is presented in Fig. 2.

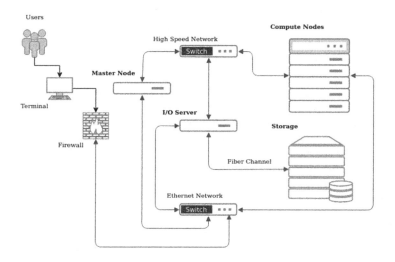

Fig. 2. General system architecture

In the age of artificial intelligence and big data, large volumes of data are common in HPC clusters, making the storage system one of the main elements to consider. The characteristics of these systems should allow for high transfer rates along with low latency, redundancy, and above all high storage capacity. Some HPC system designs typically mount the volumes created on the storage system directly on the master node, which does not incur functionality issues, but can affect performance by assigning cluster management tasks and traffic between the storage system and compute nodes. For this reason, we recommend that you have a unique I/O server that handles the transactional load on the cluster.

In relation to the above, another important element to consider is high-speed networks that are not included in many HPC clusters due to high acquisition costs but can consequently lead to network bottlenecks when there is a high demand for the network. In the implementation of this methodology, two high-speed networks have been used: Infiniband for communication and synchronization between nodes and a fiber-optic channel for the storage system and I/O node communication. It should be noted that new computing requirements and the high scalability of emerging applications make this type of high-speed network an essential part of any HPC cluster.

Finally, in the Fig. 2 shows other basic elements in any HPC cluster deployment such as ethernet switches, the master node, compute nodes, and an edge protection system for accessing the cluster from external networks.

Network Configuration. This methodology bases your network configuration on the recommendations that OpenHPC provides in your installation guide, however, we talk about general recommendations because each infrastructure differs according to the components at your disposal. Standards such as the Uptime Institute[2] recommend that all Datacenters have redundancy across all systems, including the network, but for this methodology, we assume that only the essential switches are available for each of the networks implemented in Fig. 2.

It is proposed to implement two base networks for the cluster that will be separated as two different LANs within the configuration. The first will be responsible for the communication between the master node and the compute nodes and will be for the exclusive use of the resource manager. The second network will be responsible for data traffic between the master node, compute nodes, and the I/O server. To provide Internet access to compute nodes, the gateway can be redirected to the IP of the master node, keeping in mind that the master node must have access to the Internet. This solution is not optimal, but it can simplify the administrator's work. It should be noted that this can cause network bottlenecks dedicated to resource management especially if applications running in the cluster require access to large databases available on remote servers. Therefore, the most recommended solution is the implementation of a third network that handles this external traffic, although this configuration makes it necessary to count an extra server that serves as a gateway for the output to the Internet.

Base System. In what has been described so far, a basic organization of the essential components in an HPC cluster has been shown together with the minimum network configuration required to obtain an acceptable performance and that can be considered efficient or, in other words, that performs its function in the most appropriate way.

Within this framework, the most important and essential software components for administrators have been considered, without addressing their installation and configuration. In Sect. 2.2. It was mentioned that OpenHPC has been designed to provide administrators with best practices and a software repository that allows the system base to be easily installed, configured, and updated.

---

[2] https://uptimeinstitute.com/.

However, it was not mentioned that within this repository there are several tools that perform similar tasks and that it is the administrator who must make the selection of which ones were used, taking into account the experience of this and their knowledge about them. These tools range from choosing the task handler between Slurm or PBS, to a system file system such as BeeGFS or Lustre.

The following describes the tools that were considered in the cluster deployment process using the OpenHPC repository and that serve as the basis for the implementation methodology suggested in this job:

- **NTP (Network Time Protocol):** It is an Internet protocol that is used to synchronize clocks from different computer systems on local or global networks. For the suggested configuration, the cluster master node will be used as the NTP server and will be responsible for keeping the system clock synchronized on all compute nodes and the I/O server in the cluster. Examples of the need for cluster synchronization can be seen in co-scheduling techniques in parallel applications with sensitive bulk synchronous workloads, (ii) performance analysis tools and (iii) autotuning strategies that want to exploit State-of-the-Art (SoA) high-resolution monitoring systems [12].
- **NFS (Network File System):** It is a client/server file system that allows users to access files and folders over the network and treat them as if they were local. It will be used primarily for each user's /home directory and for /opt where the platform software will be installed. These two directories belong to two logical volumes of the cluster storage system and are exported by the I/O server to the different system nodes. [19].
- **Support for Infiniband:** Infiniband is a network communication standard that provides high throughput and low latency. This type of high-speed network is not required for cluster operation, but as mentioned earlier in the network configuration section, the bottlenecks generated by high file transfer and the communication required between nodes by using inadequate networks make it an essential part of deploying an efficient cluster. In fact, OpenHPC also comes with included support for Omni-Path but Infiniband has been selected for the current cluster configuration where this methodology has been developed, but it does not mean that better results cannot be presented with Intel technology[3].
- **Memory usage limits:** Linux systems have the ability to limit the system resources that are available to user processes, and one of these limitations is the use of memory by the different components of a process that is running. Good practice in HPC is to establish new rules that allow the execution of demanding tasks by parts of users, which include new rules for memory limits and the maximum number of open files.
- **HPC modules - LMOD:** In short, a module is the setting of environment variables within a script. Each module is defined for a specified application where their respective environment variables, license files if required, are defined among the other requirements required for its successful execution.

---

[3] https://www.intel.com/content/www/us/en/high-performance-computing-fabrics/omni-path-architecture-performance-overview.html.

It should be noted that there are two types of scripts when defining modules. The first one is using TCL[4] while the second one is using LUA[5], which is distinguished from the first by using the .lua extension. Both types work for the creation of a basic application module that only requires defining the typical environment variables such as PATH, LD_LIBRARY_PATH, among others, but LUA has a number of functions[6] that allow the administrator to create more optimized modules[7]. The use of Spack[8] is also recommended, which provides the cluster with a tool for managing multiple versions and software configurations through environment modules. In the proposed implementation Spack was used instead of EasyBuild[9] due to the experience of the administrators in this tool, but it can be used both software repositories if so required and if deemed necessary by the administrator.

– **PowerShell:** It is a tool developed in Python that allows you to execute commands in parallel on all the nodes of the cluster and is highly scalable[10]. These types of tools are essential and allow simplifying routine tasks such as updates, maintenance, making copies of files and folders in directories not mounted via NFS. This tool was chosen over Clusterssh[11] motivated by the search for simplification in administrative tasks and the reduction of implementation times of a new cluster.

– **NHC (node health check):** One of the main tasks of administrators is to ensure the correct operation of each node of the HPC platform. NHC allows SLURM to monitor that each node is working properly, preventing user jobs from running on nodes marked as unhealthy. If SLURM finds any hardware failure or misconfiguration reported by NHC, the node is marked drained.

In the previous generalizations, the entire base system required for a basic implementation of a cluster is shown, keeping in mind the fundamental idea of providing those tools that improve the efficiency of the cluster. The next task to carry out is the choice of the task manager and its configuration. It was mentioned earlier that OpenHPC has two options, Slurm or PBS. The proposed implementation methodology will discuss Slurm and some configuration options that are considered necessary to improve performance and efficiency, but it does not mean that the use of PBS will incur design deficiencies or any decrease inefficiency.

SLURM. One of the most time-consuming tasks in the implementation of an HPC cluster is the installation and configuration of the task manager, especially

---

[4] https://en.wikipedia.org/wiki/Tcl.

[5] https://en.wikipedia.org/wiki/Lua_(programming_language).

[6] https://lmod.readthedocs.io/en/latest/050_lua_modulefiles.html#lua-modulefile-functions-label.

[7] https://lmod.readthedocs.io/en/latest/015_writing_modules.html.

[8] https://spack.readthedocs.io/en/latest/.

[9] https://easybuild.readthedocs.io/en/latest/.

[10] https://clustershell.readthedocs.io/en/latest/.

[11] https://github.com/duncs/clusterssh.

when you want to include certain features such as Infiniband within its configuration. Advanced administrators have the experience to easily deal with these settings, but it can still take some time to get it working properly. Therefore, it is proposed to use the SLURM and MUNGE[12] packages that come in the OpenHPC repository. Finally, it only remains to dedicate time to configuring Slurm according to the characteristics of the cluster and the policies for the task manager that are defined by the administrator.

There are a large number of configuration options in the slurm.conf file[13] that will not be detailed as they are outside the scope of this paper. However, the configuration parameters related to the SCHEDULING section will be discussed and some recommendations for their configuration will be given that will help the administrator to improve the efficiency of the use of resources.

- **SchedulerType:** Specifies the scheduler plugin to use. This parameter has two options: **schedbackfill** and **schedbuiltin**. The default option is schedbackfill and we recommended use it but the following parameters should be established to improve to the scheduler: **DefaultTime** (default job time limit), **MaxTime** (Maximum job time limit) and **OverTimeLimit** (Amount by which a job can exceed its time limit before it is killed). The optimal values of these parameters must be set according to the infrastructure and it is a task to trial and error.
- **SelectType:** Establishes how the resources of each node are used. The default option allocates nodes to jobs in exclusive mode, in other words, another job can not use the node even if resources are available. The best form to use the total resources is to set this parameter in cons_res (consumable resource) allowing manage them on a much more fine-grained basis.
- **SelectTypeParameters:** Consumable resources in our cluster. There are several values but the main consumables are the memory and the cores of the nodes, so, we set this value **CR_Core_Memory**. The rest of the configurations depend on the cluster and must be established by the systems administrator.
- **PriorityType**: By default, SLURM use FIFO (First In, First Out) to assigns the run priorities to each job. The best option in an efficient cluster is to set this value to priority/multifactor. This value depends on another series of parameters to calculate the priority of each of the jobs and they no will show in this paper but the values of these parameters are a task to trial and error [20].

It should be noted again that the detail of the SLURM configuration is not entered into because of the differentiation that must be made in the configuration depending on the hardware resources and the policies defined by the administrators. Likewise, the configuration of generic resources (GRES) such as GPU cards is not mentioned and the task/cgroup plugin is not included, but the

---

[12] https://github.com/dun/munge.
[13] https://slurm.schedmd.com/SLUG19/Priority_and_Fair_Trees.pdf.

reader is recommended to delve into this topic if its configuration requires the use of these resources[14].

Finally, it is worth remembering that within the SLURM configuration file you must specify the use of NHC after all the configuration of the nodes has been performed and their characteristics added to the slurm.conf file.

Lightweight Directory Access Protocol. Despite the fact that OpenLDAP is not an essential tool in terms of performance if it is in terms of efficiency and is mentioned here as one of the main components of a functional cluster.

LDAP is typically configured with its basic schema and is not usually modified to its tree because it is sufficient for system user management. However, we have noted that collaborative work has increased among users, leading to storage spaces shared among members of a research group or involved in the same project. Therefore, good practice in implementing LDAP is the use of dynamic groups [21] that allows you to assign different levels of access to different storage spaces within the HPC platform.

In this sense, it is understood that the LDAP service is essential and must have a mirror server that provides high availability of access to the platform. In other words, if the main access server experiences a service outage, the backup server is expected to offer the services while the main server recovers. This type of design requires a more dense infrastructure that the vast majority of small HPC labs do not have. To avoid access problems to the platform in the event of a total crash of the LDAP servers or if there is no redundant server, SSSD is used, which was explained in Sect. 2.5.

Finally, not only user access to the platform should be regulated. Storage spaces such as the user's home and project and research group folders must have restrictions that are implemented through the use of disk quotas in conjunction with LDAP.

This series of cluster implementation steps are proposed as an agile and efficient methodology that can be replicated in other HPC laboratories and that can optimize the task manager and the administration of the cluster and users by the administrator. The following section will show the results obtained from the HPL benchmark in order to show the correct operation of the cluster using the proposed methodology. However, these results are not directly related to various administrative tools that have been presented in this work and that cannot be quantitatively evaluated and are recommendations of the authors based on their experience in the implementation and administration of HPC laboratories.

4   Benchmarks and Results

HPC labs usually evaluate the performance of their clusters by running different benchmarks where the most common is Linpack and the most used implementation is HPL[15] explained in Sect. 2.6. This in turn is the tool used to position

---

[14] https://slurm.schedmd.com/SLUG19/cgroups_and_pam_slurm_adopt.pdf.

[15] https://www.netlib.org/benchmark/hpl.

the most powerful supercomputers in the world listed in the TOP500. It should be noted that these performance measures obtained and the comparison made with the five most powerful supercomputers in the world do not really show the efficiency of the cluster itself, but they do show its correct operation by using the proposed methodology.

4.1   Results and Evaluation

The cluster for which the design and implementation was carried out following the proposed methodology is made up of 14 servers

- 11 Servers:
  - ProLiant SL390s G7
  - 2 Intel Xeon E2.40 GHz processors
  - 102 GB of RAM
- 3 Servers:
  - ProLiant SL390s G7
  - 2 Intel Xeon E2.67 GHz processors
  - 102 GB of RAM
- Infiniband Mellanox Technologies MT26438 IB QDR/10GigE of Mellanox

Table 1 shows the results obtained by carrying out three tests on the cluster. Two of them were made for the Intel Xeon E5645 processor model using 6 and 11 nodes, the third test was performed on the three nodes with Intel Xeon E5640 processor. The parameter values for HPL were found using the equations presented in Sect. 2.6. The NB value was selected from the values 96, 112, 128, and 144 where the best Rpeak was for the value 112.

The $R_{peak\_cluster}$ of the cluster is obtained by multiplying the value of R_{peak} by the number of processors in a server by the number of servers used in the measurement.

Table 1 shows the results obtained by carrying out three tests on the cluster. Two of them were made for the Intel Xeon E5645 processor model using 6 and 11 nodes, the third test was performed on the three nodes with Intel Xeon E5640 processor. The parameter values for HPL were found using the equations presented in Sect. 2.6. The NB value was selected from the values 96, 112, 128, and 144 where the best Rpeak was for the value 112.

Table 1. HPL best results

Processor	Nodes	MPI Proc	NB	PxQ	N	R_{peak}	$R_{peak\_cluster}$	R_{max}	Efficiency
Xeon E5645	6	144	112	12×12	256256	57,6	691,2	556,9	0,804
	11	264	112	12×22	372512	57,6	1267,2	1035	0,8168
Xeon E5640	3	48	112	8×6	162064	42,72	256,32	215,84	0,842

Table 2 shows the performances of the first 5 supercomputing machines presented in the TOP500 in November 2019[16]. These results obtained by the implementation of the methodology described in this document show an acceptable operation by simplifying the tasks of deploying an HPC cluster.

Table 2. First HPC supercomputers - TOP500

Rank	System	R_{max}	R_{peak}	Effiency
1	Summit	148600	200749,9	0,7402
2	Sierra	94640	125712	0,7589
3	Sunway TaihuLight	93014,6	125435,9	0,7415
4	Tianhe-2A	61445,5	100378,7	0,6121
5	Frontera	23516,4	38745,9	0,6069

5 Conclusions

In conclusion, the use of the proposed methodology in the design and implementation of the cluster relying on the software repository and the best practice recommendations provided by OpenHPC simplified the tasks for the HPC laboratory start-up. In fact, the decrease in platform update times was also observed along with the complexity of installation and configuration of certain scientific applications through the use of Spack. Finally, according to the results obtained from the HPL tests, it was observed that the implementation of the cluster using the described methodology presents good performance results when executing tasks that require intensive computation.

References

1. Schulz, K.W., et al.: Cluster computing with OpenHPC. In: HPC Systems Professionals Workshop (2016)
2. Thornton, J.E.: The CDC 6600 Project. Ann. Hist. Comput. **2**(4), 338–348 (1980). https://doi.org/10.1109/MAHC.1980.10044
3. Sen, S.K., Agarwal, R.P.: Computing: birth, growth, exaflops computation and beyond. In: Flaut, D., Hošková-Mayerová, Š., Ispas, C., Maturo, F., Flaut, C. (eds.) Decision Making in Social Sciences: Between Traditions and Innovations. SSDC, vol. 247, pp. 3–47. Springer, Cham (2020). https://doi.org/10.1007/978-3-030-30659-5_1
4. Papadopoulos, P.M., Katz, M.J., Bruno, G.: NPACI rocks: tools and techniques for easily deploying manageable Linux clusters. Concurr. Comput.: Pract. Exp. **15**(7–8), 707–725 (2003)

---

[16] https://www.top500.org/lists/2019/11/.

5. Scott, S.L.: OSCAR and the Beowulf arms race for the "cluster standard". In: 2001 IEEE International Conference on Cluster Computing (CLUSTER 2001), 8–11 October 2001, p. 137, Newport Beach (2001)
6. Aydin, S., Bay, O.F.: Building a high performance computing clusters to use in computing course applications. Procedia - Soc. Behav. Sci. **1**(1), 2396–2401 (2009)
7. Hoste, K., Timmerman, J., Georges, A., Weirdt, S.D.: EasyBuild: building software with ease. In: 2012 SC Companion: High Performance Computing, Networking Storage and Analysis, Salt Lake City, UT, USA, 10–16 November 2012, pp. 572–582 (2012)
8. Gamblin, T., et al.: The spack package manager: bringing order to HPC software chaos. In: Proceedings of the International Conference for High Performance Computing, Networking, Storage and Analysis, SC 2015, Austin, TX, USA, 15–20 November 2015, pp. 40:1–40:12 (2015)
9. Yoo, A.B., Jette, M.A., Grondona, M.: SLURM: simple Linux utility for resource management. In: Feitelson, D., Rudolph, L., Schwiegelshohn, U. (eds.) JSSPP 2003. LNCS, vol. 2862, pp. 44–60. Springer, Heidelberg (2003). https://doi.org/10.1007/10968987_3
10. Wang, L., et al.: BOPS, Not FLOPS! a new metric and roofline performance model for datacenter computing (2018). http://arxiv.org/abs/1801.09212
11. Dongarra, J., Luszczek, P., Petitet, A.: The LINPACK benchmark: past, present and future. Concurr. Comput.: Pract. Exper. **15**, 803–820 (2003). https://doi.org/10.1002/cpe.728
12. Libri, A., Bartolini, A., Cesarini, D., Benini, L.: Evaluation of NTP/PTP fine-grain synchronization performance in HPC clusters. In: ACM International Conference Proceeding Series (2018)
13. Supercomputación y Cálculo Científico (SC3). https://www.sc3.uis.edu.co. Accessed 20 May 2020
14. Top500. https://www.top500.org/. Accessed 20 May 2020
15. Clustering fundamentals. https://developer.ibm.com/articles/l-cluster1/. Accessed 12 May 2020
16. Lightweight Directory Access Protocol (LDAP). http://web.mit.edu/rhel-doc/5/RHEL-5-manual/Deployment_Guide-en-US/ch-ldap.html. Accessed 5 May 2020
17. SLURM Overview. https://slurm.schedmd.com/overview.html. Accessed 8 May 2020
18. SSSD. https://access.redhat.com/documentation/en-us/red_hat_enterprise_linux/6/html/migration_planning_guide/sect-migration_guide-security_authentication-sssd. Accessed 15 May 2020
19. Network File System (NFS). https://access.redhat.com/documentation/en-us/red_hat_enterprise_linux/7/html/storage_administration_guide/ch-nfs. Accessed 20 May 2020
20. SLURM Priority Multifactor. https://slurm.schedmd.com/priority_multifactor.html. Accessed 15 May 2020
21. ZYTRAX - Configuring Dynamic Groups. https://www.zytrax.com/books/ldap/ch11/dynamic.html. Accessed 2 May 2020

Estimating the Execution Time of the Coupled Stage in Multiscale Numerical Simulations

Juan H. L. Fabian[1], Antônio T. A. Gomes[1]([⊠]), and Eduardo Ogasawara[2]

[1] Laboratório Nacional de Computação Científica (LNCC), Petrópolis, RJ, Brazil
{juanhlf,atagomes}@lncc.br
[2] Centro Federal de Educação Tecnológica Celso Suckow da Fonseca (CEFET/RJ),
Rio de Janeiro, RJ, Brazil
eogasawara@ieee.org

Abstract. Estimating the execution time of high-performance computing (HPC) applications is an issue that affects both shared computing infrastructures and their users. The goal of the present work is to estimate the execution time of simulation applications driven by multiscale numerical methods. In computational terms, these methods induce a two-stage simulation process. Fundamentally, the number of possibilities for configuring this two-stage process tends to be much larger than that of classical, one-stage numerical methods. This scenario makes it harder to provide accurate estimates of the execution time of multiscale simulations by using classical regression techniques. We propose a methodology that explores the idiosyncrasies of multiscale simulators to reduce the uncertainty of predictions. We applied it in this paper to the specific challenge of estimating the execution time of these simulators based on knowledge about the influence of each parameter of the numerical method they employ. We consider the multiscale hybrid-mixed (MHM) finite element method as a specific multiscale method to validate our methodology. We compared our proposed technique with 3 well-known regression approaches: a model-based tree (M5P), a bayesian nonparametric method (GPR), and a state-of-the-art ensemble method (Random Forest). We found that the root-mean-square error (RMSE) of the test dataset for our technique was considerably less than that obtained by these 3 approaches. We conclude that an educated consideration of the numerical parameters of the MHM method to estimate the execution time of the simulations helps to obtain more accurate models. We believe such conclusion can be easily generalized to other multiscale numerical methods.

Keywords: Multiscale simulations · Performance prediction · Machine learning

The authors thank CAPES (finance code 001), FAPERJ, and CNPq for partially funding this research.

S. Nesmachnow et al. (Eds.): CARLA 2020, CCIS 1327, pp. 86–100, 2021.
https://doi.org/10.1007/978-3-030-68035-0_7

1 · Introduction

Simulators are computational tools used to assist in the understanding of complex natural, artificial, and social-cultural phenomena. Phenomena with multiscale characteristics require the use of sophisticated numerical methods to deal with these characteristics in terms of not only the quality of approximation but also computational performance. The so-called *multiscale numerical methods* tackle both issues. These methods achieve low approximation error rates and incorporate the granularity of the new generations of massively parallel architectures. For this paper, we consider multiscale numerical methods for finite element analysis. From a mathematical viewpoint, these methods are composed of: (i) a global formulation defined in the skeleton of a mesh of elements; and (ii) a collection of local problems, element by element, guided by the problem data—which is inherently multiscale [5]. In computational terms, this formulation induces a two-stage process:

Asynchronous stage. It solves the local problems independently, without communication between the involved processors;
Coupled stage. It collects the solutions of the local problems to build a single, coupled problem that uses all available processors synchronously.

It is important to note that the computational effort to solve the problems in the asynchronous stage can be performed offline. Besides, the problem solved at the coupled stage—although it is usually carried out online—is typically smaller than that found in a classical numerical method and, therefore, computationally advantageous. The drawback of this two-stage process is that it increases the number of configuration possibilities, as there is not only an additional stage to be configured, but also the interface between the stages.

Consider the context of shared computing infrastructures, such as clusters in supercomputing centers. The configuration problem mentioned above becomes particularly important. In these clusters, workload management systems are responsible for regulating users' access to computing nodes. These systems implement scheduling strategies that arbitrate resource contention, managing queues of jobs sent by users. Typically, users and the supercomputing center benefit from job specifications that provide accurate estimates of total execution time. It enables shorter queue times and better backfill scheduling performance. Nonetheless, it is difficult to provide accurate estimates for simulations based on multiscale numerical methods. Each configuration possibility impacts the quality of approximation and computational performance achieved.

So far, research on predicting the execution time of high-performance computing (HPC) applications has sought generality, targeting general-purpose code kernels and parallel execution patterns. We believe that exploring the idiosyncrasies of specific application families—such as that of simulators based on multiscale numerical methods—helps to reduce the uncertainty of predictions.

We propose a methodology that employs machine learning to explore the aforementioned idiosyncrasies. In this paper, we applied this methodology to build models for the prediction of the execution time of multiscale simulators based on knowledge about the influence of each parameter of the numerical method they employ. We use the MHM method proposed by Araya et al. [2] as a frame of reference for training and testing the prediction models. Nevertheless, it is crucial to bear in mind that this study is also applicable to simulators based on other multiscale numerical methods; notably, the ones with the same parallel execution pattern [3, 7].

As local problems can be computed offline, we disregard their cost for predicting the execution time of MHM simulations in this work. This simplification does not make the prediction task less difficult, though. The parameters that affect the quality of approximation of the asynchronous phase also affect some characteristics related to the computational performance of the global problem, such as the matrix conditioning and the sparsity pattern of the underlying system of linear equations.

We compared the models we built in this paper for the prediction of the execution time of MHM simulations with 3 well-known regression approaches: (i) a model-based tree (M5P), (ii) a bayesian nonparametric method (GPR), and (iii) a state-of-the-art ensemble method (Random Forest). We found that our models achieved the lowest errors among them.

We organized the remainder of this paper in the following way. In Sect. 2, we analyze some related work. The MHM method, on which the proposed methodology is based, is described in Sect. 3. It also presents the problem statement for this work. In Sect. 4, we present the proposed methodology. Some experiments are analyzed in Sect. 5. Finally, in Sect. 6, we present some concluding remarks and perspectives for future work.

2   Related Work

In the last few years, there have been many initiatives that applied machine/ statistical learning for predicting the execution time of HPC applications. We describe below the most representative ones according to the data collected, techniques, and results achieved.

Matsunaga and Fortes [15] applied machine learning to predict the time and resources consumed by applications. These applications may be used in different computing infrastructures. To estimate the optimal resource usage for them is a complex task. Thus, a tree algorithm called Predicting Query Runtime (PQR) was applied to predict execution time and memory required. This algorithm enables defining different machine learning models on the leaves. Models in the leaves can be defined as linear regression or SVM. They are built from information about the application and the computing infrastructure. The approach was evaluated using two bioinformatics applications, BLAST, and RAxML, and showed good accuracy for each prediction model.

Huang et al. [11] also studied the prediction of execution time in HPC applications. They built the prediction models by using a statistical technique called sparse polynomial regression (*SPORE*). The use of this technique is justified by many predictors (*features*) considered for each application. The paper also investigated the relationship between the predictors and the target variable and which predictors were the most relevant to predict the elapsed time. Three applications (Lucene search engine and two image processing algorithms) were used to validate the method and compare it with other statistical techniques.

Tiwari et al. [19] used machine learning to model the performance of HPC *kernels*. The data was collected using a tool called PowerMon. The assessed kernels were matrix multiplication, stencil computation, and LU factorization. It used a multilayer perceptron as the machine learning technique. Models were built regarding energy usage and execution time for each *kernel*, and the authors analyzed the influence of the training dataset size on the model accuracy.

Hieu et al. [10] studied the predictions for the execution time of applications in computational fluid dynamics (CFD). Those CFD applications were executed in a cloud environment. The prediction of the execution time was executed in two steps. Firstly, a decision tree (C4.5) was built to classify the final status of the execution (executed or not). Secondly, a multilayer perceptron was built to predict the execution time. The authors assessed the models by using the accuracy measure for the classifier, and the coefficient of determination (R) and mean absolute relative error (MARE) for the regression.

Martínez et al. [13] described a process to improve the performance of stencil kernels on multicore architectures. The process used machine learning to predict the GFLOPS and execution time of this kind of kernel. It used three different data sources: configuration parameters in the stencil implementation, hardware counters, and performance metrics. The final models were built in two steps. Both were based on SVM. In the first, intermediate models were built relating configuration parameters and hardware counters. Then, final models were built using hardware counters and performance metrics. The authors considered two kernels—7-point Jacobi and seismic wave modeling—for experimentation and reported high accuracy in the performance prediction.

Tanash et al. [18] considered a supervised machine learning technique to predict needed resources in HPC systems. The authors were interested in predicting the required memory and time for a job and in improving the Slurm resource manager used in the HPC systems. HPC log files were used as input for the model. By using a Slurm simulator, the authors observed that the model could help the resource manager to use the HPC resources in a better way.

Kim et al. [12] proposed a scheme to estimate execution time in computational science and engineering simulations. The scheme, called EXTES, is based on machine learning, and it is applied to obtain efficient simulations. The authors demonstrated the use of EXTES in a web-based platform named EDISON. They considered 16 simulation programs and observed better accuracy in the models for each simulation program.

These pieces of work have in common the use of machine learning as a tool to predict the performance of diverse kinds of applications or kernels. None of them, however, considered as predictors domain-specific information about the applications or kernels. We believe the lack of such type of information in prediction models potentially reduces their accuracy. In this paper, we consider this type of information, in the specific context of multiscale numerical simulations.

3   MHM: A Multiscale Numerical Method

In this section, we briefly describe the Multiscale Hybrid-Mixed method (MHM), a type of finite element method that aims to solve large problems with multiple scales. The application of this method departs from a partial differential equation (PDE) that represents the physical problem to be simulated. A hybrid finite element formulation is proposed for this PDE that considers the continuity of its solution space using Lagrange multipliers. The hybrid formulation is then rewritten to obtain the MHM method. This rewriting leads to two types of problems: global and local. They are then discretized to obtain proper numerical approximations to the solution of the original PDE. The global problem is solved on the skeleton of a fixed finite element mesh that discretizes the domain of the PDE. The local problems are independent of each other and are solved in parallel for each element of the mesh. Each local problem considers its corresponding element of the mesh, a domain of its own. Therefore, these elements may also be discretized by a "sub-mesh". Since the local problems may be computed offline, we do not detail them in the remainder of this section.

Different physical problems can be modeled and simulated with the MHM method [2,9]. For this paper, we consider in the following the Darcy equation in a two-dimensional domain[1] defined as a boundary value problem for a diffusive process.

Diffusion Problem: Find the pressure $u : \Omega \to \mathbb{R}$ in the domain Ω s.t.:

$$\begin{cases} -\mathcal{K}\Delta u = f & \text{in } \Omega, \\ u = 0 & \text{on } \partial\Omega. \end{cases}$$

For the hybridization procedure, the MHM method first considers the decomposition of Ω into subdomains. It then defines the following function spaces:

- **V**: the space of u living over Ω; and
- **Λ**: the space of Lagrange multipliers living over the skeleton formed by the decomposition of Ω. This space is associated with the normal fluxes over the subdomains' boundaries.

The solution u can then be characterized as:

$$u = u_0 + \tilde{u} + u^\lambda, \text{ with } u_0 \in V_0, \tilde{u} \in \tilde{V}, u^\lambda \in \Lambda, \text{ and } \mathbf{V} = V_0 \bigoplus \tilde{V},$$

where V_0 is the space in which the kernel of the Laplacian operator (Δ) lives.

---

[1] Much of the description in this section also applies to a three-dimensional domain setting, if one considers faces instead of edges as composing the skeleton of the mesh that discretizes the domain.

For the discretization procedure, the MHM method first considers a regular mesh $\mathcal{T}_H$ of elements K that discretizes the domain Ω. $H > 0$ is the characteristic measure (*i.e.*, the level of refinement) of $\mathcal{T}_H$. For simplicity, let us map each K to a unique subdomain of Ω. Each element K has its boundary ∂K, and $\mathcal{E}_H = \{\partial K\}_{K \in \mathcal{T}_H}$ defines the skeleton (*i.e.*, the set of edges) of $\mathcal{T}_H$. K can be further discretized as a local sub-mesh; $h > 0$ is the characteristic measure of this sub-mesh. The approximate function spaces are then:

$$\Lambda_H = \Lambda_l^m \subset \Lambda \text{ and } \tilde{V}_h = \bigoplus_{K \in \mathcal{T}_H} \tilde{V}_K \subset \tilde{V}.$$

The parameter m in the space of Lagrange multipliers defines the number of partitions of each edge of ∂K, and the parameter l defines the degree of Lagrange polynomials in each such partition. At the local level, each K has its space $\tilde{V}_K$ formed by Lagrange polynomials of degree k. Further details about the MHM method applied to diffusion problems are in [2,8].

It is worth remarking that, on average, approximately 94% of the time spent on the global problem is due to the solution of its underlying system of linear equations. Because of MHM's hybridization procedure, this system is of the form:

$$\begin{pmatrix} A & B \\ B^T & 0 \end{pmatrix} \begin{pmatrix} \lambda \\ u_0 \end{pmatrix} = \begin{pmatrix} g_f \\ g_0 \end{pmatrix},$$

in which the dimension of A is determined by l, m, and $\#\mathcal{E}_H$, and the dimensions of B and B^T are proportional to $\#\mathcal{T}_H$.

The linear system above is a *saddle-point system*, thus presenting important challenges to linear solvers [4]. The larger the parameters l and m, and the level of refinement of the mesh, the more challenging the linear system for the solvers. Moreover, these parameters affect the linear system differently; refining the mesh—*i.e.*, increasing $\#\mathcal{E}_H$ and $\#\mathcal{T}_H$ only—increases the dimensions of the matrix, while increasing l or m makes the matrix not only bigger but also denser. The consideration of these aspects has an important impact on the quality of the predictions of the time to run simulations based on the MHM method.

4   Methodology

This paper describes part of a methodology under development, called NAZCA,[2] to assist users of multiscale simulations in the configuration of the simulations themselves and the computing resources used for these simulations. Figure 1 depicts the workflow for prediction models proposed in the NAZCA methodology.

The NAZCA methodology has two steps: learning and production. The *learning* step defines the process of building predictive models. The process departs from a set of three *parameter spaces*: (1) the characterization of the numerical method, (2) the computational architecture, and (3) the performance metrics.

---

[2] The name NAZCA was inspired by the Nazca Lines in Peru, which are sometimes related with ceremonial activities involving prediction [17].

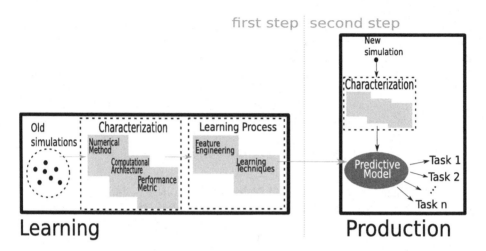

Fig. 1. NAZCA: The workflow for learning and operating prediction models.

For each intended predictive model, we need to do feature engineering in the (raw) data collected from a subset of the parameter spaces and explore diverse kinds of machine/statistical learning techniques over the data. The collected data is then used to train a model. The model typically outputs a response living in one of the parameter spaces. It is important to highlight that different combination of these parameter spaces as predictors can be used to produce different models that output different responses. In this paper, we aim to use the parameter space that characterizes the numerical method as a way to predict the execution time of a simulation. In the *production* step, predictive models are put into operation for new simulations. The feature engineering accomplished in the learning process is considered for these models as well.

A dataset in the NAZCA methodology is organized as a table with attributes as columns and samples as lines. The attributes are grouped in the three parameter spaces described above. To characterize a numerical method, we may define attributes related to the physical phenomenon, the mesh of the domain, and the numerical parameters. For the computational architecture, we may define attributes related to the number of computational nodes, the number of cores per node, and the RAM size in each node that is used in the simulation. Finally, for the performance metric, we may define attributes to analyze the performance of the numerical method (like errors in L2- and H1-norms) and of the simulation as a whole (such as success or failure, and execution time). Some of these attributes may be interrelated: for example, only when the simulation ends successfully, is it possible to obtain information on RAM usage and execution time.

Table 1 presents an example of attributes for MHM simulations.[3] These attributes were used for the proof of concept in the experiments described

---

[3] We differentiate **h** and **submesh** because the characteristic measure has an absolute value, whereas the level of refinement for the sub-mesh has local meaning.

in Sect. 5. It is also described the type of each attribute. We do not apply any attribute transformations. The users inform the values associated with the attributes in the numerical method and computational architecture parameter spaces. The attributes associated with the performance metric parameter space are collected while the simulations run.

Table 1. Attributes from different parameter spaces: Numerical Method, Computational Architecture and Performance Metric.

Parameter space	Attribute	Nomenclature	Type
Numerical method	Dimension of the domain (2D, 3D)	**Dim**	Nominal
	Physical phenomenon (diffusion, elasticity, etc.)	**Phys**	Nominal
	Characteristic measure of the mesh	**H**	Continuous
	Level of refinement for the sub-mesh	**submesh**	Discrete
	Characteristic measure of the sub-mesh	**h**	Continuous
	Degree of polynomial in the element - local problems	**k**	Discrete
	Degree of polynomial on the edge/face (2D/3D) - global problem	**l**	Discrete
	Number of divisions on the edge/face (2D/3D) - global problem	**m**	Discrete
Computational architecture	Number of computational nodes	**Nodes**	Discrete
	Number of cores per node	**Cores**	Discrete
	Total RAM in the computational nodes	**RAM**	Discrete
Performance metric	Success of the simulation	**S**	Binary
	Numerical error in the L2-norm	**L2**	Continuous
	Numerical error in the H1-norm	**H1**	Continuous
	Total execution time	**TE**	Continuous
	Partial time of the global problem	**TPG**	Continuous
	Partial time of the local problems	**TPL**	Continuous
	RAM usage in the local problems	**RAM-PL**	Discrete
	RAM usage in the global problem	**RAM-PG**	Discrete

In the learning step, the data is randomly divided into training and test datasets using the 80-20 strategy. The model is trained only using the training dataset, and it is assessed in the test dataset. We do not optimize the hyperparameters of the models, therefore, a validation set is not defined.

Estimating the Execution Time from Numerical Method Attributes. We explained in Sect. 3 that the execution time of the global problem in MHM simulations is influenced by the parameters l, m, $\#\mathcal{E}_H$, and $\#\mathcal{T}_H$. Besides, l and m are determinants for the sparse pattern of the system of linear equations associated with the global problem, affecting its computational complexity (as verified in Subsect. 5.2). We, therefore, devised a tree-based architecture that handles each possible combination of l and m. Moreover, we employed a feature engineering procedure to derive from l, m, $\#\mathcal{E}_H$, and $\#\mathcal{T}_H$ an additional attribute (GLG) that represents the total number of degrees of freedom in the linear system solved by the global problem. This new attribute is employed as the predictor of several univariate regression models, each one of them living on a different leaf of the tree. Figure 2 depicts the tree architecture.

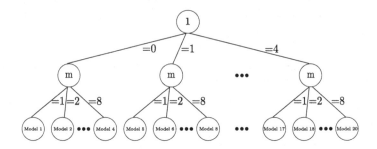

Fig. 2. Tree-based architecture for handling prediction models.

On each leaf of the model tree, we use empirical analysis to select the best univariate regression model. The empirical analysis consists of repeating the training and testing of a given model,[4] with a random division of training and test data for each repetition. We then collect for each such repetition the fitted model and its associated prediction band, and analyze two hypotheses over them:

- H_0^V: The model suffers little effect from changes in training and test data. We verify this hypothesis by ascertaining that the fitted models are confined within the area bounded by the prediction bands;
- H_0^R: The model is reliable—we verify this hypothesis by ascertaining that the data samples are all contained within some prediction band.

5 Experimental Evaluation

In this section, we describe the proof of concept of the methodology explaining the experimental part of the research. We start by defining the data used for building the prediction models, in which the attributes in the data were defined by experts. Next, we look for any possible patterns in the data. Finally, we apply our methodology for building predictive models of the execution time.

5.1 Dataset

Using Table 1 as a reference, we fixed **Dim** = '2D' and **Phys** = 'Diffusion' to match the diffusion problem described in Sect. 4. For the other parameters, we considered the combination of the values listed in Table 2. For a single combination, two different simulations were performed to enrich the dataset—each one based on a different refinement pattern for H (criss-cross and irregular). For the computational architecture, we fixed a single configuration, consisting of a workstation with two 12-core sockets and 320 GB of RAM. All the simulations that were run to collect performance metric data used 2 MPI processes. This setup amounts to a total of 1,800 simulations in our experimental dataset.

---

[4] We used 1,000 repetitions as in the traditional bootstrap setup [6].

5.2   Exploratory Data Analysis

In Fig. 3, we analyze the relation between TPG (the target variable) and GLG. We can confirm in Fig. 3(a) our assertions in Sects. 3 and 4 that there are different patterns when we combine the values of parameters l and m. Besides, we can see that for a fixed value of the parameter l, there are patterns influenced by the values in the parameter m, as we can see in Figs. 3(b) and 3(c).

Table 2. Parameters used in the experimental evaluation

Parameters	Values
Submesh	1, 2, 4, 8
m	1, 2, 4, 8
k	2, 3, 4, 5, 6
l	0, 1, 2, 3, 4

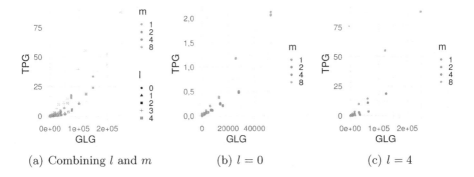

(a) Combining l and m (b) $l = 0$ (c) $l = 4$

Fig. 3. TPG vs GLG.

We show in Fig. 4 the distribution of training and test data on each of these leaves. Each time we increase the value of l and m, the amount of data available for training and test decreases. This skewed distribution is a consequence of the specific constraints of the well-posedness of a formulation in MHM,[5] and it may affect the performance of the model, as we show in the following section.

5.3   Model Building and Assessment

We consider different kinds of models for our analysis: $y = a_0 + a_1 x$ (model 1); $y = a_0 + a_1 x^{3/2}$ (model 2); $y = a_0 + a_1 x + a_2 x^{3/2}$ (model 3); $y = a_0 + a_1 x^2$ (model 4) and $y = a_0 + a_1 x + a_2 x^2$ (model 5). Models 2 and 3 were considered

---

[5] Briefly speaking, increasing l without increasing m also increases the minimal accepted value for k, thus reducing the amount of possible combinations in Table 2.

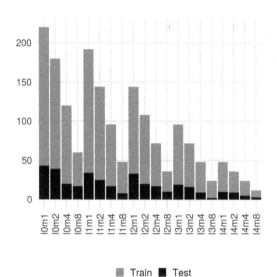

Fig. 4. Distribution of training and test data according to each case.

because we use the MUMPS parallel linear solver [1] for the global problem, and Mary [14] shows that this solver has an asymptotic time complexity of $\mathcal{O}(n^{3/2})$.

In the following, we analyze cases $l = 0, m = 2$, and $l = 4, m = 8$. In the first case, we have a filtered dataset with 200 simulations and a clear behavior for the empirical analysis (c.f. Fig. 5). In the second case, we have a filtered dataset with only ten simulations and a fuzzier behavior (c.f. Fig. 6).

As for the selection of model 2 in the example of Fig. 5, we observe that in models 1, 3, and 5, there are data points that fall out of the prediction band. For this reason, we refute the hypothesis H_0^R. Concerning the hypothesis H_0^V, we refute it in models 3, 4, and 5. We then selected model 2 because it was the only one in which we could not refute both hypotheses. As for the case shown in Fig. 6, at least one of the hypotheses was refuted by each model. In this case, our technique cannot select a proper model using empirical analysis. Thus, the strategy adopted based on Occam's razor was to select the most straightforward model (model 1). In Table 3, we summarize the models selected by our technique for each leaf of our model tree.

Table 3. Models for different values of the parameters l and m.

l	m	Model	l	m	Model	l	m	Model	l	m	Model	l	m	Model
0	1	$a_0 + a_1 x$	1	1	$a_0 + a_1 x^{3/2}$	2	1	$a_0 + a_1 x^{3/2}$	3	1	$a_0 + a_1 x^{3/2}$	4	1	$a_0 + a_1 x^{3/2}$
	2	$a_0 + a_1 x^{3/2}$		2	$a_0 + a_1 x^{3/2}$		2	$a_0 + a_1 x^{3/2}$		2	$a_0 + a_1 x^{3/2}$		2	$a_0 + a_1 x$
	4	$a_0 + a_1 x^{3/2}$		4	$a_0 + a_1 x^{3/2}$		4	$a_0 + a_1 x^{3/2}$		4	$a_0 + a_1 x$		4	$a_0 + a_1 x$
	8	$a_0 + a_1 x^{3/2}$		8	$a_0 + a_1 x^{3/2}$		8	$a_0 + a_1 x$		8	$a_0 + a_1 x$		8	$a_0 + a_1 x$

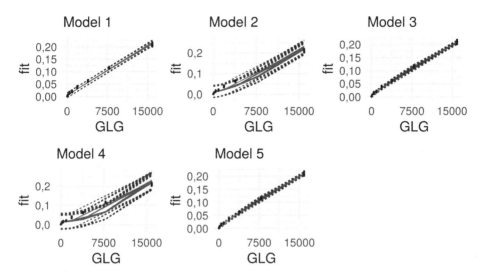

Fig. 5. An empirical analysis for $l = 0, m = 2$. We plot the data samples (dots) and the fitted models (green) with their prediction bands, upper (blue) and lower (red) bound. (Color figure online)

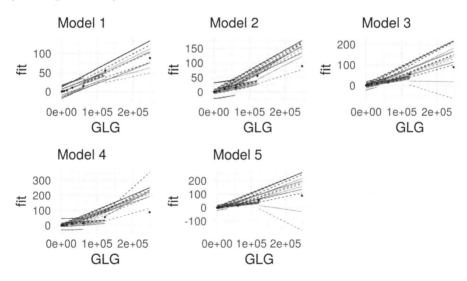

Fig. 6. An empirical analysis for $l = 4, m = 8$. We plot the data samples (dots) and the fitted models (green) with their prediction bands, upper (blue) and lower (red) bound. (Color figure online)

We calculated the error obtained in the test dataset for each leaf of our model tree. After that, we computed the error for the complete test dataset and arrived at an RMSE of 0.272. In Fig. 7, we can see the squared error for each leaf of our model tree. We can identify which of them have the higher errors. A high error

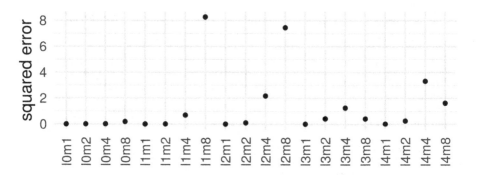

Fig. 7. Squared errors for each case during the tests.

could be caused for diverse reasons, such as a small dataset or a poor model. Reducing the errors for these cases is the subject of future work.

We compared the performance of our technique in the test dataset with 3 well-known regression approaches implemented in the WEKA workbench [21]: (i) M5P ([16, 20]), (ii) Gaussian Process Regression (GPR), and (iii) Random Forest (RF). Table 4 summarizes the results obtained for each technique.

Table 4. Comparison of regression approaches.

Technique	RMSE
NAZCA	0.272
M5P	2.111
RF	2.446
GPR	3.477

We can conclude that the considerations related to the numerical parameters proposed in our technique allowed a better generalization of the model.

6   Conclusion

Predicting the execution time of simulations based on multiscale numerical methods is complex due to their two-stage process. We presented NAZCA, a methodology capable of dealing with this situation. NAZCA aims to build prediction models for these simulations based on machine learning, benefiting both computing infrastructure providers and their users.

We applied the MHM method in a diffusion equation, and we conducted some experiments to obtain a dataset used for training and test. Different machine learning techniques are explored to build prediction models. We proposed a technique inspired in a tree, which for its building, considers some parameters of the numerical method. On each leaf of the tree, we carried out an empirical analysis for model selection. To validate our approach, we compared it with three well-known regression approaches. We concluded that our proposed technique achieves a small error of generalization compared to them.

Some future work could be considered for this research. In our proposed technique, we established some assumptions and limitations that could be tackled. Values for the numerical parameters are not limited to the experiments considered here, so another type of learning technique may be needed for this situation. In our technique, we also observed that the small amount of data influenced the achievement of accurate models, and a better analysis of how to get around this difficulty could be studied. Finally, we consider the application of the methodology described herein to other multiscale numerical methods in which the two-stage process is observed.

References

1. Amestoy, P., Duff, I.S., Koster, J., L'Excellent, J.Y.: A fully asynchronous multifrontal solver using distributed dynamic scheduling. SIAM J. Matrix Anal. Appl. **23**(1), 15–41 (2001)
2. Araya, R., Harder, C., Paredes, D., Valentin, F.: Multiscale hybrid-mixed method. SIAM J. Numer. Anal. **51**(6), 3505–3531 (2013)
3. Arbogast, T., Pencheva, G., Wheeler, M.F., Yotov, I.: A multiscale mortar mixed finite element method. Multiscale Model. Simul. **6**(1), 319–346 (2007)
4. Benzi, M., Golub, G.H., Liesen, J.: Numerical solution of saddle point problems. Acta Numerica **14**, 1–137 (2005)
5. Efendiev, Y., Hou, T.Y.: Multiscale Finite Element Methods. Springer, New York (2009). https://doi.org/10.1007/978-0-387-09496-0
6. Efron, B., Tibshirani, R.J.: An Introduction to the Bootstrap. No. 57 in Monographs on Statistics and Applied Probability. Chapman & Hall/CRC, Boca Raton (1993)
7. Guiraldello, R.T., Ausas, R.F., Sousa, F.S., Pereira, F., Buscaglia, G.C.: The multiscale robin coupled method for flows in porous media. J. Comput. Phys. **355**, 1–21 (2018)
8. Harder, C., Paredes, D., Valentin, F.: A family of multiscale hybrid-mixed finite element methods for the Darcy equation with rough coefficients. J. Comput. Phys. **245**, 107–130 (2013)
9. Harder, C., Paredes, D., Valentin, F.: On a multiscale hybrid-mixed method for advective-reactive dominated problems with heterogeneous coefficients. Multiscale Model. Simul. **13**(2), 491–518 (2015)
10. Hieu, D.N., Tieu Minh, T., Van Quang, T., Giang, B.X., Van Hoai, T.: A machine learning-based approach for predicting the execution time of CFD applications on cloud computing environment. In: Dang, T.K., Wagner, R., Küng, J., Thoai, N., Takizawa, M., Neuhold, E. (eds.) FDSE 2016. LNCS, vol. 10018, pp. 40–52. Springer, Cham (2016). https://doi.org/10.1007/978-3-319-48057-2_3
11. Huang, L., Jia, J., Yu, B., Chun, B.G., Maniatis, P., Naik, M.: Predicting execution time of computer programs using sparse polynomial regression. In: Advances in Neural Information Processing Systems 23, pp. 883–891. Curran Associates, Inc. (2010)

12. Kim, S., Suh, Y., Kim, J.: EXTES: an execution-time estimation scheme for efficient computational science and engineering simulation via machine learning. IEEE Access **7**, 98993–99002 (2019)
13. Martínez, V., Dupros, F., Castro, M., Navaux, P.: Performance improvement of stencil computations for multi-core architectures based on machine learning. Proc. Comput. Sci. **108**, 305–314 (2017)
14. Mary, T.: Block Low-Rank multifrontal solvers: complexity, performance, and scalability. Ph.D. thesis, Université Paul Sabatier - Toulouse III (2017)
15. Matsunaga, A., Fortes, J.A.B.: On the use of machine learning to predict the time and resources consumed by applications. In: 2010 10th IEEE/ACM International Conference on Cluster, Cloud and Grid Computing, pp. 495–504 (2010)
16. Quinlan, R.J.: Learning with continuous classes. In: 5th Australian Joint Conference on Artificial Intelligence, pp. 343–348. World Scientific, Singapore (1992)
17. Silverman, H.: Cahuachi in the Ancient Nasca World. University of Iowa Press, Iowa City (1993)
18. Tanash, M., Dunn, B., Andresen, D., Hsu, W., Yang, H., Okanlawon, A.: Improving HPC system performance by predicting job resources via supervised machine learning. In: Proceedings of the Practice and Experience in Advanced Research Computing on Rise of the Machines (Learning), pp. 1–8 (2019)
19. Tiwari, A., Laurenzano, M.A., Carrington, L., Snavely, A.: Modeling power and energy usage of HPC kernels. In: 2012 IEEE 26th International Parallel and Distributed Processing Symposium Workshops PhD Forum, pp. 990–998 (2012)
20. Wang, Y., Witten, I.H.: Induction of model trees for predicting continuous classes. In: Poster Papers of the 9th European Conference on Machine Learning. Springer (1997)
21. Witten, I.H., Frank, E., Hall, M.A.: Data Mining: Practical Machine Learning Tools and Techniques. Morgan Kaufmann Series in Data Management Systems, 3rd edn. Morgan Kaufmann, Amsterdam (2011)

High Performance Computing
and Artificial Intelligence

Using HPC as a Competitive Advantage in an International Robotics Challenge

Claudia Álvarez Aparicio[1], Jonatan Ginés[2], Miguel A. Santamarta[1],
Francisco Martín Rico[2], Ángel M. Guerrero Higueras[1],
Francisco J. Rodríguez Lera[1], and Vicente Matellán Olivera[3]

[1] Grupo de Robótica, Universidad de León, León, Spain
{calvaa,mgons,am.guerero,fjrodl}@unileon.es
[2] Robotics Lab, Universidad Rey Juan Carlos, Madrid, Spain
{jonatan,fmartin}@urjc.es
[3] SCAYLE - Centro de Supercomputación de Castilla y Len, León, Spain
vicente.matellan@scayle.es
http://robotica.unileon.es
http://robotica.gsyc.urjc.es
http://www.scayle.es

Abstract. Researchers in every knowledge field are moving towards the use of supercomputing facilities because the computing power they can provide is not achievable by individual research groups. The use of supercomputing centers would allow them to reduce costs and time. Additionally, there is a growing trend towards the use of GPUs clusters in HPC centers to accelerate particularly parallel codes as the ones related with the training of artificial neural networks. This paper presents a successful use case of a supercomputing facility, SCAYLE - Centro de Supercomputación de Castilla y León -(Spain) by a group of robotic researchers while participating in an international robotics competition - the ERL Smart CIty RObotic Challenge (SciRoc). The goal of the paper is to show that HPC facilities can be required to provided particular SLAs (Service Level Agreement). In the case described, the HPC services were used to train neural networks for object recognition, that could not be easily trained on-site and that cannot be trained in advanced because of the regulation of the competition.

Keywords: HPC · Robotics · Neural networks · Training

1 Introduction

The use of supercomputing facilities for training neural networks keeps growing significantly, both in academia and in the industry. Moreover, robotic researchers have lately show increasing interest on using deep learning approaches to face

Supported by SCAYLE, INCIBE and Spanish Ministry of Science and Innovation of the Kingdom of Spain (Grant RTI2018-100683-B-I00).

© Springer Nature Switzerland AG 2021
S. Nesmachnow et al. (Eds.): CARLA 2020, CCIS 1327, pp. 103–114, 2021.
https://doi.org/10.1007/978-3-030-68035-0_8

robotic challenges [5]. One way of comparing the performance of these approaches in this domain are competitions, but in those events the use of HPC facilities presents some challenges that are shown in this paper.

The case described in this paper focuses on the ERL Smart CIty RObotic Challenge (SciRoc challenge[1]), a biennial competition whose main objective is the integration of robots in smart cities. The First SciRoc Challenge was held at Milton Keynes (UK), on September 18th to 21st, 2019. In this edition, the robots had to cooperate continuously with a simulated digital infrastructure of a smart shopping mall, in order to accomplish their tasks.

The SciRoc Challenge is organized into three categories depending on the task to achieve and the type of robots involved, HRI&Mobility, Manipulation, and Emergency. These competitions aim at replicating consistent benchmarking results and have been designed to target three clear objectives: the European societal challenge of the aging population, the strengthening of the European robotics service industry and to push the state of the art in autonomous systems for emergency response [2].

The work described was carried out by Gentlebots a joint team between two Spanish universities, Universidad de León and Universidad Rey Juan Carlos. This team has participated in several competitions, such as the RoboCup, the ERL or the first edition of the SciRoc Challenge. In these competitions several robotic platforms have been used, Pepper, RB-1, TIAGo. Obtaining in some of them even the first position in the episodes.

TIAGo robot [16] was used in the SciRoc Challenge by Gentlebots team. The main components of this robot are an RGB-D camera on its head, a frontal touch screen to interact with people in the torso and a horizontal laser with a 10-meter range in its base. The internal computer is an Intel i7 CPU with 16 GB of RAM and 512 GB of SSD. As an add-on, the robot has an Nvidia Jetson TX2 on its back.

During the first edition of the SciRoc Challenge, the Gentlebots team competed in two episodes. Both episodes have the social character of robotics implicit in them but consist in solve completely different tasks.

1.1 Challenge Description

In the first episode called "Deliver coffee shop orders" (see Fig. 1a), the robot assists people in a coffee shop to serve customers, by taking orders and bringing objects to and from customers' tables. In this episode, the main functionality that is evaluated is people's and object perception, navigation and, speech synthesis and recognition [3].

In the second episode called "Take the elevator" (see Fig. 1c), the robot must take the elevator crowded with customers to reach a location in a different floor. The robot should interact with the referee to discover which floor it must reach to accomplish its task and also be capable of taking the elevator. The robot should be able to enter and exit the elevator on the right floor in the presence

---

[1] https://sciroc.eu/challenge-description-2019.

of people nearby and/or inside the elevator. To perform the episode the robot can interact with the customers in spoken language [4].

(a)   (b)   (c)

Fig. 1. Real scenarios: (a) Episode E03 - "Deliver coffee shop orders" E. (b) Real objects Episode E03. (c) Episode E04 - "Take the elevator"

The access time to the scenario and objects (Fig. 1) is very limited because many teams participate in the same episode. Time is limited in every way, there is a short period of time to get into the enclosure and examine the objects, but there is very limited time to train the computing systems before the competition.

1.2   Software Description

The base system in which the team carries out the development is ROS (Robot Operating System) the *de facto* standard for robotics nowadays. ROS is a distributed system that allows the communication between the different components of the robot easily, abstracting from the hardware and allowing focus on software development.

The implementation of the architecture used to solve the tasks is composed of two main elements: ROSPlan [1] and BICA [11]. ROSPlan is an IA planning framework, use `popf` as planner. BICA is a toolbox to create control solutions for robots. Virtually all the elements of the design are BICA components that perform different functions and is mapped to a ROS node. These components are executed concurrently in a hierarchical way in order to generate complex behaviors.

Gentlebots uses a well-known tool named YOLO [15] that integrates a neural network to carry out object recognition, a fundamental task in episode E04. A fully functional network model requires a large volume of data to train it.

The problem is how to generate that volume of data and its labeling in the very limited time since the scenario and the objects are available and the beginning of the competition. It is necessary to generate images with the objects and label them manually, which is very time-consuming. The training of the neural network with the information generated must be made as fast as possible to win time. The goal of this work is to see if the use of supercomputing is feasible in this domain.

The rest of the paper is organized as follows. The next section describes the use of neural networks for object detection, including an explanation of different technologies and why we choose YOLO. Section 3 describes the process of image labeling and neural network training. The use of SCAYLE and the obtained results are described in Sect. 4. Section 5 discusses the above results. Finally, our contribution and the next steps foreseen are presented in Sect. 6.

2   Neural Networks for Object Detection

Object recognition in real environments is a challenge that has got many applications not only robotics, and that can be solved by different methods. However, in recent years almost all efforts have been focused on the use of neural networks, in particular convolutional neural networks (CNN).

Early research such as [17] presented an integrated framework for using CNNs for classification, localization, and detection objects, introducing also a deep learning approach to their localization by learning to predict object boundaries. Other research [6] presented some improvements to CNNs based on object classification. Based on the use of CNN, the work [20] proposed a new architecture named "Inception", which was responsible for setting the new state of the art for classification and detection in the ImageNet Large-Scale Visual Recognition Challenge 2014 (ILSVRC 2014).

The work DenseNet (Dense Convolutional Network) [7], proposes a new improvement in the use of CNNs for classification, localization, and detection objects. In comparison with four highly competitive object recognition benchmark tasks, Imagenet abovementioned among other, (CIFAR-10, CIFAR-100, SVHN, and ImageNet), DenseNets obtain significant improvements over the state-of-the-art on most of them, whilst requiring less computation to achieve high performance. They showed that convolutional networks can be substantially deeper, more accurate, and efficient to train if they contain shorter connections between layers close to the input and those close to the output.

Other researchers as CBNet [10] present results that improve the detection accuracy of many state-of-the-art detectors, such as the FPN, CNN, and the mask. CBNet presents a novel composite backbone network architecture for object detection. It proposes a novel strategy for assembling multiple identical backbones by composite connections between the adjacent backbones, to form a more powerful backbone. In this way, CBNet iteratively feeds the output features of the previous backbone, namely high-level features, as part of input features to the succeeding backbone, in a stage-by-stage fashion, and finally, the feature maps of the last backbone (named Lead Backbone) are used for object detection. This study allows for increasing the quality of the neural networks to detect objects it works as an add-on to the neural network used in the system. It would be necessary to integrate it with the different options present to carry out object recognition in mobile robotics.

Researches as FoveaBox, [8] aim to carry out an improvement in the detection of objects through neural networks. This research presents an accurate, flexible, and completely anchor-free framework for object detection. FoveaBox directly learns the object existing possibility and the bounding box coordinates without anchor reference. This is achieved by predicting category-sensitive semantic maps for the object existing possibility and producing a category-agnostic bounding box for each position that potentially contains an object. By simultaneously predict the object position and the corresponding boundary, FoveaBox gives a clean solution for detecting objects without prior candidate boxes. This simplifies the computation of object detection.

Other researches in this field of object recognition are based on the study and development of new techniques for reducing training and computation times. In one hand, in the work [18] SNIPER is introduced, an algorithm for performing efficient multi-scale training in instance-level visual recognition tasks. Instead of processing every pixel in an image pyramid, SNIPER processes context regions around ground-truth instances. The research presents an algorithm for efficient multi-scale training that sampled low-resolution chips from a multi-scale image pyramid to accelerate multi-scale training by a factor of 3 times. This would reduce the training time, but would not reduce the labeling time that the team needs. In other hand, the paper [9] addresses the question of whether using the memory in computer vision systems can not only improve the accuracy of object detection in video streams but also reduce the computation time. this research is based on the human visual system that is capable of forming a rich representation of a complex environment, reaching a holistic understanding which facilitates object recognition and detection. This phenomenon is known as recognizing the "gist" of the scene and is accomplished by relying on relevant prior knowledge. The research demonstrates that the method is competitive with the state-of-the-art for mobile video object detection while enjoying a substantial speed advantage and removing the dependency on optical flow, making it effective and straightforward to deploy in a mobile setting. In mobile robotics, the reduction of computing times is essential because it is real-time systems. Thus approach would need to be adapted to an RGBD camera to test this new system on a robot.

YOLO, based on a convolutional neural network, is the system chosen by the team, has undergone several updates over the years as we see in [13–15]. Its last version allows doing object detection in real-time. The algorithm applies a single neural network to the full image, and then divides the image into regions and predicts bounding boxes and probabilities for each region. These bounding boxes are weighted by the predicted probabilities. These capabilities added to the fact that at the start time to development for the competition, it was the newest system and it was easily integrated on ROS. This made it be selected as the software base for object recognition of the team.

3   Training Neural Networks in Challenging Domains

Training YOLO requires a great number of images. First, it is necessary to generate the raw images which will be used later in the training. The easiest way to obtain the images is recording videos of the objects that the network has to detect in the real scenario. Every frame from these videos are extracted creating a large set of individual images. Then the labeling process is needed, for each raw image like Fig. 2a, it is needed to create manually a box around each object we want to process, the resultant labeled image is shown in Fig. 2b. This is one of the main problems of YOLO owing to the fact that a lot of time is required to label the images.

After these images have been labeled, some operations have been made over each of them to augment the dataset. These operations consist of rotations, contrast changes, intensity changes, brightness changes, vertical flip, horizontal flips and horizontal and vertical flip. With these operations the number of images to training the neural network increase. Two subsets are created. One of them has the images which will be used in the training. The other one is composed of the images which YOLO will use to evaluate the training in each iteration. Commonly is used 80% of the global dataset to train the neural network and the 20% to evaluate it. This way, the training set is composed of 372605 images and the validation set is composed of 79763 images.

The final step is training the neural network. This may take several hours so using HPC to train YOLO network implies an advantage. Once the convolutional neural network used by YOLO has been trained, we can use its software that allows us to identify the objects captured by the robot's camera as we can see in Fig. 2c.

(a)   (b)   (c)

Fig. 2. Objects episode E03: (a) Raw image. (b) Labeled image. (c) YOLO output after training

4   Experimentation

4.1   Hardware

SCAYLE (Supercomputing center of CAstilla y LEón) is a regional supercomputing facility providing HPC services to the research and development instutions of the region, and also at national level as part of the Spanish Supercomputing Network (Red Española de Supercomputación - RES). It is headquartered

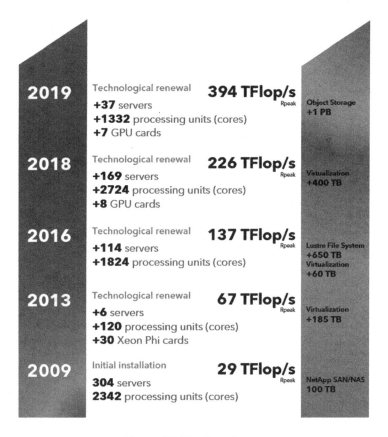

Fig. 3. SCAYLE evolution

in León (Spain) and currently is made up by more 7.000 cores of different Intel processors (Sandybridge, Broadwell, Haswell and Ivybridge).

SCAYLE was established in 2009 and since then the computing capabilities keep growing. Figure 3 shows the evolution of the intense calculus capabilities (in TeraFLOPS, left column) and in storage (right column).

The tests with the different YOLO configurations described have been carried out on SCAYLE, the node on which the tests have been carried out is composed of a server with 2 Xeon E5-2695 v4 processors with 36 cores, 384 GB RAM, 2 hard drive of 200GB each one, Infiniband FDR 56 GB/s, and 8 GPUs Nvidia V100. Also on a personal computer with an Intel Core i7-6700 3.4 GHz, a GTX 1060 6 GB GPU and 16 GB of RAM.

4.2   Parameters

The task, as previously explained, was training YOLO networks with different configurations. To launch the task to the cluster we have used slurm [19], an open-source job scheduling and cluster management system, with the configuration shown in Listing 1.1. This configuration includes the use of one process and four GPUs.

Listing 1.1. Slurm Script to launch YOLO training

```
1  #!/bin/bash
2
3  #SBATCH −−ntasks=1
4  #SBATCH −−job−name=sciroc
5  #SBATCH −−mail−type=ALL
6  #SBATCH −−output=results/sciroc/sciroc%A_%a.out
7  #SBATCH −−error=results/sciroc/sciroc%A_%a.err
8  #SBATCH −−partition=broadwellgpu
9  #SBATCH −−qos=normal
10 #SBATCH −−time=05:00:00
11 #SBATCH −−gres=gpu:4
12
13 cd ./YOLO/darknet
14 srun ./darknet detector train_cfg/sciroc.data \
15       cfg/sciroc.cfg darknet53.conv.74
```

These configurations were tested using different values of the YOLO parameters for managing the pipeline of training. On the one hand, the batch size is the number of images processed in each iteration. On the other hand, as explained in [12]; the subdivisions are the number of mini-batches used to train YOLO. For this reason the subdivision must be a divisor of the batch size. Each mini-batch is processed by the GPU in the training. For a smaller number of mini-batches, more GPU resources will be needed and faster is the training speed.

The alteration of the three parameters described has repercussions on two variables, time and loss. These variables will allow us to evaluate the effectiveness of using HPC to train neural networks. Time describes the duration of neural network training and the loss represents the error made at the end of each interaction. This way, in each iteration, after training the network, the network is evaluated with the evaluation set. This value is better the smaller it is because represents the difference between the results obtained over the desired results.

Table 1. Tests

Test ID	Iterations	Batch size	Subdivisions	Training location
personal_computer	3800	24	12	Personal computer
scayle_12	3800	24	12	SCAYLE
scayle_8	3800	24	8	SCAYLE
scayle_4	3800	24	4	SCAYLE

Table 2. Results

Test ID	Total duration	Average time	Minimum	Maximum
personal_computer	3.90 h	3.69 s	1.85 s	6.57 s
scayle_12	1.34 h	1.27 s	0.51 s	2.00 s
scayle_8	1.22 h	1.16 s	0.44 s	2.03 s
scayle_4	1.13 h	1.07 s	0.38 s	1.82 s

The tests performed are sum up in Table 1. It has been determined to carry out the study of the data on 3800 iterations, due to the fact that the training on the personal computer takes too much time. With 3800 iterations only 91200 images are processed. The batch size defines the number of samples that will be propagated through the network, which means, for example, for a set of 20 images, with a batch size of 10, the first 10 images would be processed in an iteration and then the other 10 in the next iteration. The batch size chosen for each test is the same for each test, 24, to get each test process the same number of the image in each iteration. As the batch size value is 24, tests with subdivisions of 12, 8 and 4 were performed (batch size divisors), but only in SCAYLE. As it is shown in Table 1, there is only one test in which the personal computer is used. This is because the personal computer does not have as many GPU resources as SCAYLE. Table 2 represents the results obtained from carrying out YOLO training with the parameters described in Table 1. For each training, the total training time and the minimum and maximum time per iteration is presented.

5   Discussion

The first criteria to compare the environments is the duration of each test shown in Fig. 4. Personal computer is the slowest one. Additionally, training performed in SCAYLE could be improved by decreasing the subdivisions using the larger amount of GPU memory.

Figure 5 shows the loss of the neural network at the end of each interaction whit each configuration described in Table 1. On one hand, in spite of starting with a different loss, each test tends to have the same loss. On the other hand, it is important to remark that this loss is achieved in different instants of time. Figure 6 shows that the test carried out in the personal computer needs more time to get the same loss than the tests performed in SCAYLE. It is also shown that thanks to the use of HPC more resources can be assigned to the training, which makes that the training in SCAYLE can achieve better results using other configurations that can be used in the personal computer.

The team in this type of competition plays against the time, teams are only assigned a 2 h slot in the setup day. In this slot, the team can access to the scenario to record the videos mentioned in Sect. 3 in addition to other tasks, it is important to note that the team not only prepares the object recognition on the first day but must do other tasks, such as configuring the network, creating

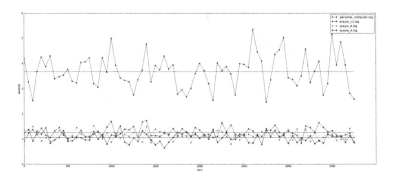

Fig. 4. Training time values

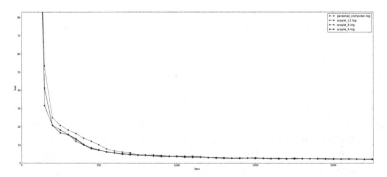

Fig. 5. Training loss values

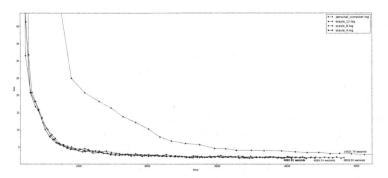

Fig. 6. Loss values over training time

maps of the scenarios, etc. Once the videos have been recorded, part of the team must start labeling the images obtained from the videos, this task took the team about 10 h. Once the images are labeled are uploaded to the cluster. The volume of images is increased, in the cluster, by the operations described in Sect. 3. Thus reducing the number of images to be uploaded to the cluster making the network consumption lower and therefore its upload faster. Finally, the training of the network starts, the training is done during the night, so the next morning the neural network model will be ready to be used in the episodes.

Tables 1 and 2 show that the use of a supercomputing facility means a reduction in the training times of the neural network used by YOLO. Compared to the 3.93 h of training on the personal computer, we have durations of 1.34, 1.22 and 1.13 respectively for training in SCAYLE. This means a reduction of the calculation times in SCAYLE compared the personal computer that oscillates between 65.91% and 71.22% respectively.

We can also see that the reduction of the number of subdivisions allows the training to be carried out at greater speed. For the scayle_12 configuration which has 12 subdivisions, the training duration is 1.34 h compared to 1.22 and 1.13 h obtained with the scyale_8 and scayle_4 configurations respectively. This represents a time reduction of 8.96% and 15.68% in the scyale_8 and scayle_4 configurations versus scayle_12 respectively. Thus, the reduction of subdivisions can only be done if powerful GPUs are available so the reduction of training times can only be done if this type of hardware is available, in the described problem the use of SCAYLE is the solution.

6   Conclusions and Further Work

This paper describes the comparative study of training an artificial neural network system in an HPC facility vs. local computer in an environment were time restrictions were significant, a robotic competition. In that environment hard real-time is not required, but deadlines (a few hours) are firm. Different configuration of the workloads was tested obtaining that the use of supercomputing in this type of competition allows us to reduce the training time of the neural network that uses YOLO by 71.22%. Furthermore, the use of SCAYLE has allowed us to discover that by reducing the value of the variable subdivisions we can reduce up to 15.68% plus the time of training within SCAYLE. As future work, the team will undoubtedly continue to use SCAYLE to carry out training of their neural networks. In addition to studying new object recognition software options and trying to find solutions to reduce image tagging time.

References

1. Cashmore, M., et al.: Rosplan: planning in the robot operating system. In: ICAPS (2015)
2. ERL: European robotics league description (2016). https://www.eu-robotics.net/robotics_league/about/the-european-robotics-league/index.html. Accessed 16 Mar 2020
3. ERL: Episode e03 - deliver coffee shop orders (2018). https://sciroc.eu/e03-deliver-coffee-shop-orders/. Accessed 16 Mar 2020
4. ERL: Episode e04 - take the elevator (2018). https://sciroc.eu/e04-take-the-elevator/. Accessed 16 Mar 2020

5. Guerrero-Higueras, Á.M., et al.: Tracking people in a mobile robot from 2D lidar scans using full convolutional neural networks for security in cluttered environments. Front. Neurorobot. **12**, 85 (2019)
6. Howard, A.G.: Some improvements on deep convolutional neural network based image classification. arXiv preprint arXiv:1312.5402 (2013)
7. Huang, G., Liu, Z., Van Der Maaten, L., Weinberger, K.Q.: Densely connected convolutional networks. In: Proceedings of the IEEE Conference on Computer Vision and Pattern Recognition, pp. 4700–4708 (2017)
8. Kong, T., Sun, F., Liu, H., Jiang, Y., Shi, J.: FoveaBox: beyond anchor-based object detector. arXiv preprint arXiv:1904.03797 (2019)
9. Liu, M., Zhu, M., White, M., Li, Y., Kalenichenko, D.: Looking fast and slow: memory-guided mobile video object detection. arXiv preprint arXiv:1903.10172 (2019)
10. Liu, Y., et al.: CBNet: a novel composite backbone network architecture for object detection. arXiv preprint arXiv:1909.03625 (2019)
11. Martín-Rico, F., Ginés, J., Vargas, D., Rodríguez-Lera, F.J., Matellán-Olivera, V.: Planning-centered architecture for RoboCup SSPL @Home. In: Fuentetaja Pizán, R., García Olaya, Á., Sesmero Lorente, M.P., Iglesias Martínez, J.A., Ledezma Espino, A. (eds.) WAF 2018. AISC, vol. 855, pp. 287–302. Springer, Cham (2019). https://doi.org/10.1007/978-3-319-99885-5_20
12. Mou, X., Cui, J., Yin, H., Zhou, X.: Tracking position and status of electric control switches based on YOLO detector. In: Yin, H., Camacho, D., Tino, P., Tallón-Ballesteros, A.J., Menezes, R., Allmendinger, R. (eds.) IDEAL 2019. LNCS, vol. 11871, pp. 184–194. Springer, Cham (2019). https://doi.org/10.1007/978-3-030-33607-3_21
13. Redmon, J., Divvala, S., Girshick, R., Farhadi, A.: You only look once: unified, real-time object detection. In: Proceedings of the IEEE Conference on Computer Vision and Pattern Recognition, pp. 779–788 (2016)
14. Redmon, J., Farhadi, A.: YOLO9000: better, faster, stronger. In: Proceedings of the IEEE Conference on Computer Vision and Pattern Recognition, pp. 7263–7271 (2017)
15. Redmon, J., Farhadi, A.: YOLOv3: an incremental improvement. arXiv (2018)
16. Robotics, P.: Tiago (2020). http://pal-robotics.com/es/robots/tiago/. Accessed 13 Apr 2020
17. Sermanet, P., Eigen, D., Zhang, X., Mathieu, M., Fergus, R., LeCun, Y.: OverFeat: integrated recognition, localization and detection using convolutional networks. arXiv preprint arXiv:1312.6229 (2013)
18. Singh, B., Najibi, M., Davis, L.S.: SNIPER: efficient multi-scale training. In: Advances in Neural Information Processing Systems, pp. 9310–9320 (2018)
19. Slurm: Slurm (2020). https://slurm.schedmd.com/overview.html. Accessed 30 Apr 2020
20. Szegedy, C., et al.: Going deeper with convolutions. In: Proceedings of the IEEE Conference on Computer Vision and Pattern Recognition, pp. 1–9 (2015)

A Survey on Privacy-Preserving Machine Learning with Fully Homomorphic Encryption

Luis Bernardo Pulido-Gaytan[1] ⃝, Andrei Tchernykh[1,2,4(✉)] ⃝,
Jorge M. Cortés-Mendoza[2] ⃝, Mikhail Babenko[3,4] ⃝, and Gleb Radchenko[2] ⃝

[1] CICESE Research Center, carr. Tijuana-Ensenada 3918, 22860 Ensenada, BC, Mexico
{lpulido,chernykh}@cicese.edu.mx
[2] South Ural State University, Prospekt Lenina 76, 454080 Chelyabinsk, Russia
{kortesmendosak,gleb.radchenko}@susu.ru
[3] North-Caucasus Federal University, Kulakova 2, 355029 Stavropol, Russia
mgbabenko@ncfu.ru
[4] The Ivannikov Institute for System Programming of the RAS, Alexander Solzhenitsyn st., 25,
Moscow, Russia

Abstract. The secure and efficient processing of private information in the cloud computing paradigm is still an open issue. New security threats arise with the increasing volume of data into cloud storage, where cloud providers require high levels of trust, and data breaches are significant problems. Encrypting the data with conventional schemes is considered the best option to avoid security problems. However, a decryption process is necessary when the data must be processed, but it falls into the initial problem of data vulnerability. The user cannot operate on the data directly and must download it to perform the computations locally. In this context, Fully Homomorphic Encryption (FHE) is considered the holy grail of cryptography in order to solve cybersecurity problems, it allows a non-trustworthy third-party resource to blindly process encrypted information without disclosing confidential data. FHE is a valuable capability in a world of distributed computation and heterogeneous networking. In this survey, we present a comprehensive review of theoretical concepts, state-of-the-art, limitations, potential applications, and development tools in the domain of FHE. Moreover, we show the intersection of FHE and machine learning from a theoretical and a practical point of view and identify potential research directions to enrich Machine Learning as a Service, a new paradigm of cloud computing. Specifically, this paper aims to be a guide to researchers and practitioners interested in learning, applying, and extending knowledge in FHE over machine learning.

Keywords: Cloud security · Fully homomorphic encryption · Machine learning as a service

1 Introduction

Cloud computing provides considerable benefits as availability, scalability, pricing, energy efficiency, application acceleration, without upfront infrastructure investment,

© Springer Nature Switzerland AG 2021
S. Nesmachnow et al. (Eds.): CARLA 2020, CCIS 1327, pp. 115–129, 2021.
https://doi.org/10.1007/978-3-030-68035-0_9

and direct active management by the user. However, it also brings security and privacy concerns, where data breaches are the top threat. Sensitive information can be released, viewed, stolen, or used by an unauthorized party. Additionally, data outsourcing implies that the user delegates the direct control of data and its processing. The user requires greater trust in the Cloud Service Provider (CSP) because dishonest behavior can compromise the data. In general, new threats appear since more data is outsourced.

Security and privacy are critical issues for preserving integrity, reliability, and availability in a cloud computing environment. Privacy and efficient data processing are important research areas in the field of outsourcing computing. Traditionally, encryption of confidential information was the standard solution before the use of the cloud model, this approach may protect the privacy of user data from a non-trustworthy third-party, but it cannot support effective ciphertext computing. In this respect, a vulnerability appears when data has to be decrypted in order to be processed. In this sense, the general idea of security is to delegate the processing of data without giving transparent access to it.

Fully Homomorphic Encryption (FHE) has been dubbed the holy grail of cryptography, an elusive goal that could solve the cybersecurity problems. FHE allows a non-trustworthy third-party to blindly process encrypted information without disclosing confidential data. Since the remote server only sees encryption of the data and never has access to the secret key, the client can be assured that it does not learn anything about their data, or the output of the computation. This is a hugely valuable capability in the world of distributed computation and heterogeneous networking.

FHE enables applying mathematical operations directly to the ciphertext in such a way that the decrypting of ciphertext results in the same answer as applying the operations to the original unencrypted data. So, the processing of confidential data can be delegated without giving away access to data. In other words, FHE enables compatibility between two critical factors in computing: cloud computing and privacy.

FHE is a promising tool for security against the quantum computer threat [1]. Current public-key cryptography is based on problems such as factoring or solving discrete logarithms. These problems, widely studied, are believed to be hard to settle on a classical computer. However, an adversary equipped with a sufficiently large quantum computer can solve them easily. While the quantum computer does not exist today, its potential is considered a threat.

Recent years of FHE development demonstrates remarkable progress. Despite the continuous improvements in the field, its implementation exhibits several limitations in performance; they suffer from complicates designs, low computational efficiency, and high computing complexity. However, the actual knowledge in the area makes their use technically feasible for real-world domains. A long-pursue application is a privacy-preserving machine learning model for predicting or classifying of confidential information. These systems can provide security and efficient accuracy at the same time, where the data and processing are always encrypted.

In this paper, current FHE schemes are comprehensively overviewed, focusing mainly on those located at the intersection of cryptography and machine learning. The objective of this survey is to give a knowledge foundation to researchers and practitioners interested in knowing, applying, and extending state-of-the-art FHE approaches.

This paper is structured as follows. The next section reviews the evolution of homomorphic schemes. The formal definition of FHE and fundamental concepts, such as bootstrapping and key-switching, are described in Sect. 3. Section 4 discusses the state-of-the-art and current directions of homomorphic ciphers and Machine Learning as a Service (MLaaS) paradigm. Section 5 presents the application of FHE in real-world problems and currents tools for its development. Finally, we conclude and discuss future works in Sect. 6.

2 Homomorphic Encryption

This section introduces the essential concepts of *Homomorphic Encryption* (HE) schemes and presents relevant works in different research areas that emerge from this approach.

HE performs operations on ciphertexts based solely on publicly available information, and in particular, without having access to any secret key. The term "homomorphic" refers to the existence of a correspondence between the space of messages and ciphertexts. In such a way, operations performed on ciphertexts are reflected in operations on the messages they encrypt. As an example, an additively homomorphic encryption scheme allows us to take a ciphertext c_1 encrypting a message m_1, a ciphertext c_2 encrypting a message m_2, and produce a ciphertext c_+ that decrypts to $m_1 + m_2$. Analogously, a multiplicatively homomorphic encryption scheme, can build a ciphertext $c_\times$ that decrypts $m_1 \times m_2$.

In this context, a *Partially Homomorphic Encryption* (PHE) scheme supports only some types of operations, but not others. For example, additively homomorphic encryption allows additions but no multiplications. RSA [2] was the first PHE scheme, being multiplicative homomorphic: given ciphertexts $c_1 = m_1^e \bmod N$ and $c_2 = m_2^e \bmod N$, one can compute a ciphertext $c_\times \leftarrow c_1 \times c_2 = (m_1 \times m_2)^e \bmod N$ that encrypts the product of the original plaintexts. However, a basic RSA is deterministic and, therefore, not even semantically secure. Some PHE approaches are described in [3–5].

The encryption process in HE requires adding an error term to guarantee a certain level of security. The reason for the error in encryption schemes relies on the hardness of solving "noisy" problems, i.e., problems where the relations are not exact but are perturbed by a moderate quantity of error [6].

A *Somewhat Homomorphic Encryption* (SHE) scheme can evaluate a certain amount of homomorphic operations before the error grows too much to maintain the correctness of the evaluation. Roughly speaking, each homomorphic operation increases the underlying noise. The message can be recovered if the error is under a certain threshold. However, the decryption process is hopeless when the error overpasses the threshold. Hence, noise growth limits the number of operations that can be accomplished.

A *Fully Homomorphic Encryption* scheme allows the evaluation of arbitrarily complex computations over encrypted data; it enables calculation on encrypted data without leaking any underlying information. A FHE scheme is more flexible than a SHE scheme because it does not set a bound on the number of homomorphic operations. The first FHE was proposed by Gentry [7]. In the last years, FHE has been an active field of research, leading to an extensive list of contributions [8–12].

In general, the research in the field of FHE can roughly be divided into four main families. The first family denotes the stemming directly from Gentry's seminal work, whose hardness is based on the *lattice reduction problem*. The second family refers to those *integer-based* approaches [8, 10], where the hardness of the schemes is based on the *Approximate of Greatest Common Divisor* (A-GCD) problem [13]. The third generation includes schemes based on *Learning with Error* (LWE) [12], and *Ring Learning with Error* (RLWE) [11], both reducible to lattice problems. Finally, the family of *Nth-Degree Truncated Polynomial Ring Unit* (NTRU) [14], and subsequent works [15, 16].

Despite the continuous improvement in the efficiency of all these schemes, their contributions involve complicated designs, too large keys, low computing efficiency, and high computing complexity. Several schemes are far from practical applications due to operations necessary to perform an addition or multiplication of integers in FHE.

For instance, any data must be homomorphically encrypted to be evaluated by a computer; the most common message space is binary $M = \{0, 1\}$ where operations of addition and multiplication correspond to a logical operator's XOR and AND, respectively. Thus, performing a 32-bit integer addition using a simple ripple-carry adder design involves 32 full adders, each requiring three XORs, two ANDs, and one OR operations, i.e., 256 operations to add two integers [17].

3   Fully Homomorphic Encryption

FHE is a solution that provides privacy and computes outsourcing data effectively in cloud environments. It allows delegating the processing of data without giving away access to it. This section introduces the formal definition of FHE and fundamental concepts, such as bootstrapping and key-switching.

The *privacy homomorphism*, a formal description of FHE, was introduced by Rivest [3] shortly after having proposed the RSA scheme [2]. In general, the idea is the arbitrarily computing on encrypted data without the decryption key [7]. Obfuscation is not a characteristic of FHE; this cybersecurity term refers to a scheme capable of hiding a program P by $P_{Encrypt}$. In such a way, a third-party can process $P_{Encrypt}(x) = P(x)$ for each input x, it prevents learning nothing about P, except the input-output relation between x and $P_{Encrypt}(x)$. In the case of FHE, the third-party cannot decrypt output $P_{Encrypt}(x)$ to get $P(x)$ from the compute of $P_{Encrypt}$ with input x.

At a high-level, the essence of FHE is simple: given ciphertexts $c_1, c_2, \ldots, c_t$ that encrypt the messages $m_1, m_2, \ldots, m_t$, FHE allows the output of a ciphertext that encrypts $f(m_1, m_2, \ldots, m_t)$ for any desired function f, as long as that function can be efficiently computed. No information about $m_1, m_2, \ldots, m_t$ or $f(m_1, m_2, \ldots, m_t)$ should leak; the inputs, output, and intermediate values are always encrypted. Figure 1 shows the expected operation of FHE based on the classic black box model in computer systems. The task is basically to find the appropriate mechanism $Evaluate_\varepsilon$ that satisfactorily leads to the output.

The following sections present the formal definition of the FHE scheme and fundamental concepts, such as bootstrapping and key-switching.

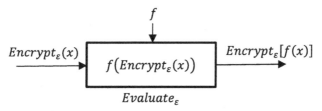

Fig. 1. Homomorphic encryption scheme

3.1 Notation

Formally, a FHE scheme ε defines a conventional public-key scheme that relies on four processes [7]: $KeyGen_\varepsilon$, $Encrypt_\varepsilon$, $Decrypt_\varepsilon$, and $Evaluate_\varepsilon$. The computational complexity of all operations must be polynomial in λ, where:

- $KeyGen_\varepsilon$ uses a security parameter λ as input and outputs a secret key sk and public key pk; pk maps from a plaintext space $\mathbb{P}$ to a ciphertext space $\mathbb{C}$ and sk in the opposite direction.
- $Encrypt_\varepsilon$ consists of taking pk and a plaintext $m \in \mathbb{P}$ as input and outputs a ciphertext $c \in \mathbb{C}$.
- $Decrypt_\varepsilon$, the opposite process of $Encrypt_\varepsilon$, receives sk and $c \in \mathbb{C}$ as input and outputs the plaintext $m \in \mathbb{P}$.
- $Evaluate_\varepsilon$ takes as input pk, a circuit $\delta \in \delta_\varepsilon$, and a tuple of ciphertexts $C = c_1, \ldots, c_t$ for the input wires of δ; it outputs a ciphertext $C' \in \mathbb{C}$, such that $Decrypt_\varepsilon\big(sk, C'\big) = \delta(m_1, \ldots, m_t)$.

Generally speaking, the desired functionality of $Evaluate_\varepsilon$ is that, if c_i encrypts m_i under pk, then $C' \leftarrow Evaluate_\varepsilon(pk, \delta, C)$ encrypts $\delta(m_1, \ldots, m_t)$ under pk, where $\delta(m_1, \ldots, m_t)$ is the output of δ on inputs $m_1, \ldots, m_t$. In this sense, the four operations establish the bases for a formal definition of a FHE scheme and fundamentals properties of correctness and compactness.

Definition 1. Correctness. A HE scheme ε is correct for circuits in δ_ε if, for any key-pair (sk, pk) output by $KeyGen_\varepsilon(\lambda)$, any circuit $\delta \in \delta_\varepsilon$, any plaintexts $m_1, \ldots, m_t$, and any ciphertexts $C = c_1, \ldots, c_t$ with $c_i \leftarrow Encrypt_\varepsilon(pk, m_i)$, it is the case that:

$$C' \leftarrow Evaluate_\varepsilon(pk, \delta, C), \text{ then } Decrypt_\varepsilon\big(sk, C'\big) \rightarrow \delta(m_1, \ldots, m_t) \qquad (1)$$

Definition 2. Compactness. A HE scheme ε is compact if there is a polynomial f such that, for every value of the security parameter λ, $Decrypt_\varepsilon$ can be expressed as a circuit D_ε of size at most $f(\lambda)$. Now, let ε be compact and also correct for all circuits in δ_ε, then ε "compactly evaluates" δ_ε.

Definition 3. Fully Homomorphic Encryption. A HE scheme ε is fully homomorphic if it compactly evaluates all circuits, i.e.:

$$Decrypt_\varepsilon(sk, Evaluate_\varepsilon(pk, \delta, c_1, \ldots, c_t)) = \delta(m_1, \ldots, m_t) \qquad (2)$$

Additionally to the formal definition of FHE, the bootstrapping process is fundamental for a FHE scheme, the next section describes its importance and sketches the process.

3.2 Bootstrapping

As previously mentioned, the encryption process and homomorphic operations require adding an error term to guarantee a certain level of security; the plaintext is hidden by noise, which can be removed by decryption. However, the error is increased with each homomorphic operation, and the decryption process is hopeless when the error reaches a threshold.

The notion of bootstrapping was introduced to limit the error growing in SHE schemes; it allows the generation of the first FHE scheme. In general, bootstrapping uses a recryption function that evaluates the decryption function homomorphically to refresh the noisy ciphertext. The recryption function encrypts a ciphertext anew and subsequently removing the inner encryption by homomorphically evaluating the doubly encrypted plaintext using the encrypted secret key [18]. In other words, recryption refers to the process of executing $Evaluate_\varepsilon$ function on $Decrypt_\varepsilon$, i.e., $Evaluate_\varepsilon(pk, D_\varepsilon, c)$, where D_ε is the $Decrypt_\varepsilon$ function expressed as a circuit of size at most $f(\lambda)$, see Algorithm 1. A scheme is called bootstrappable if it can evaluate its own decryption algorithm circuit.

Algorithm 1 defines a sufficient process to build a FHE scheme out of the SHE, see [7] for more details. Broadly, $Evaluate_\varepsilon$ function takes in the bits of sk_1 and c_1, each encrypted under pk_2, i.e., $\overline{\langle sk_{1j} \rangle}$ and $\overline{\langle c_{1j} \rangle}$, where sk_{1j} denotes the j th bit of sk_1. After, ε is used to evaluate the decryption circuit homomorphically. The output c_2 is encryption under pk_2 of $Decrypt_\varepsilon(sk_1, c_1) = m$. Since m is doubly encrypted, the inner encryption is removed through the $Evaluate_\varepsilon$ function, thus obtaining a new ciphertext with the same thing as the original one.

Algorithm 1. Recryption function in bootstrapping
Input: $pk_2, D_\varepsilon, \langle \overline{sk_{1j}} \rangle, c_1$
Output: c_2
Set $\overline{c_{1j}} \leftarrow Encrypt_\varepsilon(pk_2, c_{1j})$
$c_{2j} \leftarrow Evaluate_\varepsilon(pk_2, D_\varepsilon, \langle\langle \overline{sk_{1j}} \rangle, \langle \overline{c_{1j}} \rangle\rangle)$

Self-reference has been proven impossible at times. In this context, bootstrapping is a homomorphic encryption scheme able to decrypt itself. The next section provides additional information about this characteristic.

3.3 Key-Switching

The notion of bootstrapping refers to a process that allows the encryption/decryption procedure to be executed homomorphically. In algorithmic terms, bootstrapping can be defined as:

$$C'' = Encrypt_\varepsilon\left(pk_2, Decrypt_\varepsilon\left(sk_1, C'\right)\right) \tag{3}$$

According to Eq. (3), a fresh ciphertext C'' is generated with less noise than the original C'. sk_1 and C' are encrypted under a public key pk_1 and C'' under pk_2. The encryption of sk_1 is usually referred to as bootstrapping key bk. bk is a fundamental piece for the correct operation of the process. The quality in the selection and development of bk is directly proportional to the performance carried out by bootstrapping and, therefore, of the FHE scheme.

There are two alternatives to define bk: encrypt the secret key sk under itself $Encrypt_\varepsilon(sk, sk)$, or under another key $Encrypt_\varepsilon(sk', sk)$. The first possibility implies that the refreshed ciphertext C'' is encrypted under the same key as the original ciphertext C', it requires *circular security* [11] assumption to avoid handling a key collection.

The second alternative, also known as *key-switching*, has the advantage of not requiring *circular security*. Hence, it handles multiple keys. Likewise, the number of keys is a fundamental limitation of *key-switching*, i.e., n available keys allow to perform n bootstrapping operations, thus achieving only a leveled homomorphism.

A combination of both alternatives is a possible solution to these problems, a *circular security* scheme with *key-switching*. As an example, the following sequence of keys: $sk_1 \to sk_2 \to \ldots sk_n \to sk_1$ and so on, i.e., using a collection of keys iteratively. These schemes have been widely used in different domains. The next section presents the last advance in the field of HE and MLaaS.

4   Last Advances in the Field of HE

This section presents a comprehensive review of the last advances in the field of FHE on the MLaaS domain. First, we highlight the gap in the related literature on both topics, a lack of a specialized study of contributions to machine learning models. Later, we identify general limitations, introduce the latest approaches, and establish the current research in the area.

4.1   Related Work

This section presents a brief description of surveys in the literature related to HE schemes; the main idea is to emphasize the contribution of each work and provide an extensive bibliography reference in the field of FHE and machine learning.

Since Gentry [7] presented the first bootstrapping technique to transform a SHE scheme into a FHE, multiple contributions to performance improvement, new approaches, and applications have appeared in the literature. At the same time, various surveys consolidate the work carried out and gave a clear knowledge foundation to researchers interested in applying and extending FHE approaches.

Fundamental concepts related to implementation and development in HE, particularly in FHE, are addressed in [18]. The authors present the last advances in the field and discuss relevant terminology and notions.

In [19, 20], the benefits of real-world applications with the use of FHE or SHE are exhibited, the authors analyze the practical use of applications in medical, financial, and advertising domains, and present their significant limitations in computational cost.

An exhaustive literature review in the field and open research directions to essential contributions are described in [21]. Likewise, the topic is presented from an engineering perspective in [22], the state-of-the-art approaches are analyzed and compared with respect to performance and security. Also, several works [23–26] cover developments in homomorphic encryption, aimed mainly at mathematicians or expert readers rather than practitioners.

Other works focused on specific domains can be found in the literature. For example, signal processing applications [27], cloud applications [28], or hardware implementation solutions of FHE schemes [29].

The extensive literature review exhibits the absence of a specialized survey in the domain of MLaaS and FHE schemes. We mean a classified compendium of contributions related to the design of machine learning modules for processing confidential information using homomorphic ciphers over encrypted data.

4.2 FHE on Machine Learning as a Service Paradigm

In this section, we introduce the MLaaS paradigm and show its potential use with FHE. Both approaches enable the classification or prediction process over encrypted data without leaking any underlying information. Also, we review the current state-of-the-art in the field and present future research directions in the privacy-preserving evaluation of these models.

In a nutshell, MLaaS refers to a cluster of services that offer machine learning tools as a component of cloud computing services [30]. MLaaS has emerged as a flexible and scalable solution to run predictive models remotely. However, the multiple benefits of MLaaS can generate inherent security and privacy concerns. For example, prediction or classification models involve highly sensitive information: medical, advertising, financial data, among others.

FHE offers an elegant way to solve this apparent paradox by allowing encrypted data to be blindly processed by a remote server, i.e., the third-party does not learn anything about the data, or output of the computation. According to the notation used in previous sections, the desired operation is as follows: given an scheme ε, a model α, and an input pattern encrypted $Encrypt_\varepsilon(p)$, a FHE scheme returns a ciphertext c such that $Decrypt_\varepsilon(c) = \alpha(p)$, i.e., the evaluation of the model α on the input p.

Under this premise, many cryptographic systems have focused on implementing machine learning models for the prediction or classification of confidential information using homomorphic ciphers [31].

Naehrig et al. [19] considered a logistic regression model with private prediction where training data are protected in the generation of the regression coefficients. The model enables an efficient message encoding where n independent encryptions of bits can be packed into a single ciphertext that encodes a degree-$(n - 1)$ polynomial.

Regarding classification models, Khedr et al. [32] implement Bayesian filters and decision trees on encrypted data using FHE, supporting ciphertexts multiplication without requiring *key-switching*.

Some researches delve into FHE schemes capable of enriching the MLaaS paradigm, those contributions are dedicated to the design of efficient frameworks for the arbitrary evaluation of complex Neural Networks (NN) over encrypted data.

CryptoNets [33] was the first approach to address the challenge of achieving a blind non-interactive classification. The NN over ciphertexts applies a SHE scheme into the inputs and propagates the signals across the network homomorphically. Nevertheless, the replacement of the sigmoid activation function and the computational overhead limit its performance.

Several subsequent works in literature try to improve the CryptoNets approach:

Chabanne et al. [34] addressed the limitations of CryptoNets by taking advantage of the batch normalization principle. The implementation enables a homomorphic evaluation of deeper NNs and achieves an accuracy similar to the best non-secure versions.

Badawi et al. [35] presented a convolutional NN for image classification with properties of FHE on GPUs, the AlexNet accelerates the classification process and maintains security and accuracy, it is a way towards efficient MLaaS.

Zhang et al. [36] proposed a privacy-preserving deep learning model for big data feature learning. The model uses a Brakerski-Gentry-Vaikuntanathan (BGV) homomorphic scheme [11] to support a back-propagation algorithm training on the cloud.

Other approaches propose to restructure the network:

Takabi et al. [37] worked over decentralized scenarios, where the datasets are distributed across multiple parties. They use a polynomial approximation as an activation function to train a NN.

Phong et al. [38] introduced an additively HE with asynchronous stochastic gradient descent on a Deep Neural Network (DNN). The approach keeps intact the accuracy and adds a tolerable overhead to the conventional deep learning system.

Wagh et al. [39] proposed a novel secure three-party protocol for multiple NNs building blocks. This model enables the training and inference of several NNs architectures without learning about the data.

Notwithstanding, FHE schemes still suffer from performance problems. For instance, any HE is capable of natively supporting division operations or comparisons, such as the test of equality/inequality. Number comparison or sign determination are essential operations for the implementation of cryptographic algorithms and cloud computing [40]. Consequently, many algorithms appear out of reach without substantial redevelopment [17].

In this way, efforts have focused on designing approximate methods to address these limitations. Babenko et al. [40] introduced a technique for numerical comparison in the Residue Number System (RNS) without requiring resource-consuming non-modular operations.

Table 1 presents a comparison between the main approaches of this nature, emphasizing its operational characteristics, objectives, ML approach, and implemented scheme. The classification of the implemented scheme is based on the four families presented in Sect. 2. According to Table 1, the majority of current works in FHE focus on security and efficiency. However, both objectives are in conflict, a higher level of security, greater computing resources are needed, and, therefore, less efficiency.

Table 1. Comparative of HE approaches

Reference	Year	Operations			ML approach					Scheme						Objective	
		Addition	Multiplication	Other	Logistic regression	Neural Networks	Deep Neural Networks	Decision Trees	Discrete Fourier Transform	Ideal Lattice-based	Integer-based	(R) LWE	NTRU	Two-party	Multi-party	Security	Efficiency
[2]	1978		•											•		•	
[4]	1985		•											•		•	
[5]	1999	•												•		•	
[7]	2009	•	•							•				•		•	
[19]	2011	•	•		•						•			•		•	
[14]	2014	•	•										•	•			•
[41]	2014	•	•		•						•			•		•	
[31]	2015	•	•						•		•			•		•	
[32]	2015	•	•						•		•			•		•	
[37]	2016	•	•				•				•				•	•	•
[33]	2016	•	•			•					•			•		•	
[42]	2016	•	•								•			•		•	
[43]	2016	•	•		•							•		•		•	
[36]	2016	•	•				•				•				•	•	
[1]	2017	•	•									•		•		•	•
[34]	2017	•	•				•				•			•		•	
[44]	2017	•	•						•			•		•		•	
[45]	2018	•	•		•							•		•		•	
[38]	2018	•					•				•				•	•	•
[46]	2018	•	•				•				•			•		•	
[35]	2018	•	•				•				•			•		•	•
[6]	2018	•	•				•				•			•		•	
[39]	2019	•	•					•			•				•	•	
[40]	2019	•	•	•										•		•	•

The literature review exposes three main directions in FHE's research and development:

i. Optimization of the bootstrapping procedure, the major bottleneck in a FHE implementation. The aim is to improve data processing speed and its recurrent evaluation in a circuit, both intricate tasks. Moreover, although noise needs to be controlled through bootstrapping, approaches capable of reducing noise generation are also required.

ii. Improving the technical characteristics and expanding the scope of the homomorphic ciphers. A higher number of operations in FHE can benefit the security of more real-world applications. For instance, the comparison of numbers, or determine the sign of a number are operations that can define how far is the practical usage of FHE.

iii. Designing and implementing machine learning models. A small number of primitives have been developed for predicting, and classifying confidential information using FHE schemes. The main goal is to enrich the MLaaS paradigm.

5 Applications and Tools

In this section, we outline the potential of FHE in real-world applications and present current tools for its development. Instead of including an exhaustive applications list, we evidence the importance of FHE and the breadth of domains that can benefit from it.

The traditional security model proposes to encrypt confidential information before being transferred to a server to protect data from non-trustworthy third-parties. However, a vulnerability appears when data have to be processed because the server needs unencrypted access to the data to compute on it. The traditional model is literally used in all computer applications that need security; this situation enables a wide range of potential application lines to develop FHE schemes in almost any domain. In other words, a computing environment without significant benefit from this kind of constructions is challenging to identify.

Considering the strongly applied nature of FHE schemes, theoretical research should be complemented with high-quality implementations, thus feeding back current efforts and identifying remaining limitations. In this sense, it is currently possible to find implementations in areas such as genomics, smart cities, medical diagnosis, spam filtering, image processing, advertising, financial privacy, etc. (see more details in [18–20]). A promising long-pursue application is a search without disclosure where the engine does not know what it is looking for, but it does. In a nutshell, we can encompass all these tasks in a single one: computation delegation.

Several homomorphic encryption libraries have been released over the years by numerous authors, mostly for specific implementations. We focus on those that allow the reader to develop solutions in a broad spectrum of possibilities.

Simple Encrypted Arithmetic Library (SEAL) [47] is a well-documented open-source HE tool powered by Microsoft. SEAL owns high popularity in the field and important affordability for experts and practitioners with a limited background.

Homomorphic-Encryption Library (HElib) [48] is one of the most widely used libraries in applications, HElib is characterized by executing homomorphic operations efficiently, but with limited bootstrapping performance.

Faster Fully Homomorphic Encryption (TFHE) [9] is a library that features the bootstrapping procedure in a fraction of second. This improvement is due to the implementation of an alternative representation of the LWE problem over the torus.

PALISADE [49] is an open-source HE software library, the project provides implementations of lattice cryptography building blocks and leading HE schemes following security standards for HE.

cuHE [50] is a CUDA GPU library to accelerate evaluations with homomorphic schemes, where the optimizations take full advantage of the mass parallelism and high memory bandwidth GPUs.

Homomorphic Encryption for Arithmetic of Approximate Numbers (HEAAN) [51] is a library with supports of fixed-point arithmetic. HEAAN supports approximate operations between rational numbers.

Homomorphic Encryption transformer for nGraph (HE transformer) [52] is a graph compiler for NN powered by Intel; the project is a proof-of-concept for HE on local machines with the goal of measure performance of various HE schemes for deep learning.

6   Conclusion

A large number of works in the field of homomorphic encryption have been proposed due to its strongly applied nature in real-world problems and significant privacy benefits. The increasing use of cloud computing makes full homomorphic encryption an ideal candidate to solve security problems, so the development of a specialized survey in the intersection of both domains appears to be an essential task.

This paper intends to be a reference guide for researchers and practitioners interested in learning, applying, and extending the knowledge on homomorphic encryption and machine learning. The manuscript covers theoretical concepts, state-of-the-art, capabilities, limitations, potential applications, and useful development tools of both fields. Moreover, we highlight the limitations from a theoretical and a practical point of view, identifying potential research directions to enrich the new paradigm of machine learning as a service.

In this sense, our work can serve as guidelines with the goal of blindly process, classify or predict encrypted information by non-trustworthy third-parties without disclosing confidential data. However, further study is required; this will be the subject of future work.

Acknowledgment. This work was partially supported by the Ministry of Education and Science of Russian Federation (Project 075-15-2020-788).

References

1. Player, R.: Parameter selection in lattice-based cryptography. Royal Holloway, University of London, Ph.D. Thesis (2017)
2. Rivest, R., Shamir, A., Adleman, L.: A method for obtaining digital signatures and public-key cryptosystems. Commun. ACM **21**, 120–126 (1978). https://doi.org/10.1145/359340.359342
3. Rivest, R.L., Dertouzos, M.L., Adleman, L.: On data banks and privacy homomorphisms. Found. Secur. Comput. **4**, 160–179 (1978)
4. ElGamal, T.: A public key cryptosystem and a signature scheme based on discrete logarithms. IEEE Trans. Inf. Theory **31**, 469–472 (1985). https://doi.org/10.1109/TIT.1985.1057074
5. Paillier, P.: Public-key cryptosystems based on composite degree residuosity classes. In: Stern, J. (ed.) EUROCRYPT 1999. LNCS, vol. 1592, pp. 223–238. Springer, Heidelberg (1999). https://doi.org/10.1007/3-540-48910-X_16

6. Minelli, M.: Fully homomorphic encryption for machine learning. PSL Research University, Ph.D. Thesis (2018)
7. Gentry, C.: A fully homomorphic encryption scheme. Stanford University, Ph.D. Thesis (2009)
8. van Dijk, M., Gentry, C., Halevi, S., Vaikuntanathan, V.: Fully homomorphic encryption over the integers. In: Gilbert, H. (ed.) EUROCRYPT 2010. LNCS, vol. 6110, pp. 24–43. Springer, Heidelberg (2010). https://doi.org/10.1007/978-3-642-13190-5_2
9. Chillotti, I., Gama, N., Georgieva, M., Izabachène, M.: Faster fully homomorphic encryption: bootstrapping in less than 0.1 seconds. In: Cheon, J.H., Takagi, T. (eds.) ASIACRYPT 2016. LNCS, vol. 10031, pp. 3–33. Springer, Heidelberg (2016). https://doi.org/10.1007/978-3-662-53887-6_1
10. Brakerski, Z., Vaikuntanathan, V.: Efficient fully homomorphic encryption from (standard) LWE. In: IEEE 52nd Annual Symposium on Foundations of Computer Science, pp. 97–106 (2011)
11. Brakerski, Z., Gentry, C., Vaikuntanathan, V.: (Leveled) fully homomorphic encryption without bootstrapping. In: Proceedings of the 3rd Innovations in Theoretical Computer Science Conference - ITCS 2012, pp. 309–325 (2012)
12. Gentry, C., Sahai, A., Waters, B.: Homomorphic encryption from learning with errors: conceptually-simpler, asymptotically-faster, attribute-based. In: Canetti, R., Garay, J.A. (eds.) CRYPTO 2013. LNCS, vol. 8042, pp. 75–92. Springer, Heidelberg (2013). https://doi.org/10.1007/978-3-642-40041-4_5
13. Gentry, C.: Computing arbitrary functions of encrypted data. Commun. ACM **53**, 97–105 (2010). https://doi.org/10.1145/1666420.1666444
14. Rohloff, K., Cousins, D.B.: A Scalable implementation of fully homomorphic encryption built on NTRU. In: Böhme R., Brenner M., Moore T., Smith M. (eds.) Financial Cryptography and Data Security, FC 2014, pp. 221–234 (2014)
15. Hiromasa, R., Abe, M., Okamoto, T.: Packing messages and optimizing bootstrapping in GSW-FHE. In: Katz, J. (ed.) PKC 2015. LNCS, vol. 9020, pp. 699–715. Springer, Heidelberg (2015). https://doi.org/10.1007/978-3-662-46447-2_31
16. Alperin-Sheriff, J., Peikert, C.: Faster bootstrapping with polynomial error. In: Garay, J.A., Gennaro, R. (eds.) CRYPTO 2014. LNCS, vol. 8616, pp. 297–314. Springer, Heidelberg (2014). https://doi.org/10.1007/978-3-662-44371-2_17
17. Aslett, L.J.M., Esperança, P.M., Holmes, C.C.: A review of homomorphic encryption and software tools for encrypted statistical machine learning (2015)
18. Armknecht, F., et al.: A guide to fully homomorphic encryption. IACR Cryptology ePrint Archive (2015)
19. Naehrig, M., Lauter, K., Vaikuntanathan, V.: Can homomorphic encryption be practical? In: 3rd ACM Workshop on Cloud Computing Security Workshop - CCSW 2011, pp. 113–124 (2011)
20. Archer, D., et al.: Applications of homomorphic encryption (2017)
21. Acar, A., Aksu, H., Selcuk Uluagac, A., Aksu, H., Uluagac, A.S.: A survey on homomorphic encryption schemes: theory and implementation. ACM Comput. Surv. **51**, 1–35 (2018). https://doi.org/10.1145/3214303
22. Martins, P., Sousa, L., Mariano, A.: A survey on fully homomorphic encryption: an engineering perspective. ACM Comput. Surv. **50**, 33 (2017). https://doi.org/10.1145/3124441
23. Parmar, P.V., et al.: Survey of various homomorphic encryption algorithms and schemes. Int. J. Comput. Appl. **91**(8), 26–32 (2014)
24. Vaikuntanathan, V.: Computing blindfolded: new developments in fully homomorphic encryption. In: IEEE 52nd Annual Symposium on Foundations of Computer Science, Palm Springs, pp. 5–16 (2011)

25. Sobitha Ahila, S., Shunmuganathan, K.L.: State of art in homomorphic encryption schemes. Int. J. Eng. Res. Appl. **4**, 37–43 (2014)

26. Gentry, C.: Computing on the edge of chaos: structure and randomness in encrypted computation. In: Proceedings of the International Congress of Mathematicians (2014)

27. Aguilar-Melchor, C., Fau, S., Fontaine, C., Gogniat, G., Sirdey, R.: Recent advances in homomorphic encryption: a possible future for signal processing in the encrypted domain. IEEE Signal Process. Mag. **30**, 108–117 (2013). https://doi.org/10.1109/MSP.2012.2230219

28. Hrestak, D., Picek, S.: Homomorphic encryption in the cloud. In: 37th International Convention on Information and Communication Technology, Electronics and Microelectronics (MIPRO 2014), pp. 1400–1404 (2014)

29. Moore, C., O'Neill, M., Hanley, N., O'Sullivan, E.: Accelerating integer-based fully homomorphic encryption using Comba multiplication. In: IEEE Workshop on Signal Processing Systems, SiPS, pp. 1–6. IEEE (2014)

30. Hunt, T., Song, C., Shokri, R., Shmatikov, V., Witchel, E.: Chiron: privacy-preserving machine learning as a service (2018)

31. Bost, R., Popa, R.A., Tu, S., Goldwasser, S.: Machine learning classification over encrypted data. In: Network and Distributed System Security Symposium (2015)

32. Khedr, A., Gulak, G., Member, S., Vaikuntanathan, V.: SHIELD: scalable homomorphic implementation of encrypted data-classifiers. IEEE Trans. Comput. **65**, 2848–2858 (2015). https://doi.org/10.1109/TC.2015.2500576

33. Dowlin, N., Gilad-Bachrach, R., Laine, K., Lauter, K., Naehrig, M., Wernsing, J.: CryptoNets: applying neural networks to encrypted data with high throughput and accuracy. In: 33rd International Conference on Machine Learning, pp. 201–210 (2016)

34. Chabanne, H., De Wargny, A., Milgram, J., Morel, C., Prouff, E.: Privacy-preserving classification on deep neural network (2017)

35. Badawi, A.Al., et al.: The AlexNet moment for homomorphic encryption: HCNN, the first homomorphic CNN on encrypted data with GPUs (2018)

36. Zhang, Q., Yang, L.T., Chen, Z.: Privacy preserving deep computation model on cloud for big data feature learning. IEEE Trans. Comput. **65**, 1351–1362 (2016). https://doi.org/10.1109/TC.2015.2470255

37. Takabi, H., Hesamifard, E., Ghasemi, M.: Privacy preserving multi-party machine learning with homomorphic encryption. In: 29th Annual Conference on Neural Information Processing Systems (2016)

38. Phong, L.T., Aono, Y., Hayashi, T., Wang, L., Moriai, S.: Privacy-preserving deep learning via additively homomorphic encryption. IEEE Trans. Inf. Forensics Secur. **13**, 1333–1345 (2018). https://doi.org/10.1109/TIFS.2017.2787987

39. Wagh, S., Gupta, D., Chandran, N.: SecureNN: 3-party secure computation for neural network training. Proc. Priv. Enhancing Technol. **2019**, 26–49 (2019). https://doi.org/10.2478/popets-2019-0035

40. Babenko, M., et al.: Positional characteristics for efficient number comparison over the homomorphic encryption. Program. Comput. Softw. **45**(8), 532–543 (2019). https://doi.org/10.1134/S0361768819080115

41. Bos, J.W., Lauter, K., Naehrig, M.: Private predictive analysis on encrypted medical data. J. Biomed. Inform. **50**, 234–243 (2014). https://doi.org/10.1016/j.jbi.2014.04.003

42. Xu, C., Chen, J., Wu, W., Feng, Y.: Homomorphically encrypted arithmetic operations over the integer ring. In: Bao, F., Chen, L., Deng, R.H., Wang, G. (eds.) ISPEC 2016. LNCS, vol. 10060, pp. 167–181. Springer, Cham (2016). https://doi.org/10.1007/978-3-319-49151-6_12

43. Aono, Y., Hayashi, T., Phong, L.T., Wang, L.: Scalable and secure logistic regression via homomorphic encryption. In: 6th ACM Conference on Data and Application Security and Privacy - CODASPY 2016, pp. 142–144 (2016)

44. Costache, A., Smart, N.P., Vivek, S.: Faster homomorphic evaluation of discrete fourier transforms. In: Kiayias, A. (ed.) FC 2017. LNCS, vol. 10322, pp. 517–529. Springer, Cham (2017). https://doi.org/10.1007/978-3-319-70972-7_29

45. Kim, A., Song, Y., Kim, M., Lee, K., Cheon, J.H.: Logistic regression model training based on the approximate homomorphic encryption. BMC Med. Genomics **11**, 83 (2018). https://doi.org/10.1186/s12920-018-0401-7

46. Coron, J.-S., Lepoint, T., Tibouchi, M.: Scale-invariant fully homomorphic encryption over the integers. In: Krawczyk, H. (ed.) PKC 2014. LNCS, vol. 8383, pp. 311–328. Springer, Heidelberg (2014). https://doi.org/10.1007/978-3-642-54631-0_18

47. Chen, H., Laine, K., Player, R.: Simple Encrypted arithmetic library (2019)

48. Halevi, S., Shoup, V.: Design and implementation of a homomorphic-encryption library (2013)

49. PALISADE. https://palisade-crypto.org/community

50. Dai, W., Sunar, B.: cuHE: a homomorphic encryption accelerator library. In: Pasalic, E., Knudsen, Lars R. (eds.) BalkanCryptSec 2015. LNCS, vol. 9540, pp. 169–186. Springer, Cham (2016). https://doi.org/10.1007/978-3-319-29172-7_11

51. Cheon, J.H., Kim, A., Kim, M., Song, Y.: Homomorphic encryption for arithmetic of approximate numbers. In: Takagi, T., Peyrin, T. (eds.) ASIACRYPT 2017. LNCS, vol. 10624, pp. 409–437. Springer, Cham (2017). https://doi.org/10.1007/978-3-319-70694-8_15

52. Boemer, F., Lao, Y., Cammarota, R., Wierzynski, C.: NGraph-HE: a graph compiler for deep learning on homomorphically encrypted data. In: Proceedings of the 16th ACM International Conference on Computing Frontiers, pp. 3–13 (2019)

Distributed Greedy Approach for Autonomous Surveillance Using Unmanned Aerial Vehicles

Santiago Behak, Giovani Rondán, Martín Zanetti, Santiago Iturriaga[✉],
and Sergio Nesmachnow

Universidad de la República, Montevideo, Uruguay
{santiago.behak,giovani.rondan,martin.zanetti,
siturria,sergion}@fing.edu.uy

Abstract. This article presents a distributed approach for autonomous exploration and surveillance using unmanned aerial vehicles. The proposed solution applies the agent-oriented paradigm to implement a cooperative approach to solve the problem efficiently. A specific state machine is proposed for unmanned aerial vehicles to implement the coordination needed to explore and monitor a set of points of interest without a centralized infrastructure. The system is conceived to be applied in low-cost commercial unmanned aerial vehicles, to provide an affordable solution for the problem. The experimental evaluation is performed over real and synthetic scenarios. Relevant metrics are studied, including coverage of the explored area and surveillance of the defined points of interest, considering the flight autonomy limitations due to the battery charge. Results demonstrate the validity and applicability of the proposed distributed approach and the effectiveness of the greedy exploration strategy to fulfill the considered goals.

Keywords: Computational intelligence · Distributed agents · Unmanned aerial vehicles · Surveillance

1 Introduction

Unmanned Aerial Vehicles (UAVs) have emerged as a useful tool in many application areas, e.g., agriculture (field fertilization, measurements, and analysis of soil and crops) [8], military applications (e.g., reconnaissance and offensive missions), security (surveillance [17] and support for rescue tasks [2]), logistics, and other relevant applications. Currently, most of the existing applications are based on remote control (by a human operator) of UAVs that do not fly autonomously. In general, UAVs require a pilot to control them directly, or to at least carry out follow-up tasks. Few systems have been proposed for completely autonomous operation, via system-on-a-chip or single-(on)board computers.

One of the main limitations of UAVs is their flight autonomy. The flight range of an UAVs is the maximum distance (or time) it can fly on a full charge

© Springer Nature Switzerland AG 2021
S. Nesmachnow et al. (Eds.): CARLA 2020, CCIS 1327, pp. 130–145, 2021.
https://doi.org/10.1007/978-3-030-68035-0_10

of its battery. While sophisticated UAVs provide a reasonable flight range, they are also very expensive. On the other hand, low-cost commercial UAVs provide an appropriate solution for simple tasks, but their flight range is limited. Specifically, the autonomy of most commercial UAVs does not exceed 25–30 min. Furthermore, a full charge of the UAV battery is a slow process that takes about an hour. These two drawbacks pose severe limitations to the practical operation of low-cost commercial UAVs in tasks that requires a constant presence, such as the surveillance of a terrain. These problems can be mitigated using a fleet of multiple UAVs instead of a single one. A fleet improves the efficiency of the system, allowing cooperation among several agents (the UAVs in the fleet) that operate in parallel. It also provides a solution for covering the duties of any single UAV that must recharge its battery, to maintain a constant presence in the air. For these reasons, studying intelligent methods to guarantee autonomous flight of UAV fleets has become and interesting subject in the area [18].

In this line of work, this article studies a cooperative approach for autonomous UAVs operation. The main goal is to develop a system to allow controlling a fleet of low-cost commercial UAVs in a completely autonomous and distributed manner, to fulfill two goals: exploration and surveillance. In particular, the problem to be solved has the following characteristics: i) UAVs in the fleet must operate autonomously, without control of a human operator or a central server; ii) UAVs must be able to communicate with each other to exchange information; iii) the system must focus on maximizing the covered area in the minimum time possible; and iv) certain points of interest (POI) are defined in the area to be explored, which have priority over other locations, and must be monitored regularly.

The proposed system is implemented over low-cost commercial UAVs (Parrot Bebop 2), using an environment for programming each UAV to have an autonomous behavior. This is a specific contribution of the reported research, since low-cost commercial UAVs do not include this type of environment, or just offer a simple API that only allows controlling the UAV remotely. In turn, all the functionalities needed to perform basic actions (communication between UAVs, determining their location in space, navigation) are implemented. The logic of the system is implemented in a state machine, and a specific distributed greedy algorithm is proposed to determine the flight planning. The experimental evaluation determines the capabilities of the proposed approach to successfully perform the exploration and surveillance tasks, and the proposed greedy algorithm is compared to other planning strategies over different realistic scenarios, considering different dimensions of the studied area, obstacles, and different surveillance requirements for POIs. Results show that the developed system is effective to fulfill the goals of the problem. The capabilities of the autonomous system to meet the exploration goals is highlighted, in addition to the reduced response time for monitoring the considered POIs. Furthermore, the implemented planning algorithm is able to react to information collected in real time, which allows taking into account situations that vary during the system operation, such as already explored areas and POIs that require to be visited.

The article is organized as follows. Section 2 describes the problem of autonomous flight of UAVs. Section 3 describes the proposed distributed approach for exploration and surveillance. The experimental evaluation and results are reported and discussed in Sect. 4. Finally, the conclusions and the main lines for future work are presented in Sect. 5.

2 Exploration and Surveillance Using Autonomous UAVs

This section describes the problem of autonomous flight of unmanned aerial vehicles for exploration and surveillance and reviews related works.

2.1 Autonomous Exploration and Surveillance

The problem to be solved consists of efficiently exploring and surveil a territory using a fleet of UAVs that fly autonomously. A set of different POIs is considered within the area to explore/surveil. POIs require to be periodically monitored, thus they are prioritized in the surveillance. The exploration goal implies that UAVs should maximize the area covered in the shortest time possible, to overcome low flight autonomy due to limited battery charge.

Several subproblems are considered. The exploration goal involves a global path planning problem to efficiently cover the area. In turn, the priority of the considered POI imposes constraints on the possible paths computed for exploration. The computed paths must consider the flight autonomy, since UAVs must return to a charging dock to allow a continuous operation of the system. All these subproblems have to be addressed cooperatively by UAVs in the fleet, without considering a centralized infrastructure (e.g., a central server) that controls the UAVs or even has global visibility of the fleet. Thus, an agent-based approach must be applied, where each UAV includes the logic to communicate and cooperate with other UAVs in the fleet. Then, a new subproblem arises when considering that UAVs must establish an ad-hoc network, so that communication can be performed independently of requiring an external network infrastructure.

Finally, the problem poses a significant additional challenge, because the target vehicles are low-cost commercial UAVs. This decision is motivated by the goal of providing a scalable and cost-efficiently solution, that can be implemented in practice for surveillance of small and medium-size areas (e.g., educational, industrial, or commercial facilities). This requirement implies that all the logic must be implemented in the UAVs, using the available hardware infrastructure and software able to run over it.

2.2 Related Works

Several recent articles have addressed different variants of the exploration problem using UAVs, providing different autonomy levels and developing solutions for diverse objective platforms.

Mufalli et al. [12] applied an optimization approach for military reconnaissance of target installations (whose location is known in advance), by UAVs equipped with sensors. Two subproblems were considered: assigning sensors to UAVs and routing them to fulfill the mission goals. A purely mathematical approach was applied, using CPLEX for problem instances modeling simple missions and heuristics to address larger missions. The approach applying Column Generation was able to compute the best solutions. No specific implementation was proposed to be developed and operated in UAVs.

Cesare et al. [3] proposed an algorithm for coordinating a team of UAVs in order to explore previously unknown territory, considering battery limitations and unreliable communications. A state machine of five states (explore, meet, sacrifice, relay, and go home) is proposed: exploration is based on defining borders between explored space and unknown space; meet is used for sharing data in a known location; relay state lands the UAV; and go home sends a UAV to a base location. The (unrealistic) sacrifice state commands the UAV to explore disregarding its remaining battery. The proposed approach was evaluated in a small safe area (office exploration) using two custom-built quadcopters. The proposal is based on the premise that UAVs do not need to return to a base location, thus it is not practical for realistic surveillance scenarios.

Grøtli and Johansen [6] solved the (offline) path planning of UAVs via Mixed Integer Linear Programming, minimizing fuel consumption and maximizing connectivity between UAVs and considering communication and terrain avoidance constraints. Data from the SPLAT! service for radio communications were used to estimate connectivity levels. Experiments were performed for a case study considering two UAVs to form a communication chain from a base station to a target station and considering a no-fly zone in the studied area. No specific implementation on UAVs was proposed. Shang et al. [16] proposed a hybrid algorithm to maximize benefits from UAVs surveillance subject to flight autonomy. Genetic Algorithm, Ant Colony Optimization, and Path Relinking (PR) were combined to provide a flexible optimization method for the theoretical approach presented. No practical application was proposed or developed.

Previous work from our research group [5] explored the application of evolutionary algorithms and agent-oriented programming to solve the static off-line planning of a fleet of UAVs to achieve compromise values between the explored area, the proximity of the UAVs, and surveillance metrics. Results indicated that the proposed techniques are capable of computing effective flight plans to be used as input for more sophisticated navigation methods to be implemented in the UAVs [4]. Schleich et al. [15] proposed a control approach for a fleet of UAVs to patrol an area, relying on communications for surveillance and connected coverage model that reinforces successful paths for other UAVs to follow. The mobility model was compared with a random strategy to select destinations, regarding coverage and connectivity in simulations with up to 20 UAVs. Results showed a reduced negative impact on coverage, but connectivity is significantly improved. The model does not apply computational intelligence and does not include the reactive navigation component provided by agent-oriented programming.

Some other articles focused specifically on communications. Kopeikin et al. [9] analyzed the characteristics of the communication channels established on ad-hoc networks of UAVs and concluded that proper control of the network is critical for a distributed system to function properly. Bekmezci et al. [1] introduced the concept of flying ad-hoc network, which is critical for autonomous operation, and described the main design challenges and protocols. A recent analysis was presented in the survey by Oubbati et al. [14], including classification and comparative description of existing routing protocols.

The analysis of related works allows concluding that several researches focused on autonomous flight and surveillance models for UAV fleets, with emphasis on cooperative models using ad-hoc communication networks. However, few proposals have included specific distributed agent-based approaches to be implemented in real UAVs. No proposals for low-cost commercial UAVs were found, mainly because of the intrinsic difficulties of software development on the limited API provided. Thus, there is room to contribute to this line of research by implementing and evaluating distributed agent-based flight control systems.

3 The Proposed Distributed Cooperative Approach for Exploration and Surveillance

This section describes the proposed distributed cooperative approach for exploration and surveillance using autonomous low-cost commercial UAVs.

3.1 Overall Description

The proposed research posed several challenges to design and implement a robust system to be used in practice over real low-cost commercial hardware. One of the first difficulties was determining alternatives that allow the execution of a software program directly on the UAV hardware. This was the first issue solved, since it has a direct impact on the implementation of the other components of the system, including the exploration algorithms, the communications network, and the control/positioning mechanism. In addition, several limitations generated at software level by the operating system (OS) that runs on the UAVs were addressed. After that, the implementation of flight instructions was addressed. In turn, the communication components of the proposed solution were developed, which were needed for the next stage, that involved the development of the logic for autonomous flight control via a specific state machine and exploration strategies. These components and stages are described in the following subsection.

3.2 Hardware and Software

Hardware. The research was developed using low-cost commercial Parrot Bebop 2 UAVs, which have several useful features, including a strong and simple design, a good quality camera, GPS positioning, and flight stabilization systems. On the other hand, the Bebop 2 model has an important limitation: its hardware was not designed for directly executing programs implemented by third parties.

Table 1 presents the main features of low-cost commercial Parrot Bebop 2 UAVs. Bebop 2 features the ARMv7 RISC architecture, which is not compatible with x86 processors of desktop computers. Thus, specific systems are needed to compile programs to be used in Bebop 2 UAVs. Next subsection describes different alternatives proposed to overcome the limitations presented by the ARMv7 architecture and the custom OS in Bebop 2.

Table 1. Main features of low-cost commercial Parrot Bebop 2 UAVs.

Feature	Description
Rotor system	Four rotors (diameter: 5 cm), three blades per helix
Max. speed	18 m/s (horizontal), 6 m/s (vertical)
Signal range	300 m
Battery	2.700 mAh
Flight autonomy	20–25 min
Front camera	14 megapíxeles
Dimensions	$33 \times 30 \times 10$ cm
Memory	8 GB
Weight	480 g
CPU architecture	ARMv7
Sensors (accessible via SDK)	Digital camera (1080 dpi), GPS sensor, altimeter
Sensors (not accessible via SDK)	Accelerometer, gyroscope, compass
Operating system	Unix (Busybox)

Software. Bebop 2 UAVs use Busybox, a specific Unix distribution modified by Parrot to prevent users from executing certain tasks (e.g., network connection, accessing the file system, executing privileged operations); it only grants access to a limited part of the memory and does not allow new programs to be installed or compiled directly from the UAV. Several alternatives were evaluated to compile a program for ARMv7. Cross-compiling between x86 and ARM was analyzed, but many drawbacks emerged do to the limited capabilities of the OS and libraries installed in the UAVs. The use of the Qemu emulator to execute a custom OS was also studied, but its installation/configuration are also difficult. A third alternative was adopted: programs were compiled in (general purpose) Raspberry Pi, which features the ARM architecture. This approach provides a simpler solution, without requiring emulators or cumbersome techniques. In any case, compiling and installing programs on the UAV is a complex and time-consuming task, so we decided to install the minimum number of programs.

A software development kit (SDK) is provided by Parrot to develop simple software for controlling the UAV remotely, e.g., FreeFlightPro, an application to control the Bebop 2 manually. Using the Parrot SDK directly to develop/run programs is a complex task, so `pyparrot` (pypi.org/project/pyparrot), a Python library that implements an interface to the Parrot SDK was used.

Pyparrot offers a variety of control options (e.g, connect/disconnect, take-off/landing, camera control, sensor reading, etc., but it was not designed to be used for a fleet of UAVs. Thus, several modifications were needed to operate a fleet and implement the proposed strategies for exploration and surveillance. The original version of the *connect* method provided to establish the connection between pyparrot and the UAV, randomly connects one when many are flying around. To solve this problem, the method was extended to receive a specific IP address to identify the connected UAV and modified to handle several of them operating in a fleet. Connect also starts the flow of data from the sensors. Several additional modifications were performed for control and communications, as described in the following subsection.

3.3   Control and Positioning System

Geolocalization. Geolocalization is essential for the correct operation of several functionalities, such as take-off/landing, collecting data, maintaining the state of the map, evading obstacles, etc. Studied alternatives for geolocalization include:

- *relative positioning*: determines the UAV position based on the location of the starting point and a record of its movements. This method does not require using external sensors or other equipment, but it heavily depends on the precision of movements, which accumulates inaccuracies in practice.
- *GPS positioning*: uses information from the GPS sensor to estimate latitude and longitude coordinates of each UAV. GPS positioning has several drawbacks, including interference, delays (up to a few minutes) for satellite connection and about 10 seconds for updating, dependence on the weather, and a margin of error of approximately 5 m.
- *Wi-Fi Positioning System* (WPS): uses trigonometry to estimate the UAV position, measuring the signal strength of nearby Wi-Fi access points (AP). Theoretically, only three AP are needed, but in practice at least five are recommended [10]. Databases owned by IT companies are needed to get information (intensity, decay rate, AP location), which either are not free or do not provide enough accuracy for operating in medium-size areas.
- *positioning using camera images*: computes the relative position with respect to the known location of other objects, e.g. using a marker-based technique [4]. This method is accurate, but requires placing markers in the area and also demands computational resources for image processing.

The Parrot Bebop 2 do not have distance sensors, just a height sensor, and the SDK does not provide access to accelerometer or gyroscope information. Thus, developing a custom geolocation system is hard. WPS require three antennas to reduce the multipath effect, which the Bebop 2 does not have. Some functionalities require accuracy, e.g., landing in the charging pad, thus GPS positioning cannot be used. On the other hand, relative positioning can be implemented using the pyparrot relative flight mode and the information from the proposed navigation/exploration system.

Navigation. Two navigation modes were implemented: *lateral movements* and *rotation and forward translation*. Using only lateral movements is simpler and more accurate, but limits the view of the camera, which always points in the same direction. This can be mitigated by pointing the camera downwards, but the viewing area is less than pointing the camera tangentially at the ground. The rotation+translation mode allows the camera to be in a more natural position, close to 45° with respect to the horizontal, giving a larger, more natural viewing area for filming, but offering only one horizontal angle. On the other hand, rotation involves making an extra movement every time the UAV moves, which doubles the number of movements required. In addition, a mechanism in needed to allow the value of the rotation angle to be accurately determined, which is as costly as accurately determining the position of the UAV. These difficulties make the option of using rotations slow and imprecise.

3.4 Connectivity and Communications

Two alternatives were developed for establishing the communication network between UAVs: i) *ad-hoc master/managed network*, since the integrated network card in Bebop 2 (Broadcom BCM4360) only includes drivers for master/managed modes, the network is established by configuring a leader UAV in master mode and the others in managed mode; and ii) *WiFi network*, UAVs communicates using a WiFi covering the exploration area, without making one of them a single-point-of-failure. The default UAV configuration is changed to allow the managed mode, include an IP address, the name of the access point, and a password (a script was installed on each UAV to allow changing the interface mode).

A specific information exchange protocol was established between the UAVs through the established communication channel (see next subsection).

3.5 State Machine

The implemented control is based on the agent-oriented programming paradigm, to allow the collaboration of UAVs in the fleet. Each UAV executes the logic defined in the state machine presented in Fig. 1, which accounts for a specific exploration strategy, the considered PoI in the surveilled area, the communication protocol between UAVs, and the monitoring of the battery charge.

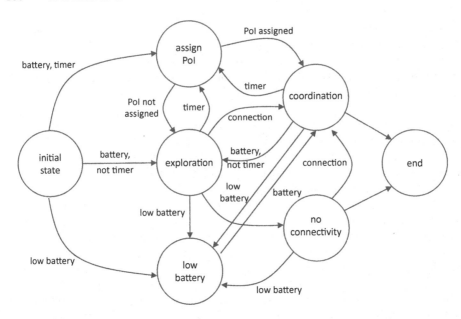

Fig. 1. State machine of the proposed distributed exploration system

Initial State. The initial state loads relevant parameters from a configuration file, including the dimensions of the explored area, the location of PoI, WiFi and video streaming parameters, etc. A synchronization algorithm is executed to coordinate the internal timers of each UAV to consider for POI surveillance. After that, all UAVs move to the exploration state.

Exploration State. A specific procedure is applied to determine the next area to visit, by dynamically defining movements using data collected in real time to determine the path of each UAV. Two strategies were implemented: *greedy* strategy and *by regions* strategy. Both strategies divide the area to explore in regular (square) zones. The greedy strategy (Algorithm 1) only considers neighboring zones in the search, visiting them according to the times of the last visit. On the other hand, the regions strategy (Algorithm 2) considers all zones, grouped in four regions (NW, NE, SE, and SW, clockwise). The coverage of each region is evaluated and the zone with the minimum time of last visited in the least covered region is selected. After performing a movement, the internal map of the UAV is updated, registering the current position as visited. Once this stage is completed, if the UAV can establish a connection with another one in the fleet, a *Coordination* is performed to implement the collaborative exploration system; otherwise the *No Connectivity* state of the machine is executed.

Algorithm 1 . Greedy exploration strategy

1: **for each** neighbor zone Z **do**
2:     timer = GetTimeLastVisit(Z)
3:     min = GetThreshold()
4:     **if** timer ¡ min **then**
5:         min = timer
6:         selectedZone = Z
7:     **end if**
8: **end for**
9: **return** selectedZone

Algorithm 2. Regions exploration strategy

1: **for each** region Z **do**
2:     coverage = GetCoverage(R)
3:     **if** coverage ¡ minCoverage **then**
4:         minCoverage = coverage
5:         selectedRegion = R
6:     **end if**
7: **end for**
8: **for each** zone Z in R **do**
9:     timer = GetTimeLastVisit(Z)
10:     min = GetThreshold()
11:     **if** timer ¡ min **then**
12:         min = timer
13:         selectedZone = Z
14:     **end if**
15: **end for**
16: **return** selectedZone

Assign PoI State. UAVs execute this state when the time since the last visit of a given zone is above a predefined threshold. A collaborative algorithm is then applied to select a UAV to attend the unattended PoI. A consensus algorithm based on the classical Paxos method for fault-tolerant distributed systems [11] is used. The proposed negotiation involves five steps: i) all available UAVs (battery charged and not assigned to any prioritized task) exchange messages to announce the participation on the decision process for a given PoI; a time window is defined by each UAV and all time windows are synchronized to avoid inconsistencies; ii) participating UAVs exchange message stating their distance to the PoI; iii) each UAV proposes the closest UAV to the PoI to be assigned to attend it; iv) each UAV revises the received proposals and the one with the most votes is selected; this step is repeated until just one candidate exists; v) the decision is communicated to the selected UAV; which is monitored by the other members of the fleet to assure that the mission is accepted and accomplished.

All UAVs act as leaders in the consensus algorithm (until the final step), benefiting from autonomy and reducing the impact of errors due to no-connectivity. All UAVs act as proposers and can be selected as acceptors. The considered PoI is the client, which issues a request to the distributed system, and waits for a response. In the case of a tie, the UAV with the greatest IP address is selected. The robustness of the method is guaranteed since distance is an absolute value for all UAVs and IP addresses are unique. UAVs not selected for PoI surveillance return to *Exploration* state. The selected UAV must prioritize visiting the assigned PoI, thus their movements are redirected. Two cases are distinguished: if the alert is not critical or the timer does not exceed the threshold value for a critical visit, the UAV returns to *Exploration* state but considering only zones that allow approximating to the assigned PoI. Otherwise, the UAV flies directly to the zone of the assigned PoI. To determine the shortest path to reach the destination, the A* pathfinding algorithm [7] is used, considering the Manhattan distance. When a PoI is visited, a message is sent to all UAVs to reset their timer for that PoI.

Low Battery State. This state is executed if the UAV charge is below a configurable threshold. Similar to the previous state, two cases are distinguished: if the battery charge is not critical (i.e., it allows performing more movements than those required to reach the charging platform from its current location), the UAV continues exploring, but considering only zones that allows approximating the charging platform. Otherwise, the UAV flies directly to the charging platform, considering the shortest path computed using the A* algorithm and the Manhattan distance. Once the UAV battery is charged, it rejoins the fleet.

Coordination State. In this state, UAVs send messages using the connection established in the initial state. Information about the current location is shared among UAVs and timers are updated accordingly. To check status mission each UAV tries to establish a connection with the assigned UAV to each PoI; when an ack is received, a message is sent to all other UAVs to warn that the mission is being carried out normally and UAVs move to *Exploration* state. If no member of the fleet receives a response from the UAV with the assigned mission, all UAVs return to the *assign PoI* state to reassign the PoI to an available UAV.

A specific protocol was defined over TCP/IP and queues are used to store messages waiting to be processed in the corresponding state for each UAV.

No Connectivity State. In case the UAV cannot establish a communication channel with any other member of the fleet, an off-line exploration is performed prioritizing visiting those zones where connection was previously established with other UAVs. If it has a PoI assigned, the mission is canceled. In turn, an offline update of the map is performed and the corresponding information is stored to be shared with the rest of the fleet after re-connection. If a re-connection is not possible, the UAV lands in the base and moves to the end state.

End State. At the end of the execution of the system, the UAV is landed in the base, close the communication channel and all relevant information of the execution is stored in CSV files.

4   Experimental Evaluation

This section describes the experimental evaluation of the proposed distributed approach for a UAV fleet.

4.1   Evaluation Methodology, Validation Problem and Instances

Methodology. Experiments were performed considering a fleet of three UAVs. The flight height was defined to 10 m. The (non-rotation) lateral displacement navigation mode was used, providing vision over an area of 10×18 m. Thus, each scenario is represented as a grid of rectangles of dimension 10×18 m. The maximum flying time of each UAV was set to 20 min (slightly shorter than the flight autonomy of Bebop 2 UAVs) and the total time of the mission is 120 min. The departing location is at the bottom left corner of the area. PoI generate standard and critical alerts that must be considered by the UAVs. Critical alerts have precedence over standard and must be attended first.

Metrics. Several metrics are proposed to evaluate the proposed exploration strategies. These metrics account for the two main objectives of the problem: cover the area to be explored and properly surveil the PoIs, with the least possible delay. The studied metrics are:

- percentage of the map covered (cov); a zone is considered covered if it is visited in the last 10 min;
- percentage of the map covered per time (cpt), based on samples taken every 10 s;
- average/best/worst response time (rt) to attend a standard PoI alert;
- average/best/worst response time to attend a critical PoI alert

A random walk is used as a baseline method to compare the results of the proposed exploration strategies. All results correspond to average values computed over 50 executions of each algorithm performed for each scenario.

Scenarios and Instances. Three realistic scenarios were considered in the evaluation, accounting for different dimensions and position of obstacles. Scenario 1 is based on a real facility to be surveilled using UAVs, from a company in Montevideo. This scenario was studied with real UAVs. In turn, two larger scenarios were built and studied using a distributed simulation approach, implemented over Sphinx, the official simulator for Parrot UAVs, based on Gazebo robotics software for 64-bit Linux. Experiments were executed on Xeon Gold 6138 processors with 128 GB of RAM memory and Nvidia Tesla P100 GPUs (12 GB memory), from National Supercomputing Center (Cluster-UY), Uruguay [13], following a Multiple-Instruction-Multiple-Data (MIMD) parallel approach.

For each scenario, ten instances are created varying the PoI locations (uniform distribution in the exploration zone) and the requests to be attended (uniform distribution between one and ten minutes). Overall, thirty problem instances are considered. Five executions are performed for each instance, and average/standard deviation values are reported for each metric. Details of the considered scenarios are provided in Fig. 2.

4.2   Numerical Results

Coverage. The greedy exploration strategy computed the best results for all scenarios. Improvements over random walk were 31.3% in average and up to 39.4% in the best case, while improvements over the regions strategy were 22.9%

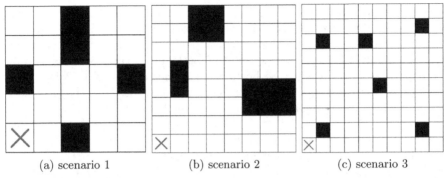

(a) scenario 1   (b) scenario 2   (c) scenario 3

attribute	scenario 1	scenario 2	scenario 3
description	small shed	medium-size lot	large terrain
dimensions	70 m×70 m	100 m×100 m	141 m×141 m
area, grid	5000 m² (5×5)	10000 m² (8×8)	20000 m² (10×10)
#PoI	1	3	5
obstacles	wall	buildings	trees, houses, etc.

Fig. 2. Evaluated scenarios: ✕–starting point, ■–obstacle, ☐–exploration zone.

Table 2. Coverage results for the studied exploration strategies.

Scenario	Metric	Exploration strategy		
		Greedy	Regions	Random walk
Scenario 1	Average coverage	100.00%	83.25%	79.75%
	Average coverage per time	10.0	5.2	5.3
	Δ coverage	1.00	1.06	1.16
scenario 2	average coverage	93.50%	66.90%	54.12%
	Average coverage per time	9.4	8.9	6.8
	Δ coverage	1.09	1.25	1.26
scenario 3	Average coverage	66.46%	41.23%	32.31%
	Average coverage per time	16.6	12.7	9.2
	Δ coverage	1.12	1.37	1.34

in average and up to 26.6%. These results implies that the greedy algorithm provides a better coverage and speed for exploring the considered scenarios.

Regarding the coverage of the map as a function of time, all algorithms showed the same trend: coverage increased progressively until reaching a certain limit and then remains relatively stable until the end of the execution. This limit varies significantly for each algorithm and for each scenario (Table 2).

Coverage results of the greedy algorithm demonstrated a high robustness. The percentual standard deviation of the coverage results distribution was $\sigma < 0.08$, and the maximum difference between coverage obtained for any scenario (Δ coverage) was just 0.12 for scenario 3.

PoI Surveillance. Regarding PoI surveillance, the greedy algorithm computed the best values for average and maximum rt, as reported in Table 3. Small differences were detected between the regions algorithm and the random walk, suggesting that the regions strategy is not useful for surveillance in practice. Results are not as consistent between the instances of the same scenario as in the case of coverage. When comparing the results obtained for each scenario, it is highlighted that the rt metrics are significantly affected by the distribution of POIs for each instance. No special pattern is detected regarding the distribution of POIs generates the best results.

Table 3. PoI surveillance results for the studied exploration strategies.

Scenario	Metric	Exploration strategy		
		Greedy	Regions	Random walk
Scenario 1	*Average rt a standard PoI*	65.74	78.35	104.63
	Δrt standard PoI	1.23	1.25	1.25
	Average rt critical PoI	27.68	36.76	52.49
	Δrt critical PoI	1.62	1.40	1.32
Scenario 2	*Average rt standard PoI*	93.89	112.85	132.92
	Δ rt standard PoI	1.15	1.19	1.15
	Average rt critical PoI	45.29	67.56	75.32
	Δ rt critical PoI	1.38	1.22	1.20
Scenario 3	*Average rt standard PoI*	114.18	158.01	179.19
	Δrt standard PoI	1.12	1.13	1.11
	Average rt critical PoI	58.8	104.66	121.94
	Δrt critical PoI	1.23	1.12	1.14

Results for critical PoIs were somehow similar to the ones computed for standard PoIs. The greedy algorithm remains the one with the best results regarding both average and maximum rt metrics. Improvements of greedy over random walk were 34.3% in average and up to 37.2% for standard PoIs, and 46.2% in average and up to 51.8% for critical PoIs. Improvements of greedy over the regions strategy were 20.2% in average and up to 27.7% for standard PoIs, and 33.8% in average and up to 43.8% for critical PoIs. These results indicate that the time for an effective surveillance reduced between one third and one half when using the greedy algorithm. Furthermore, both the consistency of results and the differences in rt metrics between greedy and the other algorithms increased with the size of the map, suggesting that greedy is more adaptable and scalable to face more complex situations.

5   Conclusions and Future Work

This article presented a distributed approach for autonomous exploration and surveillance using low-cost unmanned aerial vehicles, a relevant problem with several social and economic applications.

The agent-oriented paradigm was applied to implement an efficient cooperative solution to the problem. Coordination is achieved by a state machine that allows exploring and monitoring a set of points of interest without using a centralized infrastructure. The system is conceived to be applied in low-cost commercial Parrot Bebop 2 UAVs, in order to provide an affordable solution for the problem.

The experimental evaluation performed over a real and several synthetic scenarios considered coverage of the explored area and surveillance metrics for the defined PoIs. The proposed greedy exploration strategy was able to consistently obtain the best results on both coverage and surveillance metrics, when compared with a region-oriented exploration algorithm and a random walk method used as a reference baseline. Furthermore, results computed by the greedy exploration strategy were robust and properly scaled to the largest scenarios. These results demonstrate the applicability of the proposed distributed approach and the effectiveness of the greedy exploration strategy to fulfill the considered goals.

The main lines for future work are related to extending the evaluation of the proposed methodology and including more sophisticated intelligent mechanisms for navigation (e.g., via online analysis of camera images) and exploration (including learning methods to detect common patterns from different scenarios). The applicability of the proposed approach to other commercial UAVs must be studied too.

References

1. Bekmezci, İ., Sahingoz, O., Temel, Ş.: Flying ad-hoc networks (FANETs): a survey. Ad Hoc Netw. **11**(3), 1254–1270 (2013)
2. Cacace, J., Finzi, A., Lippiello, V.: Multimodal interaction with multiple co-located drones in search and rescue missions. In: Italian Workshop on Artificial Intelligence, pp. 54–67 (2015)
3. Cesare, K., Skeele, R., Yoo, S.H., Zhang, Y., Hollinger, G.: Multi-UAV exploration with limited communication and battery. In: 2015 IEEE International Conference on Robotics and Automation (ICRA) (2015)
4. Díaz, S., Garate, B., Nesmachnow, S., Iturriaga, S.: Autonomous navigation of unmanned aerial vehicles using markers. In: II Iberoamerican Congress on Smart Cities (2020)
5. Gaudín, A., et al.: Autonomous flight of unmanned aerial vehicles using evolutionary algorithms. In: Crespo-Mariño, J.L., Meneses-Rojas, E. (eds.) CARLA 2019. CCIS, vol. 1087, pp. 337–352. Springer, Cham (2020). https://doi.org/10.1007/978-3-030-41005-6_23
6. Grøtli, E.I., Johansen, T.: Path planning for UAVs under communication constraints using SPLAT! and MILP. J. Intell. Robot. Syst. **65**(1–4), 265–282 (2011)
7. Hart, P., Nilsson, N., Raphael, B.: A formal basis for the heuristic determination of minimum cost paths. IEEE Trans. Syst. Sci. Cybern. **4**(2), 100–107 (1968)
8. Ju, C., Son, H.: Multiple UAV systems for agricultural applications: control, implementation, and evaluation. Electronics **7**(9), 162 (2018)
9. Kopeikin, A., Ponda, S., Inalhan, G.: Control of communication networks for teams of UAVs. In: Valavanis, K., Vachtsevanos, G. (eds.) Handbook of Unmanned Aerial Vehicles, pp. 1619–1654. Springer, Netherlands (2014)

10. Kotaru, M., Joshi, K., Bharadia, D., Katti, S.: SpotFi. ACM SIGCOMM. Comput. Commun. Rev. **45**(4), 269–282 (2015)
11. Lamport, L.: Paxos made simple. ACM SIGACT News **32**(4), 51–58 (2001)
12. Mufalli, F., Batta, R., Nagi, R.: Simultaneous sensor selection and routing of unmanned aerial vehicles for complex mission plans. Comput. Oper. Res. **39**(11), 2787–2799 (2012)
13. Nesmachnow, S., Iturriaga, S.: Cluster-UY: collaborative scientific high performance computing in uruguay. In: Torres, M., Klapp, J. (eds.) ISUM 2019. CCIS, vol. 1151, pp. 188–202. Springer, Cham (2019). https://doi.org/10.1007/978-3-030-38043-4_16
14. Oubbati, O., Atiquzzaman, M., Lorenz, P., Tareque, H., Hossain, S.: Routing in flying ad hoc networks: Survey, constraints, and future challenge perspectives. IEEE Access **7**, 81057–81105 (2019)
15. Schleich, J., Panchapakesan, A., Danoy, G., Bouvry, P.: UAV fleet area coverage with network connectivity constraint. In: 11th ACM International Symposium on Mobility Management and Wireless Access, pp. 131–138 (2013)
16. Shang, K., Karungaru, S., Feng, Z., Ke, L., Terada, K.: A GA-ACO hybrid algorithm for the multi-UAV mission planning problem. In: 14th International Symposium on Communications and Information Technologies (2014)
17. Singh, A., Patil, D., Omkar, S.: Eye in the sky: real-time drone surveillance system (DSS) for violent individuals identification using scatternet hybrid deep learning network. In: IEEE Computer Vision and Pattern Recognition Workshops, pp. 1629–1637 (2018)
18. Tahir, A., Böling, J., Haghbayan, M.H., Toivonen, H.T., Plosila, J.: Swarms of unmanned aerial vehicles—a survey. J. Ind. Inf. Integr. **16**, 100–106 (2019)

Electricity Demand Forecasting Using Computational Intelligence and High Performance Computing

Rodrigo Porteiro[1,2(✉)] and Sergio Nesmachnow[2]

[1] UTE, Paraguay, Uruguay
[2] Universidad de la República, Montevideo, Uruguay
rporteiro@ute.com.uy, sergion@fing.edu.uy

Abstract. This article presents the application of parallel computing for building different computational intelligence models applied to the forecast of the hourly electricity demand of the following day. The short-term forecast of electricity demand is a crucial problem to define the dispatch of generators. In turn, it is necessary to define demand response policies related with smart grids. Computational intelligence models have emerged as successful methods for prediction in recent years. The large amount of existing data from different sources and the great development of supercomputing allows to build models with adequate complexity to represent all the variables that improves the prediction. Parallel computing techniques are applied to obtain two artificial neural network architectures and its related parameters to forecast the total electricity demand of Uruguay for the next day. These techniques consists in train and evaluate models in parallel with different architectures and sets of parameters using grid search techniques. Furthermore each model is trained using Tensorflow with finite-grained GPU parallelism. Considering the high computing demands of the applied techniques, they are developed and executed on the high performance computing platform provided by National Supercomputing Center (Cluster-UY), Uruguay. Standard performance metrics are applied to evaluate the proposed models. The experimental evaluation of the best model reports excellent forecasting results. This model has a mean absolute percentage error of 4.3% when applied to the prediction of unseen data.

Keywords: Computational intelligence · Forecasting · Parallel training

1 Introduction

In recent years, a wide variety of measurement devices have been incorporated into electrical systems. Many of these instruments have been installed to assist the management of new electricity generation technologies, such as wind and solar generation. Useful information for short term electricity demand forecasting

© Springer Nature Switzerland AG 2021
S. Nesmachnow et al. (Eds.): CARLA 2020, CCIS 1327, pp. 146–161, 2021.
https://doi.org/10.1007/978-3-030-68035-0_11

is related to natural variables and can be obtained from this type of devices. The corresponding information obtained from instruments related to base sources is often incorporated in prediction models for decision making [10].

To improve decision making for economic optimization, a large number of stochastic variables must be taken into account. Hardware infrastructure to perform computations on large volumes of data has developed strongly last years, so the increase in complexity associated with the number of variables can be mitigated by using such infrastructures.

The energy industry faces the challenge of harnessing new sources of information by developing appropriate intelligent systems. Traditional tools, that were useful for making predictions some decades ago, have many limitations. In this new context, computational intelligence methods have presented excellent forecasting accuracy in different areas of research in recent years. These methods have proven to be able to learn the most relevant features of the data considered to provide an accurate forecast, excluding non-relevant information and focusing on the most useful data [14].

This article presents the application of two prediction models based on computational intelligence to forecast the total electricity demand of Uruguay. Both models uses artificial neural networks (ANN), a network of nodes called neurons which perform numerical manipulations and are interconnected in a specific order determining the network architecture. The first model uses a combination of long short term memory cells (LSTM) [5] and Dropout Layers [23]. The second model improves the first one by adding convolutional neural networks layers (CNN) [11] and a vector to encode input data. Both models are compared with an Extra-Trees Regressor model applied to the same data. Both models are implemented using a two-level parallel model. The upper level consists of parallelizing the training of different neural networks at a coarse-grained level, to determine the best architectures and parameters for the problem. In turn, in the lower level, each of the models is individually parallelized with fine-grained GPU parallelism using Tensorflow. The main results of the experimental evaluation indicate that the best model found, based on CNN+LSTM, allowed obtaining a prediction error of 4.3%, outperforming existing models for the same problem. The parallel model was effective too, allowing to perform the parameter search to find the best model in 7.5 h, up to 24× faster than using a sequential approach. Once trained, the computation of the next 24-h forecast with the best model is instantaneous.

Overall, the major contributions of this article are: *i*) the evaluation and comparison of computational intelligence models applied to forecasting the total demand of Uruguay, and *ii*) the implementation of a parallel strategy to optimize the proposed models using the high performance computing infrastructure of the National Supercomputing Center, in Uruguay.

The article is organized as follows. Section 2 presents the electricity demand forecasting problem, forecasting techniques, and a review of related works. Section 3 describes the approach to solve the problem. Section 3.3 presents the implementation of the architectures considered and the description of the parallel model. Section 5 reports the experimental analysis of the developed models. Conclusions and future work are formulated in Sect. 6.

2   Forecasting Energy Demand

This section describes typical forecasting techniques applied to the problem of energy demand forecasting and reviews related works.

2.1   General Considerations

Energy demand forecasting studies usually are classified in three categories. The applied categories are related to the forecasting horizon.

The *short-term forecast* category refers to time horizons ranging from one hour to one week. This type of forecast is usually applied to optimize the distribution network, make decisions related to demand management, or to operate generators. When considering the planning of investments in the transmission network or the design of commercial rates, it is necessary to study *medium-term forecasting*, for time horizons that vary from one month to five years. Finally, investment planning and resource management to define the expansion of the electricity system require *long-term forecasting* and simulations. Among other stochastic variables, in this case is necessary to simulate demand scenarios. This scenarios are generated using long-term forecasting models.

Depending on the time horizon of the model, different variables must be considered for forecasting. For instance, in a short-term model it is very important to consider the last measured energy demand values and taking into account the gross domestic product is almost useless. However, when considering long-term scenarios, having a model of the evolution of GDP is crucial. Hence, there is a real need of developing models for different time horizons, depending on the goals.

On the one hand, in the residential sector, power consumption profiles are variable. Power profiles depend mainly on the time of the day and the day of the week. They also depend on occasional events, such as holidays, and other factors [2]. On the other hand, stability is the main feature of industrial and commercial power profiles [19]. This article focuses on short-term energy demand forecasting considering the aggregated total demand of Uruguay. Therefore, industrial, commercial, and residential components are considered within the power consumption, and all their main features are taken into account to develop the forecasting models.

There are two strategies to address the development of forecast models to predict energy demand: causal and historical models [22]. Causal models consider the cause and effect relationship between some input variables, such as climate or economic factors, and energy consumption. Models based on historical data use past values of a variable to predict future values. One the one hand, computational intelligence techniques such as ANN are generally applied for causal models. On the other hand, econometric models such as ARMA, ARIMA, SARI-MAX are used for historical models. This article proposes an strategy combining features of both models, by considering computational intelligence models, but also including a recurrent component that takes into account the temporal correlation.

2.2 Problem Formulation

The study reported in this article applies ANN to develop a model for electricity hourly demand forecast of the next day. Combining casual and historical strategies described in Sect. 2.1 imply to consider historical past demand values and other correlated variables such as temperature, day of the week, season, etc. In the proposed approach, a one-model multiple-output strategy is adopted. Multiple output models can learn the dependence structure between inputs and outputs as well as between outputs at the same time. However, they are slower to train than single output models and require more data to avoid overfitting. The sufficient amount of data gathered from the National Institute of Meteorology and the total hourly demand of Uruguay, and the fact that models are estimated on the high performance computing platform provided by National Supercomputing Center allows overcoming the aforementioned difficulties.

In the proposed approach, the output of the model consists of 24 components: $pred_{(t+1,...,t+24)} = M(d_{t-1}, ..., d_{t-24}, t_{t+1}, ..., t_{t+24}, feat_1, ..., feat_m)$. Each component of $pred_{(t+1,...,t+24)}$ represents the hourly demand forecast for the next day. The input consists in hourly demand data of the previous day $(d_{t-1}, ..., d_{t-24})$, hourly temperature forecast of the next day $(t_{t+1}, ..., t_{t+24})$, and features that characterizes the next day such as weekday, holiday, etc. $(feat_1, ..., feat_m)$.

2.3 Related Works

Several recent articles have proposed applying different variants of computational intelligence approaches for electric load forecasting. Such models include ANN [3,8,21], fuzzy inference models [13], and kernel-based models [6].

Khwaja et al. [9] used hourly temperatures and electric demand from the New England region (USA) to train an ANN for short-term load forecasting. The results confirmed that the proposed model outperformed other existing techniques. Ertugrul [3] studied a recurrent model applying extreme learning machine to forecast electric demand. Empirical results demonstrated that the recurrent ANN had success in forecasting with comparison to feed forward ANNs. The previously commented work guided our research towards the use of recurrent neural networks as a component of the models addressed.

Although ANN can significantly improve forecasting performance, computational intelligence approaches suffer from some intrinsic drawbacks. Some of the main issues related to these models include the difficulty to set the parameters that define the underlying architecture [24]. Also, ANN training may incur in premature convergence problem, i.e., get stuck in local optimal value [1]. To mitigate some of the aforementioned drawbacks, parallel models have been applied. Li [12] proposed a simple and robust parameter optimization, which exploits parallelism and aggressive early-stopping. Other established parallel methods for parameter tuning include population based training [7] and Vizier [4]. More insights into the application of computational intelligence models in forecasting electric loads are in the studies of Sapankevych and Sankar [20] and Panapakidis and Dagoumas [17].

The analysis of related works allows concluding that is possible to apply fine and coarse grained parallel techniques to improve parameter optimization of computational intelligence models. Thus, there is room to contribute in short term electricity load forecasting by applying parallel techniques to build different computational intelligence models.

3   The Proposed Approach for Day Ahead Hourly Demand Forecasting

This section describes the design of the model applied to solve the problem of hourly electricity demand forecasting, described in Sect. 2.2. The treatment of the input data and implementation of the ANN architectures addressed for building a short-term forecasting model of total electricity demand in Uruguay are also described.

3.1   Data Description

The information required to build the proposed models is related, on the one hand, to historical energy records, and on the other hand, to meteorological information. Regarding meteorological information, hourly data collected by the National Institute of Meteorology, Uruguay (www.inumet.gub.uy) between January 2010 and February 2020 is used. Regarding the total electricity demand of Uruguay, hourly data collected by the National Electricity Market Administration (adme.com.uy) from January 2010 to February 2020 is used.

The following fields are considered in each measurement representing the 53 features for each individual day: *Year*, is the year on which the measure was taken. *Month*, is the month on which the measure was taken. *Day*, is the day on which the measure was taken. *Daytype*, represents whether the measure was taken in a holiday or not. *Dayofweek*, is the day on which the measure was taken. *Temperature forecast* (24 values), indicating the temperature prediction for each hour of the forecasted day. *Demand* (24 values), the demand value for each hour of the previous day.

3.2   Data Preparation

A data cleansing process was carried out, following the urban data analysis paradigm [15], to improve the quality of the models to be trained. First, a few invalid measurements (only 0.01%) were replaced by the average of neighboring measurements. After that, a standard detection and treatment of outliers was performed. Demand values that deviates from the mean by more than three times the standard deviation are considered outliers. Detected outliers were replaced by the value of the mean, substracting three times the standard deviation if the outlier is smaller than the mean or adding three times the standard deviation if the outlier is greater. Finally, feature standardization was applied to the input dataset to avoid typical scale issues that emerge when using ANN models. The evaluation using the proposed metrics did not show significant changes after the data cleaning process, possibly due to very little anomalous data corrected in this process.

3.3   Implementation

This subsection describes the two base ANN architectures considered for the implementation of the proposed approach.

Overall Description. The set of parameters of the ANN structure was explored to find the best configuration for each architecture. Architectures are built connecting different layers. A layer is a container that receives weighted inputs, transforms them by applying a set of functions, and then passes the results as output to the next layer. The first and last layers in a network are called input and output layers, respectively; all layers in between are called hidden layers.

Typical layers used in ANNs are fully connected layers, which connects every neuron in one layer to every neuron in the next layer; LSTM layers, capable of learning long-term dependencies; convolutional layers, which applies a set of filters (convolution) and pass the result to the next layer; pooling layers, which perform a subsampling on the input by combining multiple outputs of a previous layer into a single value in the next layer; and dropout layers, which ignore units at random during the training phase with probability $1 - p$ or kept them with probability p, to prevent overfitting. Dropout can also be applied in the other types of layers. When ANN are applied to time series, a standard practice is to define an architecture that treats the temporal component and another architecture that, prior to the temporal component, performs a coding of the features. The description of the two base architectures studied in this article according to the aforementioned practice is presented next.

LSTM Model. This model is composed by an input layer, four hidden layers, and an output layer. In the first hidden layer, multiple LSTM are combined to capture the time dependency. The output of this layer is connected to a series of three fully connected layers, that compose the set of hidden layers. An output layer completes the architecture. Figure 1 represents a general outline of the structure of the proposed model.

Each component includes the following elements:

– *Input layer*, consisting of a matrix of $53 \times l$ units according to the input data defined in Sect. 3.1. The dimension l represents the number of days back considered to capture the time dependence for the forecast.
– *LSTM layer* with L_1 LSTM units using the *relu* activation function.

– *Fully connected layers with dropout*, including three fully connected layers with FC_1, FC_2 and FC_3 units respectively, using the *relu* activation function and dropout with probability $prob_d$.
– *Output layer* with 24 units representing the output, using a linear activation function.

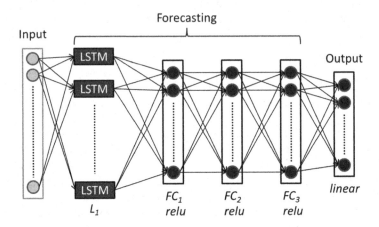

Fig. 1. Architecture of the proposed LSTM model.

CNN+LSTM Model. This model was built based on the previously described LSTM architecture. In CNN+LSTM, the input is connected to a feature extraction module based on convolution filters combined with a max pooling layer and a vector flattening procedure. The goal of this module is to encode all the relevant features for prediction into a single vector. This vector is supplied to the forecast component that has the LSTM structure already presented. Figure 2 presents the complete CNN+LSTM architecture.

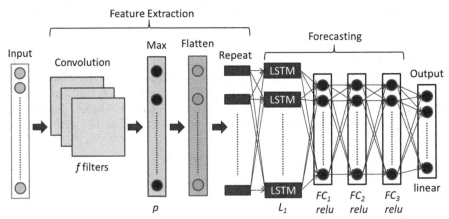

Fig. 2. Architecture of the CNN+LSTM model.

The architecture of the CNN+LSTM model includes the following elements:

- *Input layer*, consisting of $53 \times l$ units, according to the input data described in Sect. 3.1. 53 features are considered for each individual day and l represents the number of days back considered to capture the time dependence for the forecast.
- *CNN layer* using f convolutional filters of size 3 and *relu* activation function.
- *Max pooling layer* with pool size p.
- *Flatten layer* that reshapes the output matrix of the previous layer in a vector, which represents an encoding of the original features.
- *Repetition layer*, which is the interface between the feature extraction module and the forecasting module presented in Fig. 2. The function of the repetition layer is to copy the output vector of the previous layer 24 times. The 24 copies generated are passed to the next layer.
- *LSTM layer* with L_1 LSTM units with *relu* activation function.
- *fully connected layers with dropout*, including three dense layers with FC_1, FC_2 and FC_3 units respectively, using the *relu* activation function and dropout with probability $prob_d$.
- *Output layer* with 24 units representing the output, using a linear activation function.

4 Parallel Model

A two-level parallel model is applied in the proposed implementation for configuring and training each forecasting model described in the previous subsection. The main details of the applied parallel model are provided next.

4.1 Upper Level: Architecture and Parameter Configuration

On the one hand, the upper level applies a Multiple-Instruction-Multiple-Data (MIMD) parallel model to study the most important configuration parameters of the proposed model. Each model defined in the previous subsection has a series of parameters that define their learning behavior. First, several parameters define the architecture: f, p, L_1, FC_1, FC_2 and FC_3. In turn, once a particular set of the parameters that define the architecture is determined, other parameters related to the training process (e.g., learning rate, optimizer type, size of the batch of samples used in each iteration).

A configuration grid is defined, by combining parameters that define the architecture and the parameters that characterize the training process. Then, a domain decomposition is performed, using distributed memory to process subsets for each studied architecture, and shared memory to explore the learning parameters configurations. A multithreading approach is implemented for the parameter configuration on the upper level, by using the `threading` module of python. This module builds higher-level threading interfaces on top of the low-level primitives for working with multiple threads provided by the `thread` module. Easy-to-implement primitives are used to define locking mechanism for workload assignment and threads synchronization.

The pseudocode in Algorithm 1 presents a schema of the multithreading approach implemented.

Algorithm 1 Multithread processing for parameter configuration

---

1: **procedure** THREAD-TRAIN(par)
2:     global bestMAPE, bestModel
3:     model = BuildModel(P)   ▷ Model construction
4:     model.train()   ▷ Model training in GPU
5:     MAPE = model.evaluate()
6:     **if** MAPE < bestMAPE **then**
7:         bestMAPE = MAPE
8:         bestModel = model
9:
10: global bestMAPE = Inf, bestModel = {}
11: **for each** i in range(1,#conf/#threads) **do**
12:     threads = list()   ▷ Create pool of threads
13:     **for each** index in range(#threads) **do**
14:         x = threading.Thread(target=thread-train, args=(par))
15:         x.start()
16:         **for each** index, thread in enumerate(threads) **do**
17:             thread.join()

4.2 Lower Level: Parallel Training on GPU

The lower level applies an implicit asynchronous parallel model for ANN training, where different worker processes train using different portion of the input data. Synchronization is applied to aggregate gradients of the backpropagation method at each training step. An all-reduce pattern is applied by all processes.

Parallel training in GPU is accomplished via pilot jobs, which allow implementing a multilevel scheduling approach where a specific resource of the HPC platform is reserved by an application and specific tasks are scheduled in that resource directly. This method allows avoiding using a local job scheduler, thus reducing the waiting times in the queues used by the resource manager of multipurpose systems. Figure 3 presents a diagram of the proposed parallel model for ANN models for hourly electricity demand forecasting.

5 Experimental Evaluation

This section describes the experimental analysis for the proposed computational intelligence methods for forecasting the total electricity demand of Uruguay.

5.1   Computational Platform and Software

The proposed models were implemented on the Python programming language, using Tensorflow due to the flexibility it provides to define ANN architectures. The experimental analysis was performed in the high performance computing infrastructure of National Supercomputing Center, Uruguay (Cluster-UY) [16]. The hardware environment consists on a HP ProLiant DL380 G9 high end server with two Intel Xeon Gold 6138 processors (20 cores each) and 128 GB RAM.

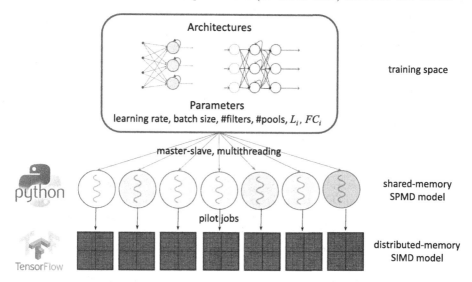

Fig. 3. Diagram of the proposed parallel model

5.2   Validation Problem and Instances

This subsection introduces the metrics used for evaluation of the proposed approach and describes the methodology applied for training of the studied models.

Metrics Used for Evaluation. Two standard metrics are used for the experimental evaluation of the forecasting accuracy of the studied models:

- Mean absolute percentage error (*MAPE*), defined in Eq. (1)
- Root mean square error (*RMSE*), defined in (Eq. 2).

$$MAPE = 100 \times \frac{\sum_{i=1}^{n} \left| \frac{act_i - pred_i}{act_i} \right|}{n} \quad (1) \quad RMSE = \sqrt{\frac{\sum_{i=1}^{n} (act_i - pred_i)^2}{n}} \quad (2)$$

In both equations, act_i represents the measured value for $t = i$, $pred_i$ represents the predicted value, and n represents the predicted horizon length.

Model Training. The methodology applied for training of the studied ANN applies the backpropagation algorithm. Backpropagation is a classical algorithm used to effectively train a neural network through applying the chain rule to compute the partial derivatives of the loss function with respect to each input. After each forward pass computation through a neural network, backpropagation performs a backward pass while adjusting the parameters of the model (weights and biases) to minimize the loss function defined.

The following procedure was applied for training and evaluation of the studied ANN models:

1. Training and validation sets were generated considering real energy consumption data from the last ten years in Uruguay obtained from ADME, Uruguay. The training set is composed of data from 2010 to 2017 and the validation set is composed of data from 2018 to 2020. The proportion between training set and validation set is 4:1.
2. The experimental evaluation compares the proposed methods between them, and an ExtraTrees Regressor model is also used as a baseline method for the results comparison. The ExtraTrees Regressor model consists of an estimator to fit several randomized decision trees on different subsets of the dataset of the considered problem. This method is used as baseline because have shown to be the most accurate for energy demand forecasting in industrial facilities in previous works [18,19].
3. A set of several configurations for the model were generated by choosing different parameters that define the underlying ANN architectures and parameters related to the training algorithm.
4. *MAPE* and *RMSE* metrics were evaluated to determine the best model. *MAPE* results were considered as the main factor for results evaluation, since it allows performing a scale-independent and easy to interpret numerical anlysis. In turn, *RMSE* metric was also evaluated, taking into account that it can provide an insight on the forecasting efficacy of the proposed models in those scenarios where *MAPE* produces infinite or undefined values for zero or close-to-zero actual values.

5.3   Numerical Results

Parameters Configuration. The parameters evaluated in the configuration experiments for each model are described in Table 1.

Table 1. Parameters and candidate values for the studied ANN models

LSTM and CNN+LSTM	
Parameter	*Candidate values*
Number of days back (l)	$1, 10$
LSTM units on the first layer (L_1)	$64, 128$
Units on hidden layers (FC_1, FC_2, FC_3)	$32, 64$
Dropout probability ($prob_d$)	$0.01, 0.05$
Learning rate (lr)	$0.01, 0.05, 0.1$
Batch size	$64, 128$
Only CNN+LSTM	
Convolutional filters (f)	$3, 5$
Pool size (p)	$2, 3$

The size of the parameter space is $2^7 \times 3 = 384$ points for the LSTM model and $2^9 \times 3 = 1536$ points for the CNN+LSTM model. Each point represents a different model to be trained.

From the results obtained in the parameters analysis, the best configuration for each studied ANN corresponds to:

- LSTM: $l = 1$, $L_1 = 128$, $FC_1 = 64$, $FC_2 = 64$, $FC_3 = 64$, $prob_d = 0.05$, $lr = 0.01$, batch size $= 128$.
- CNN+LSTM: $l = 1$, $L_1 = 128$, $FC_1 = 64$, $FC_2 = 64$, $FC_3 = 64$, $prob_d = 0.05$, $lr = 0.01$, batch size $= 128$, $f = 3$, $p = 2$.

Forecasting Precision. Table 2 reports the obtained results for rhe studied LSTM and CNN+LSTM ANNs, regarding the forecasting accuracy metrics defined in Subsect. 5.2. Results are compared with the baseline ExtraTrees Regressor model and the best model is highlighted in bold font.

Table 2. Comparison of the proposed ANN models and the baseline ExtraTreesRegressor after parameter tuning.

Model	*MAPE*	*RMSE*	$\Delta MAPE$	$\Delta RMSE$
ExtraTrees	5.17%	131.83	-	-
LSTM	4.76%	123.12	-0.41%	-8.71
CNN+LSTM	**4.30%**	**109.06**	**-0.87%**	**$- 22.77$**

The obtained results indicate that CNN+LSTM was the best model, obtaining a *MAPE* of 4.30%. Improvements over LSTM were 0.46% (*MAPE*) and 14.06 (*RMSE*), while improvements over the baseline ExtraTreesRegressor were 0.87% (*MAPE*) and 22.7 (*RMSE*). Improvements of CNN+LSTM over LSTM indicate that the explicit feature extraction module allows focusing on those features that are more relevant for a correct forecasting. The LSTM model strives to learn nonexistent correlations between weak features and the output, getting stuck in worse forecast values. The results of CNN+LSTM represent an excellent forecasting accuracy, considering the complexity of the problem. Furthermore, results improve over the official models currently used by ADME for next day electricity demand forecasting, which have an average *MAPE* of 5%.

Figure 4 presents a graphical comparison between the actual hourly demand and the values predicted by the CNN+LSTM model for a typical day.

Computational Efficiency. The proposed parallel model allowed reducing the overall execution time. Figure 5 summarizes the comparison between the sequential and parallel execution times and reports the speedup (S_{24}) over the considered computational platform.

The CNN+LSTM model has the highest computing demands, thus it profits properly from parallelism. On the other hand, the LSTM model did not scaled properly in the performed experiments, possible due to the sequential structure of LSTM layers that are not completely parallelizable in contrast with the CNN component of the other architecture. A negligible overhead was observed for

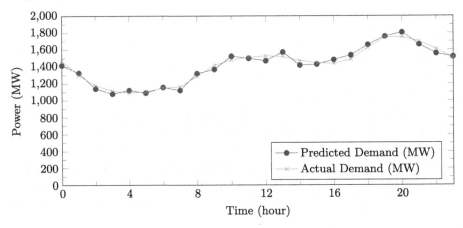

Fig. 4. Predicted demand and actual demand for a typical day.

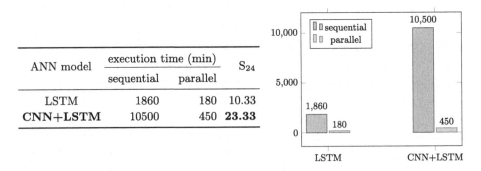

ANN model	execution time (min)		S_{24}
	sequential	parallel	
LSTM	1860	180	10.33
CNN+LSTM	10500	450	**23.33**

Fig. 5. Execution times of the sequential and parallel versions of the studied ANNs for energy demand forecasting

the CNN+LSTM model, mainly because using the pilot jobs paradigm allows reducing the impact of the time waiting on the system queues.

Furthermore, training times of the CNN+LSTM model are appropriate, especially considering the complexity of the addressed problem. Once trained, the model prediction time is negligible. Thus, according to the reported execution times, the CNN+LSTM model can be trained every day to allow incorporating data from the last day, update weather predictions, etc., and executed operatively to analyze diverse scenarios.

6 Conclusions and Future Work

This article presented a proposal for using computational intelligence and high performance computing to develop accurate forecasting models for short-term electricity demand, applied to the total demand of Uruguay.

ANNs were considered as forecasting tool, according to their capabilities in relevant related works. The proposed design applies a two-level parallel approach to efficiently obtain the best forecasting model. At the upper level, a parameter search was performed on two base ANN architectures considering long-short-term memory and a convolutional model. At the lower level, each model to be evaluated was trained using fine-grained parallelism on GPU. For each ANN architecture, the best configuration of parameters was found.

The experimental evaluation considered real data of hourly electricity demand of Uruguay gathered in the period January, 2010–February, 2020. The studied techniques were developed and executed on the high performance computing platform provided by National Supercomputing Center, Uruguay.

The $MAPE$ metric was used for evaluating the forecasting accuracy of the studied models. Results showed that CNN+LSTM had the best forecasting capabilities over the studied data, reporting a value of $MAPE = 4.3\%$. This result is very promising for addressing the addressed forecasting problem, even outperforming the results of models currently used by the National Administration of the Electric Market of Uruguay, which report $MAPE$ values of 5%.

In terms of computational efficiency, the approach applying computational intelligence and high performance computing was useful to solve the problem. Parallel implementation for grid search parameter configurations allowed improving the forecasting capabilities of ANN-based models. Furthermore, a properly utilization of the available computing resources in a scientific computing platform reduced the execution times, up to 24× for the best efficiency result of the studied parallel model.

The main lines for future work are related to extend the analysis to long-term demand forecasting including relevant variables such as gross domestic product, insertion of electric vehicles, smart grid devices or air conditioning to the network, etc. Another line of future work consists in generating different demand scenarios for each node of the transmission grid, which together represent the aggregate demand. This distributed demand model is key when planning the expansion of the transmission network. The importance of scenarios generation that includes more stochastic variables also makes it necessary to improve the parallel model, which constitutes another future line of work.

References

1. Aras, S., Kocakoç, İ.: A new model selection strategy in time series forecasting with artificial neural networks: Ihts. Neurocomputing **174**, 974–987 (2016)
2. Chavat, J., Graneri, J., Nesmachnow, S.: Household energy disaggregation based on pattern consumption similarities. In: Nesmachnow, S., Hernández Callejo, L. (eds.) ICSC-CITIES 2019. CCIS, vol. 1152, pp. 54–69. Springer, Cham (2020). https://doi.org/10.1007/978-3-030-38889-8_5
3. Ertugrul, Ö.: Forecasting electricity load by a novel recurrent extreme learning machines approach. Inte. J. Electr. Power Energy Syst. **78**, 429–435 (2016)
4. Golovin, D., Solnik, B., Moitra, S., Kochanski, G., Karro, J., Sculley, D.: Google vizier: a service for black-box optimization. In: 23rd ACM International Conference on Knowledge Discovery and Data Mining, pp. 1487–1495 (2017)
5. Hochreiter, S., Schmidhuber, J.: Forecasting electricity load by a novel recurrent extreme learning machines approach. Neural Comput. **9**(8), 1735–1780 (1997)
6. Hua, J., Noorian, F., Moss, D., Leong, P.H., Gunaratne, G.: High-dimensional time series prediction using kernel-based Koopman mode regression. Nonlinear Dyn. **90**(3), 1785–1806 (2017). https://doi.org/10.1007/s11071-017-3764-y
7. Jaderberg, M., et al.: Population based training of neural networks. Preprint arXiv:1711.09846 (2017)
8. Kelo, S., Dudul, S.: A wavelet Elman neural network for short-term electrical load prediction under the influence of temperature. Int. J. Electr. Power Energy Syst. **43**(1), 1063–1071 (2012)
9. Khwaja, A., Zhang, X., Anpalagan, A., Venkatesh, B.: Boosted neural networks for improved short-term electric load forecasting. Electric Power Syst. Res. **143**, 431–437 (2017)
10. Lazos, D., Sproul, A., Kay, M.: Optimisation of energy management in commercial buildings with weather forecasting inputs: a review. Renew. Sustain. Energy Rev. **39**, 587–603 (2014)
11. LeCun, Y., Bengio, Y.: Convolutional networks for images, speech, and time series. Handb. Brain Theory Neural Netw. **3361**(10), 1–8 (1995)
12. Li, L., Jamieson, K., et al.: A system for massively parallel hyperparameter tuning. In: 3rd Conference on Machine Learning and Systems (2020)
13. Lou, C., Dong, M.: A novel random fuzzy neural networks for tackling uncertainties of electric load forecasting. Int. J. Electr. Power Energy Syst. **73**, 34–44 (2015)
14. Luján, E., Otero, A., Valenzuela, S., Mocskos, E., Steffenel, A., Nesmachnow, S.: An integrated platform for smart energy management: the CC-SEM project. Revista Facultad de Ingeniería Universidad de Antioquia (2019)
15. Nesmachnow, S., Baña, S., Massobrio, R.: A distributed platform for big data analysis in smart cities: combining intelligent transportation systems and socioeconomic data for montevideo, uruguay. EAI Endorsed Trans. Smart Cities **2**(5), e3 (2017)
16. Nesmachnow, S., Iturriaga, S.: Cluster-UY: collaborative scientific high performance computing in uruguay. In: Torres, M., Klapp, J. (eds.) ISUM 2019. CCIS, vol. 1151, pp. 188–202. Springer, Cham (2019). https://doi.org/10.1007/978-3-030-38043-4_16

17. Panapakidis, I., Dagoumas, A.: Day-ahead electricity price forecasting via the application of artificial neural network based models. Appl. Energy **172**, 132–151 (2016)
18. Porteiro, R., Hernández-Callejo, L., Nesmachnow, S.: Electricity demand forecasting in industrial and residential facilities using ensemble machine learning. Revista Facultad de Ingeniería Universidad de Antioquia (2020)
19. Porteiro, R., Nesmachnow, S., Hernández-Callejo, L.: Short term load forecasting of industrial electricity using machine learning. In: Nesmachnow, S., Hernández Callejo, L. (eds.) ICSC-CITIES 2019. CCIS, vol. 1152, pp. 146–161. Springer, Cham (2020). https://doi.org/10.1007/978-3-030-38889-8_12
20. Sapankevych, N., Sankar, R.: Time series prediction using support vector machines: a survey. IEEE Comput. Intell. Mag. **4**(2), 24–38 (2009)
21. Singh, P., Dwivedi, P.: Integration of new evolutionary approach with artificial neural network for solving short term load forecast problem. Appli. Energy **217**, 537–549 (2018)
22. Sriram, L., Gilanifar, M., Zhou, Y., Ozguven, E., Arghandeh, R.: Causal Markov Elman network for load forecasting in multinetwork systems. IEEE Trans. Ind. Electron. **66**(2), 1434–1442 (2018)
23. Srivastava, N., Hinton, G., Krizhevsky, A., Sutskever, I., Salakhutdinov, R.: Dropout: a simple way to prevent neural networks from overfitting. J. Mach. Learn. Res. **15**(1), 1929–1958 (2014)
24. Suykens, J., Vandewalle, J., De Moor, B.: Optimal control by least squares support vector machines. Neural Netw. **14**(1), 23–35 (2001)

Parallel/Distributed Generative Adversarial Neural Networks for Data Augmentation of COVID-19 Training Images

Jamal Toutouh[1]([∅]) [iD], Mathias Esteban[2] [iD], and Sergio Nesmachnow[2] [iD]

[1] Massachusetts Institute of Technology, Cambridge, MA, USA
toutouh@mit.edu
[2] Universidad de la República, Montevideo, Uruguay
{mathias.esteban,sergion}@fing.edu.uy

Abstract. This article presents an approach using parallel/distributed generative adversarial networks for image data augmentation, applied to generate COVID-19 training samples for computational intelligence methods. This is a relevant problem nowadays, considering the recent COVID-19 pandemic. Computational intelligence and learning methods are useful tools to assist physicians in the process of diagnosing diseases and acquire valuable medical knowledge. A specific generative adversarial network approach trained using a co-evolutionary algorithm is implemented, including a three-level parallel approach combining distributed memory and fine-grained parallelization using CPU and GPU. The experimental evaluation of the proposed method was performed on the high performance computing infrastructure provided by National Supercomputing Center, Uruguay. The main experimental results indicate that the proposed model is able to generate accurate images and the 3×3 version of the distributed GAN has better robustness properties of its training process, allowing to generate better and more diverse images.

Keywords: Computational intelligence · Learning · Generative Adversarial Networks · Data augmentation · COVID-19

1 Introduction

Computational intelligence and automated learning have been successful tools for a wide range of applications [4]. In particular, generative models are powerful methods for learning and gaining knowledge about data, data distributions, and other valuable information. Generational models have been one of the most versatile unsupervised learning techniques in recent years [22,23].

Generative Adversarial Networks (GANs) [5] are powerful methods originally proposed to train generative models by using unsupervised learning. Nowadays, they have been extended to consider other approaches, including semi-supervised

© Springer Nature Switzerland AG 2021
S. Nesmachnow et al. (Eds.): CARLA 2020, CCIS 1327, pp. 162–177, 2021.
https://doi.org/10.1007/978-3-030-68035-0_12

and fully supervised learning, and reinforcement learning. GANs propose a method for learning and estimate the distribution of data from a training set, to produce new information units that approximate the original set. Two artificial neural networks (ANN) are used (a generator and a discriminator), and adversarial learning is applied to optimize the learning process and the resulting outcome. GANs have been successfully applied to many problems, especially those concerning multimedia information (e.g., images, sound, and video), in science, design, art, games, and other areas [13]. Even complex tasks such as autonomous driving [20] and medical assistance [9] have been addressed using GANs. In fact, medical assistance provides a very interesting application area for GANs, since they can provide new insights to the interpretation process of medical information stored in different media (radiography, ultrasound, etc.).

In this line of work, this article presents a parallel/distributed GAN approach for image data augmentation, applied to generate COVID-19 training samples for computational intelligence methods. This is a relevant problem nowadays, considering the recent COVID-19 pandemic. The proposed approach is based on a two-level parallel model for training and configuration, and co-evolutionary training considering a dataset of real X-rays chest images. The proposed model is implemented and executed in the high performance computing infrastructure provided by National Supercomputing Center (Cluster-UY), Uruguay.

The main contribution of the research reported in this article include: i) a proposal for applying GANs to the data augmentation problem for medical images, to assist COVID-19 diagnosis; ii) a two-level parallel model developed to take advantage of high performance computing facilities; and iii) the experimental evaluation of the proposed distributed parallel/distributed GAN approach considering a dataset of real X-rays images.

The article is organized as follows. Section 2 describes the data augmentation problem to assist COVID-19 detection and reviews related works. Section 3 describes the proposed parallel/distributed approach. The experimental evaluation and results are reported and discussed in Sect. 5. Finally, the conclusions and the main lines for future work are presented in Sect. 6.

2   Data Augmentation for Medical Images to Assist COVID-19 Detection

This section describes the problem of data augmentation for medical images, its application to assist COVID-19 detection and reviews related works.

2.1   Data Augmentation for Medical Images and COVID-19 Detection

The technique of medical imaging consists of creating visual representations of the human body for clinical analysis to help diagnosing and treating diseases. Using this technique, physicians and organizations gather useful information to build databases of both normal and pathological images to identify physiological anomalies. To that end, several imaging technologies are applied, including radiography (X-rays), magnetic resonance, ultrasound, thermography, and others.

In recent years, computational intelligence methods have been increasingly applied to assist medical diagnostics. This way, learning models have been applied to provide a new insight to the process of medical image interpretation, which was previously limited to radiologists. However, learning models require significantly large datasets for training. Within this context, an important problem arises: expanding the base of knowledge about medical conditions in order to perform a proper training of computational intelligence/learning methods.

Image data augmentation [17] allows overcoming the difficulties associated to having few data to build training datasets for learning methods. The augmentation technique is useful to expand the size of a given training dataset, by creating modified versions of existing images. Then, learning models trained with the expanded dataset are able to produce better models and improve detection results, considering that more information can be extracted from the original dataset through augmentations. Useful, transfer learning and generalization are applied to broaden the applicability of built models.

Traditional approaches for image data augmentation are based on applying image operations, like point processing and frame transformations, geometric (resize, crop) and color transformations, merging, equalization, etc. On the other hand, deep learning approaches include adversarial training, neural style transfer, and GAN-based data augmentation.

Nowadays, there is an increasing interest on learning approaches to help dealing with outbreaks, like the recent COVID-19 pandemic.

2.2 Related Works

Computational intelligence have been applied for medical image processing, to address disease detection, help and guide diagnostics, and to improve medical imaging research [11].

Kovalev and Kazlouski [9] studied the generation of artificial biomedical images to be used as a substitute for real image datasets, focusing on generating realistic chest X-ray images using Deep Convolutional GAN and Progressive Growing GAN (growing both generator and discriminator continuously). A benchmark classification problem was solved using real and synthetic images for the problem of detecting breast tumor, using data from the lymph node database (image size: 256×256). The classification accuracy dropped between 2.2%–3.5% (considered as "acceptable for practical applications"), improving between two and four times the results of Loopy Belief Propagation and Random Forest.

The application of GANs in radiology, specifically for detecting congestive cardiac failure on chest radiographies, was studied by Seah et al. [16]. A generative model (Generative Visual Rationales, GVR) was trained on an unlabeled subset of a frontal chest radiographies set and a traditional ANN encoder was trained on a·labeled subset. The experimental evaluation considered a custom overfitted model developed for comparison and classification by experts. The main results allowed to conclude that features by ANN can be identified using GVR, thus allowing detection of bias and overfitted models. The preprint article by Khalifa et al. [8] also explored the use of GANs and transfer learning, but in this cases focusing on a more general pneumonia disease. Several deep transfer learning models were studied to detect the pneumonia from images, using a training set of just 10% of real data and the other 90% generated using a GAN. No computational efficiency evaluation was reported, but authors worked under the assumption of including few layers in the underlying GANs, to reduce memory consumption and execution time. The main results showed that using GANs as augmentation technique allows improving the robustness of the proposed model, making it less prone to overfitting. Thus, using the proposed method, better images can be generated.

Regarding data augmentation of medical images, Bhagat and Bhaumik [2] proposed a method for generating synthetic chest X-ray images of patients with pneumonia, using GANs. Generator and discriminator started with low-resolution images (4×4) and the resolution increased step-by-step when including more layers (up to 128×256 and 256×128). A deep convolutional neural network was trained using the generated images, to solve the classification problem. The prediction accuracy improved when considering the augmented database.

Several recent articles have extended previous approach to help addressing the problem of coronavirus disease detection. Loey et al. [10] applied GAN and deep transfer learning for COVID-19 detection considering chest X-ray images as input, extending the proposal by Khalifa et al. [8]. Deep transfer models were studied over a training dataset containing images of four classes (COVID-19, normal, pneumonia bacterial, and pneumonia virus). GANs were applied as subordinate method for expanding the training dataset to contribute improving the detection accuracy. Waheed et al. [21] developed an auxiliary classifier GAN to overcome the problem of limited images available for COVID-19 detection when using convolutional neural networks (CNNs). The main results demonstrate that using synthetic images produced by the auxiliary classifier GAN allows improving the COVID-19 detection accuracy of CNN from 85% to 95%.

On the other hand, some recent advances have been developed on applying parallel computing to speed-up the training process of GANs and their effectiveness. Im et al. [7] recognized the difficulties of GAN training in practice, and proposed the Generative Adversarial Parallelization (GAP) framework for the simultaneous training of several GANs that share their discriminators. This approach extends the two-player generative adversarial game into a multi-player game, thus transforming the training from being a tightly-coupled problem (between generator and discriminator) to a more loosely one. Multiple models are required, each one with its own parameters, which are structured in a bipartite layout for competence. Instead of applying a traditional data-parallel approach on the parameter space, GANs are trained randomly swapping different discriminators/generators to produce synergy. The model was implemented in Theano and executed in GPU, without transfers through host memory (to reduce communication overheads). Empirical results showed that the GAP model allows improving mode coverage, convergence, and quality. No efficiency or execution time analysis was reported. Up to now, no parallel GAN training for COVID-19 detection has been proposed.

The analysis of related works allows concluding that no previous proposals have explored the application of parallel computing to implement efficient and accurate IA models for COVID-19 detection. This article contributes in this line of research, by applying a two-level parallel model for GANs training and configuration, applied to data augmentation for medical images to contribute in COVID-19 research.

3   The Proposed Parallel/distributed GANs for COVID-19 Data Augmentation

This section describes the proposed approach applying parallel/distributed GANs for COVID-19 data augmentation.

3.1   Generative Adversarial Networks

GANs are computational intelligence methods that intends to learn the specific distribution of a given training dataset, to synthesize samples using the estimated distribution. GANs consist of two ANNs, a generator and a discriminator, that applies adversarial learning to optimize their parameters. The discriminator try to learn how to distinguish the natural/real samples from the artificial/fake samples produced by the generator. The generator is trained to transform its inputs from a random latent space into artificial/fake samples to deceive the

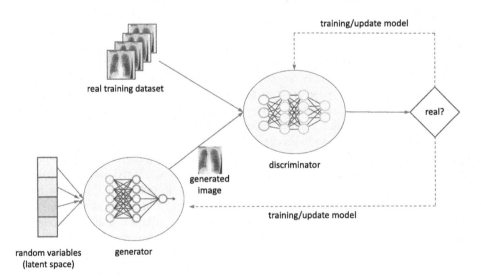

Fig. 1. General diagram of a generative adversarial network

discriminator (see Fig. 1). The GAN training problem is formulated as a minmax optimization problem by the definitions of generator and discriminator. In the last years, GANs have demonstrated to be efficient methods for learning [5].

3.2 Distributed GAN Training

The proposed approach applies the methodology introduced by Lipizzaner [15] and Mustangs [19]. A distributed GAN training is performed by applying co-evolutionary algorithms (coEA).

In the co-evolutionary distributed GAN training, two populations are evolved, one for generators and one for discriminators. These two populations are trained by competition between them. Individuals in each population are located in a spatial structure, an underlying toroidal grid. The concept of neighborhood is applied to define those individuals that participate in the training phase for both generators and discriminators.

The approach using distributed coEAs has shown to be effective overcoming the main pathologies in GAN training, namely modal collapse, vanish gradient, and non-convergence. Futhermore, cellular training allows implementing a data-parallel approach where each cell is trained using reduced subsets without affecting the overall quality of the implemented GANs, considering the difference between the probability distributions of generated samples and the original samples (or the similarity of generated images, when used with that goal). The data-parallel approach also allows improving the computational efficiency of the training process, since a smaller amount of training data batches are needed [18]. Figure 2 presents a diagram of the proposed distributed training for GANs implemented in Lipizzaner.

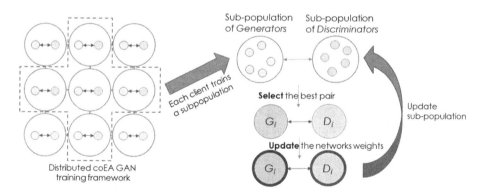

Fig. 2. Diagram of the distributed training for GANs proposed by Lipizzaner

4 Distributed GANs for COVID-19 Images Generation

This section describes the proposed approach for data augmentation of COVID-19 datasets using GANs.

4.1   Overall Description

The proposed approach for data augmentation of the COVID-19 image dataset applies the generative paradigm previously applied for generating new images of handwritten digits, small object photograph, and faces.

The approach consist in sampling from an existing database of real chest X-ray images to train the discriminator, while the generator uses a random variable from a Gaussian distribution, $z \sim \mathcal{N}(0,1)$. Then, generator and discriminator are trained using the distributed co-evolutionary approach. Figure 3 shows two sample real chest X-ray images used for training.

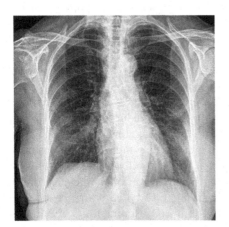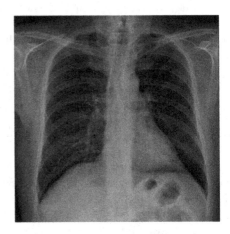

Fig. 3. Sample chest X-ray images used for GAN training

4.2   Implementation Details

Both the generator and discriminator models were implemented as Multilayer Perceptrons (MLP). MLP are one of the classical and most used types of neural network [6]. A MLP is comprised of perceptrons or neurons, organized on layers. At least two layers are used: input layer, which receives the problem data as input and output layer, and output layer, which produces the results. In between, one or more hidden layers can be included to provide different levels of abstraction to help with the learning goal. MLP are feedforward ANNs, meaning that connections between neurons do not form a cycle; information moves in only one direction (forward) from neurons on the input layer, through neurons on the hidden layers (if they exist) and finally to neurons in the output layer. Except for the input neurons, all other neurons use a nonlinear activation function, which separates MLP to simpler linear perceptrons. This feature makes MLP able to distinguish not linearly separable data. MLP are usful for dealing with structured data (e.g., tables), classification/prediction problems whith labeled inputs, regression problems, etc. Furthermore, MLP hava a high flexibility and applicability to learn any mapping function from inputs to outputs. Their flexible nature allows MLP to be applied to other types of data, e.g., pixels of an image, such as proposed for medical images in this article.

To deal with the proposed problem, the proposed approach explores the use of MLPs using four and five layers as underlying ANN architectures for both generators and discriminators. The generators and discriminators have the same input and output sizes. The generator input from the latent space has size 64 and the output has size 16384 (to encode 128×128 gray-scale images). The discriminator has input size of 16384 (an image) and output size of one to encode the truth value (real or fake). Both type of MLP use linear layers. Hidden layers apply the leaky version of a rectified linear unit (LeakyRelu) as activation function, the generators output layer the hyperbolic tangent (Tanh), and the discriminator output layer the sigmoid function. Table 1 report the main features of the MLP architectures in both generators and discriminators.

Table 1. Main features of the MLP architectures used in generators and discriminators of the proposed GAN for COVID-19 images generation

Layers	Four-layer MLP GAN		Five-layer MLP GAN	
	Generator	Discriminator	Generator	Discriminator
First hidden layer	64×256	16384×256	64×256	16384×512
Second hidden layer	256×256	256×256	256×256	512×256
Third hidden layer	–	–	256×512	256×256
Output	256×16384	256×1	256×16384	256×1

One of the key components of GANs is the `DataLoader` function, which allows performing the domain decomposition by dividing the training data in batches to be processed iteratively. In the proposed implementation, the Dataloader function reads the images from the training set and encodes each pixel with a real number in (0,1). Since gray-scale images are used, a single number is enough to provide the needed encoding (0 represents white and 1 represents black). After that, since images have different size because they come from different databases or have been possibly acquired using different devices, a resize transformation is applied in order to convert them to a unique resolution (set as an input parameter, in the reported research it is 128×128). The resulting vector of 16 384 positions is stored in memory. After all images are read, a tensor of $16\,384 \times \#TD$ is transferred to GPU, where $\#TD$ is the size of the training dataset.

4.3   Parallel Model

A three-level parallel model is applied in the proposed implementation, following the idea of the parallel/distributed implementation of cellular training for GANs proposed in our previous work [14].

The upper level applies a Multiple-Instruction-Multiple-Data (MIMD) parallel model to study one of the most important parameters of the model proposed by GANs: the architecture of the underlying ANN. A domain decomposition approach is applied on the space of candidate architectures, defined ad-hoc for the problem, and the space of relevant parameters (p_i) and a set of candidate values (v_i). A parallel master-slave model is followed, using a distributed memory paradigm implemented in the MPI for Python package. Considered architectures and parameter sets are assigned on-demand to a set of distributed processes, executed according to the availability of computational resources. A dynamic load balancing procedure is applied.

In turn, the medium level applies a distributed training approach, according to the parallel co-evolutionary model proposed by Lipizzaner. In the Lipizzaner algorithm, the population of generators and discriminators are distributed using a logical spatial grid and applying a cellular parallel model for EAs [1]. Parameters of the training process are explored and optimized competitively, in an asynchronous parallel execution of all cells in the grid defined by Lipizzaner. A master process performs the data distribution, by assigning populations to grid cells, and defines the communication channels according to the neighborhood topology, accounting for the grid size. Communications between processes are performed to exchange relevant information along the evolution.

Finally, the lower level applies the parallel training of the studied GANs in GPU, applied a Single-Instruction-Multiple-Data approach. This parallel training is implemented using the `PyTorch` open source machine learning library, widely employed for applications related to multimedia/image processing and computer vision. Unlike other libraries for ANN training like TensorFlow, PyTorch does not include a specific library for execution on GPU. Thus, the training dataset is loaded, a tensor is created (dimension #images × image width × image height × #channels). That tensor is transferred to GPU and processed in batches.

A schema of the proposed parallel model is presented in Fig. 4 (the sets of parameters and values on which the parameter sweep is performed could be different for different architectures).

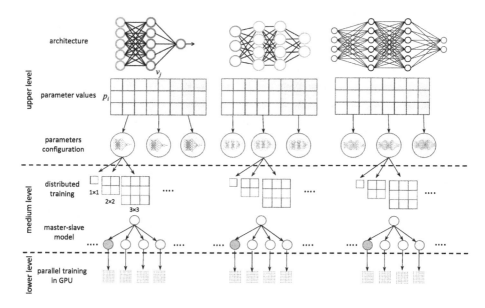

Fig. 4. Diagram of the three-levels parallel model for GANs training

5   Experimental Evaluation

This section describes the experimental evaluation of the proposed approach using GANs for COVID-19 images generation.

5.1   Evaluation Methodology, Training and Validation Instances

Methodology. The experimental evaluation is focused on analyzing the parameter configuration of the learning method and the quality of the generated images. The stop condition is 1000 *training epochs*. One training epoch is the number of iterations required to feed all batches in the training dataset to the generator.

Regarding the proposed approach using Lipizzaner, three configurations of the distributed learning method are studied: 1×1 grid, 2×2 grid, and 3×3 grid.

Metrics and Parameters. The metric considered in the evaluation is the inception score, which is commonly used for evaluating images generated by GANs. It aims at objectively assessing the quality of generated images via two relevant properties that are evaluated simultaneously: likeliness to a specific object to be generated and diversity. Inception score is within the range $(1.0, M)$, being M the highest inception score for the considered dataset. The computational efficiency of the proposed parallel model is also evaluated. In turn, the quality of generated images is also evaluated by examination of representative samples.

The studied parameters are the ANN architecture, the batch size, the Gaussian mutation probability (p_M), and the initial learning rate (l_0). All reported

Table 2. Inception score results for the studied configuration parameters.

Parameter	Value	Minimum	Median	Iqr	Max
Network architecture	Four layers perceptron	1.43	**1.68**	0.14	1.88
	Five layers perceptron	1.00	**1.68**	0.27	**2.25**
Batch size	50	1.00	**1.70**	0.14	2.05
	75	1.00	1.69	0.16	**2.25**
	100	1.00	1.64	0.18	2.07
p_M	0.3	1.00	1.66	0.18	1.95
	0.4	1.00	**1.69**	0.18	**2.25**
	0.5	1.00	1.68	0.19	2.07
l_0	0.00010	1.26	1.65	0.18	1.94
	0.00025	1.04	**1.73**	0.12	1.93
	0.00050	1.00	1.66	0.34	**2.25**

results correspond to 14 independent executions of the proposed GAN performed for each parameter configuration.

Training and Validation Instances. The training of the proposed model was performed using images from the open repository created by Cohen et al. [3], publicly available at https://github.com/ieee8023/covid-chestxray-dataset. The same dataset is considered for computing the inception score.

Development and Execution Platform. The proposed parallel/distributed GAN implementation was implemented in Python3 using pytorch (pytorch.org).

The experimental analysis was performed on National Supercomputing Center (Cluster-UY), Uruguay [12]. Cluster-UY offers up to 30 computing servers, each of them with Xeon Gold 6138 processors with 40 cores, Nvidia Tesla P100 GPUs (12 GB memory), 128 GB of RAM memory, and 300 GB of SSD storage for temporary files, interconnected by Ethernet at 10 Gbps.

5.2   Numerical Results

Quality of Generated Images: Inception Score. Table 2 reports the inception score values obtained for the studied configuration parameters. Results do not follow a normal distribution, thus values of median and interquartile range (Iqr.) are reported as relevant estimators. Figure 5 shows the corresponding boxplots for the parameters with more impact in the inception score values.

Computational Efficiency. Table 3 reports the execution time of the proposed GANs for the two configuration parameters that affect the most to the execution time. Execution parameters that impact the computational efficiency of the training process are the network architecture and the batch size. Other parameters impact on the result quality, but not on the efficiency. Results do not follow

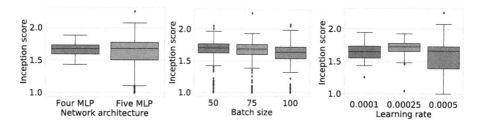

Fig. 5. Inception score boxplots for the studied configuration parameters

Table 3. Execution time for the studied network architectures and batch sizes.

Parameter	Value	Minimum	Median	Iqr	Max
Network architecture	Four layer perceptron	8.15	12.68	5.20	19.38
	Five layer perceptron	10.42	17.22	7.62	27.12
Batch size	50	9.42	15.68	3.73	27.12
	75	8.57	13.95	9.37	21.05
	100	8.15	12.53	4.52	19.38

a normal distribution, thus values of median and interquartile range (Iqr.) are reported as relevant estimators. The non-parametric Wilcoxon test was applied to analyze the results distributions and results confirmed that the differences are statistically significant (p-value < 0.01). Boxplots are presented in Fig. 6.

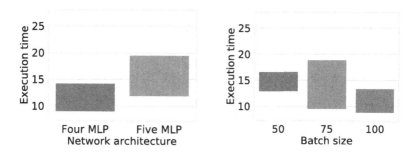

Fig. 6. Execution time boxplots for the studied values of network architecture and batch size parameters

Overall Analysis. Figure 7 presents a 2D graphical comparison of the inception score results and the execution time required for training. The well-known trade-off between results quality and execution time is observed. Considering that the time for a single execution of the proposed GAN model are very reasonable, the configurations that allowed computing the best inception score results were selected for execution of the distributed 2×2 and 3×3 GANs using Lipizzaner. The selected configurations are: *best median* (five layers perceptron, batch size 50, $p_M = 0.4$, and $l_0 = 0.00025$, whose results are marked with a red star in Fig. 7) and *best maximum* (five layers perceptron, batch size 75, $p_M = 0.4$, and $l_0 = 0.0005$, whose results are marked with a blue diamond). These configurations significantly outperformed the inception score results obtained by all others.

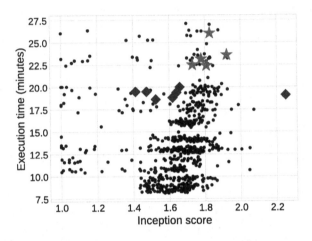

Fig. 7. Inception score vs. execution time (Color figure online)

Distributed GANs. Inception score results for 2×2 and 3×3 grids are reported in Table 4. In turn, Fig. 8 presents the evolution of loss during the training of generator (red line) and discriminator (blue line) for one representative client of Lipizzaner, using 2×2 grid (left) and 3×3 grid (right).

Table 4. Inception score results for the different grid sizes

Grid	Best maximum configuration			Best median configuration		
	Minimum	Median	Maximum	Minimum	Median	Maximum
2×2	1.53	1.66	1.68	1.61	1.63	1.68
3×3	1.34	1.58	1.73	1.80	1.83	1.86
Overall	1.34	1.63	1.73	1.61	1.74	1.86

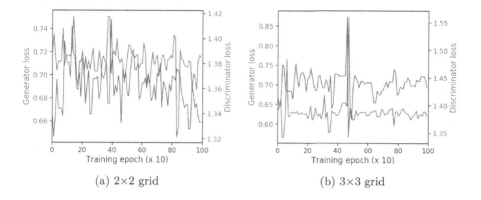

(a) 2×2 grid   (b) 3×3 grid

Fig. 8. Loss during the training for one representative client of Lipizzaner (Color figure online)

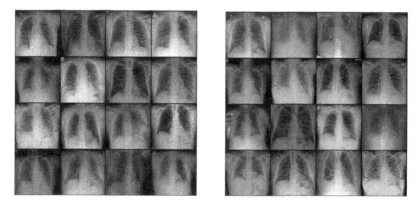

Fig. 9. Sample images generated by the proposed distributed GAN approach

Results reported in Table 4 indicate that the 3×3 grid trained better generators, able to create better samples (higher inception scores). Loss evolution in Fig. 8 show that the 3×3 grid also provides a more robust behavior of the resulting GAN, confirmed by a the loss function with fewer peaks and smoother variations, when compared with the one computed using the 2×2 grid. This result implies a better training, less prone to typical pathologies of GANs, thus producing better and more diverse images.

Sample Generated Images. Figure 9 shows two sample generated images using the proposed GAN approach.

6   Conclusions and Future Work

This article presented parallel/distributed GANs for image data augmentation, applied to the relevant problem of generating X-rays chest COVID-19 samples.

The proposed implementation applies a parallel model in three levels to combine Single-Program-Multiple-Data paralellism for parameters configuration, a masteer slave model to implement a distributed co-evolutionary training, and Single-Instruction-Multiple-Data using pytorch for training in GPU.

The experimental methodology was oriented to evaluate the image quality, considering the required execution time. The high performance computing infrastructure of National Supercomputing Center, Uruguay, was used.

The main results indicate that the proposed model is able to generate accurate images. The distributed GAN using a 3×3 neighborhood computed the best results, achieving a more robust training and generating better and more diverse images. These results allow concluding that the proposed method is useful for generation of synthetic COVID-19 images.

The main lines for future work are related to extend the evaluation of the proposed approach by studying larger training datasets, other synthetic methods for augmentation and different ANN architectures for both generator and discriminator in the proposed model.

Acknowledgment. The work of S. Nesmachnow is partly supported by ANII and PEDECIBA, Uruguay. J. Toutouh has been partially funded by EU Horizon 2020 research and innovation programme (Marie Skłodowska-Curie grant agreement No 799078), by the Spanish MINECO and FEDER projects TIN2017-88213-R and UMA18-FEDERJA-003, and the Systems that learn initiative at MIT CSAIL.

References

1. Alba, E., Luque, G., Nesmachnow, S.: Parallel metaheuristics: recent advances and new trends. Int. Trans. Oper. Res. **20**(1), 1–48 (2012)
2. Bhagat, V., Bhaumik, S.: Data augmentation using generative adversarial networks for pneumonia classification in chest Xrays. In: 5th International Conference on Image Information Processing (2019)
3. Cohen, J., Morrison, P., Dao, L.: COVID-19 Image Data Collection (2020). Preprint arXiv:2003.11597v1
4. Engelbrecht, A.: Computational Intelligence: An Introduction. Wiley, Hoboken (2007)
5. Goodfellow, I., et al.: Generative adversarial nets. In: Advances in Neural Information Processing Systems, pp. 2672–2680 (2014)
6. Hastie, T., Tibshirani, R., Friedman, J.: The Elements of Statistical Learning. Springer, New York (2009). https://doi.org/10.1007/978-0-387-84858-7
7. Im, D., Ma, H., Kim, C., Taylor, G.: Generative adversarial parallelization (2016). Preprint arXiv:1612.04021
8. Khalifa, N., Taha, M., Hassanien, A., Elghamrawy, S.: Detection of Coronavirus (COVID-19) Associated Pneumonia based on Generative Adversarial Networks and a Fine-Tuned Deep Transfer Learning Model using Chest X-ray Dataset (2020). arXiv preprint 2004.01184. Accessed June 2020
9. Kovalev, V., Kazlouski, S.: Examining the capability of GANs to replace real biomedical images in classification models training. In: Ablameyko, S.V., Krasnoproshin, V.V., Lukashevich, M.M. (eds.) PRIP 2019. CCIS, vol. 1055, pp. 98–107. Springer, Cham (2019). https://doi.org/10.1007/978-3-030-35430-5_9

10. Loey, M., Smarandache, F., Khalifa, N.: Within the lack of chest COVID-19 x-ray dataset: a novel detection model based on GAN and deep transfer learning. Symmetry **12**(4), 651 (2020)
11. Morra, L., Delsanto, S., Correale, L.: Artificial Intelligence in Medical Imaging. CRC Press (2019)
12. Nesmachnow, S., Iturriaga, S.: Cluster-UY: collaborative scientific high performance computing in Uruguay. In: Torres, M., Klapp, J. (eds.) ISUM 2019. CCIS, vol. 1151, pp. 188–202. Springer, Cham (2019). https://doi.org/10.1007/978-3-030-38043-4_16
13. Pan, Z., Yu, W., Yi, X., Khan, A., Yuan, F., Zheng, Y.: Recent progress on generative adversarial networks (GANs): a survey. IEEE Access **7**, 36322–36333 (2019)
14. Perez, E., Nesmachnow, S., Toutouh, J., Hemberg, E., O'Reily, U.: Parallel/distributed implementation of cellular training for generative adversarial neural networks. In: 10th IEEE Workshop on Parallel Distributed Combinatorics and Optimization (2020)
15. Schmiedlechner, T., Yong, I., Al-Dujaili, A., Hemberg, E., O'Reilly, U.: Lipizzaner: a system that scales robust generative adversarial network training. In: 32nd Conference on Neural Information Processing Systems (2018)
16. Seah, J., Tang, J., Kitchen, A., Gaillard, F., Dixon, A.: Chest radiographs in congestive heart failure: visualizing neural network learning. Radiology **290**(2), 514–522 (2019)
17. Shorten, C., Khoshgoftaar, T.M.: A survey on image data augmentation for deep learning. J. Big Data **6**(1) (2019)
18. Toutouh, J., Hemberg, E., O'Reilly, U.-M.: Data dieting in GAN training. In: Iba, H., Noman, N. (eds.) Deep Neural Evolution. NCS, pp. 379–400. Springer, Singapore (2020). https://doi.org/10.1007/978-981-15-3685-4_14
19. Toutouh, J., Hemberg, E., O'Reilly, U.M.: Spatial evolutionary generative adversarial networks. In: Genetic and Evolutionary Computation Conference, pp. 472–480 (2019)
20. Uřičář, M., Křížek, P., Hurych, D., Sobh, I., Yogamani, S., Denny, P.: Yes, we GAN: applying adversarial techniques for autonomous driving. Electron. Imaging **2019**(15), 48-1–48-17 (2019)
21. Waheed, A., Goyal, M., Gupta, D., Khanna, A., Al-Turjman, F., Pinheiro, P.R.: CovidGAN: data augmentation using auxiliary classifier GAN for improved Covid-19 detection. IEEE Access **8**, 91916–91923 (2020)
22. Wang, Z., She, Q., Ward, T.: Generative adversarial networks: a survey and taxonomy. preprint arXiv:1906.01529 (2019)
23. Wu, X., Xu, K., Hall, P.: A survey of image synthesis and editing with generative adversarial networks. Tsinghua Sci. Technol. **22**(6), 660–674 (2017)

Analysis of Regularization in Deep Learning Models on Testbed Architectures

Félix Armando Mejía Cajicá[1](✉) ⓘ, John A. García Henao[2](✉) ⓘ,
Carlos Jaime Barrios Hernández[1](✉) ⓘ, and Michel Riveill[2] ⓘ

[1] SC3UIS, CAGE, Universidad Industrial de Santander, Bucaramanga, Santander, Colombia
fmejia2067165@correo.uis.edu.co, cbarrios@uis.edu.co
[2] Laboratoire I3S, Université Côte d'Azur, 06900 Nice, SA, France
henao@i3s.unice.fr, michel.riveill@unice.fr

Abstract. Deep Learning models have come into significant use in the field of biology and healthcare, genomics, medical imaging, EEGs, and electronic medical records [1–4]. In the training these models can be affected due to overfitting, which is mainly due to the fact that Deep Learning models try to adapt as much as possible to the training data, looking for the decrease of the training error which leads to the increase of the validation error. To avoid this, different techniques have been developed to reduce overfitting, among which are the Lasso and Ridge regularization, weight decay, batch normalization, early stopping, data augmentation and dropout. In this research, the impact of the neural network architecture, the batch size and the value of the dropout on the decrease of overfitting, as well as on the time of execution of the tests, is analyzed. As identified in the tests, the neural network architectures with the highest number of hidden layers are the ones that try to adapt to the training data set, which makes them more prone to overfitting.

Keywords: Deep learning · Dropout · Overfitting

1 Introduction

Artificial Intelligence (AI) is the attempt to imitate human intelligence by creating programs and mechanisms that can display behaviors considered intelligent. An AI system can analyze large volumes of information (big data), identifying patterns and trends and from these, making predictions automatically with speed and precision. Pattern recognition refers to information processing to solve a wide range of problems, such as the classification of objects into classes, where these objects can be images, sounds, smells, in general [5]. Deep learning (DL) is a case of a neural network characterized by having multiple layers of neurons connected to each other, where data processing is carried out in a hierarchical way. Neural networks obtain increasingly meaningful representations of data through layered learning.

Among the best-known applications that use DL are those that estimate risk based on the input data that is injected and the output data that is indicated is of greater interest. The computer is doing more than approaching human capabilities, as it is finding new

© Springer Nature Switzerland AG 2021
S. Nesmachnow et al. (Eds.): CARLA 2020, CCIS 1327, pp. 178–192, 2021.
https://doi.org/10.1007/978-3-030-68035-0_13

relationships that are not so evident to humans and that are present in the data. For this reason, there is great fervor in the use of AI and especially DL in the field of medicine.

Medicine is one of the sciences that has benefited most from DL algorithms since they take advantage of the great computational capacities that allow the analysis of large amounts of information to predict the risks of death, the duration of hospitalization and the length of stay in intensive care units, among others [6].

The field of medicine has been supported by the DL through the analysis of medical images taken with different techniques. Researchers have seen in new technologies such as AI an indispensable support that facilitates and speeds up their work [7], since it will significantly improve quality, efficiency, and results. The total volume of medical data is increasing, it is said that every three years it doubles, making it difficult for doctors to make good use of it, so digital processing of the information is necessary.

DL models with a large number of parameters are very powerful machine learning systems, however, sometimes the problem of overfitting occurs, to avoid this, some randomly selected neural network records are discarded in the training, this prevents over adaptation by significantly reducing overfitting and providing a significant improvement in model regularization, in addition to analyze what impact this has on execution time and to determining that it is better to have a deep network or a wide network.

This research deals with how the DropOut regularization method [8] behaves in the supervised DL models, which avoids overfitting and provides a way to combine approximately different neural network architectures. The DropOut works by probabilistically keeping active the inputs to a layer, which can be either input variables in the data sample or triggers from a previous layer. As neurons are randomly kept active in the network during training, other neurons will have to intervene and handle the representation needed to make predictions about the missing neurons. It is believed that this results in the network learning multiple independent internal representations. The effect is that the neuronal network becomes less sensitive to the specific weights of the neurons. This in turn results in a network that is capable of better generalization and less likely to overfitting.

2 Related Work

The representative power of the artificial neuronal network becomes stronger as the architecture gets deeper [9]. However, millions of parameters make deep neural networks easily accessible through fit. Regularization [10, 11] is an effective way to obtain a model that generalizes well.

The networks become more powerful as the network gets deeper and as it has more parameters overfitting begins to occur. By means of regularization, there is an effective way to generalize a model. There are many techniques that allow regularizing the training of deep neural networks, such as weight decay [12], early stopping [13], data augmentation, dropout, etc. The dropout is a technique in which randomly selected neurons are ignored during training, that is, they are "dropped out" at random. This means that their contribution to the activation of the neurons below is temporarily eliminated in the forward pass and any weight update is not applied to the neuron in the backward pass.

As a neural network learns, the weights of the neurons settle into their context within the network. The weights of the neurons are tuned for specific characteristics that provide some specialization. Neighboring neurons become dependent on this specialization, which if taken too far can result in a fragile model that is too specialized for training data. This dependence on the context of a neuron during training refers to complex co-adaptations.

Srivastava [14] and Warde-Farley [15] demonstrated through experiments that the weight scaling approach is a precise alternative for the geometric medium and for all possible subnetworks. Gal et al. [8] stated that deep neural network training with Dropout is equivalent to making a variational inference in a deep Gaussian Process. Dropout can also be considered as a way of adding noise to the neural network.

At the same time, academy and industry groups are working on high-level frameworks to enable scale out to multiple machines, extending well known deep learning libraries (like tensorflow, pytorch and others).

Keras is an open-source neural-network library written in Python. It can run on top of TensorFlow, Microsoft Cognitive Toolkit, R, Theano, or PlaidML [16–18]. Designed to enable fast experimentation with deep neural networks, it focuses on being user-friendly, modular, and extensible. It was developed as part of the research effort of project ONEIROS (Open-ended Neuro-Electronic Intelligent Robot Operating System), [19] and its primary author and maintainer is François Chollet, a Google engineer. Chollet also is the author of the XCeption deep neural network model [20]. Horovod [21] is a high-level library made over tensorflow, that implements a ring all reduce as gradient update synchronization and uses MPI to communicate the workers, providing an alternative method for coordinating the parameters instead of PS. Whose scalability is linear until 256 GPUs for small neural networks as Inception V3, but presents task-granularity issues when the dimension of the neural network increases as VGG-16, the performance decreases. Mesh-tensorflow [22], implements synchronous data-parallelism with replicated parameters and the mini-batch is divided into sub-batches (one for each processor), in which the gradients update broadcast to all processors, then each processor updates its own copy of the parameters. This approach uses a WMT14 neural network to scale until 512 cores, but it did not support accelerators. Nevertheless, these approaches are tested with well-tuned AI benchmarks (as MLPerf), masked the workflow needs for implementing applications in the HDA ecosystem. DiagnoseNET [23] as a modular framework that enables the application-workflow management and the expressivity to build and finetune deep neural networks, while its runtime abstracts the distributed orchestration of portability and scalability from a GPU workstation to multi-GPUs and multi-nodes computational platforms. In which the inpatient-diagnostic workflow is being optimized for training deep neural networks on low power consumption platforms (Domain framework).

3   Methodology

The use of GPU in DL is mainly due to their enormous capacity compared to CPUs, because the latter have a few cores optimized to process sequential tasks, instead the GPU have a parallel architecture that has thousands of smaller, more efficient cores designed to multitask. To determine the relationship between regularization and batch size, dropout value and network architecture, an experimental methodology was used, using the Framework DiagnoseNet [23], developed at Sophia Antipolis (I3S) Computer, Systems and Signals Laboratory in France and as input data a set of clinical admission and hospital data which has an average of 116831 hospital patient records, which has records of the activities of hospitals in the south-ern region of France, which contains information on morbidity, medical procedures, admission details and other variables [24].

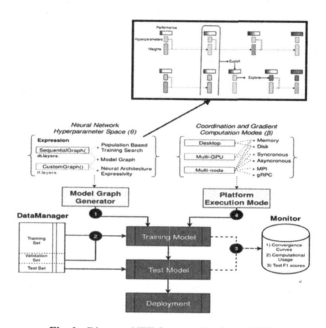

Fig. 1. DiagnoseNET framework scheme [23].

DiagnoseNET was designed to harmonize the deep learning workflow and to automatize the distributed orchestration to scale the neural network model from a GPU workstation to multi-nodes. Figure 1 shows the schematic integration of the DiagnoseNET modules with their functionalities.

The first module is the deep learning model graph generator, which has two expression languages: Sequential Graph API designed to automatize the hyperparameters search and a Custom Graph which support the TensorFlow expression codes for sophisticated neural networks. In this module, for optimized the computationals resources, in DiagnoseNet Framework was implemented the Population based training starts like parallel search, randomly sampling hyperparameters and weight initializations. However, each training run asynchronously evaluates its performance periodically. If a model in the population is under-performing, it will explore the rest of the population by replacing itself with a better performing model, and it will explore new hyperparameters by modifying the better model's hyperparameters, before training is continued. This process allows hyperparameters to be optimized online, and the computational resources to be focused on the hyperparameter and weight space that has most chance of producing good results. The result is a hyperparameter tuning method that while very simple, results in faster learning, lower computational resources, and often better solutions [25]. The second module is the data manager, compose by three classes designed for splitting, batching and multi-task any dataset over GPU workstations and multi-nodes computational platforms. The third module extends the enerGyPU monitor for workload characterization, constitute by a data capture in runtime to collect the convergence tracking logs and the computing factor metrics; and a dashboard for the experimental analysis results [26]. The fourth module is the runtime that enables the platform selection from GPU workstations to multi-nodes whit different execution modes, such as synchronous and asynchronous coordination gradient computations with gRPC or MPI communication protocols [23].

The methodology of experimentation consists of four phases as shown in Fig. 2: the first phase receives the patient's records. The second phase establishes the architecture of the neural network, batch size, dropout value, number of peak periods, computer architecture. With these parameters the training and validation of the DL model is initiated. The third phase is the analysis phase in which the overfitting, execution time, convergence curves, computational use and F1 score variables are verified.

Once the analysis stage is finished, the results are verified and other runs are executed with a new combination of parameters, to examine the relationship between the dropout and the overfitting in order to determine which combination of parameters is the best to achieve the reduction of the overfitting.

To establish the architectures of the neural networks, the same number of neurons was maintained in each of the architectures, only modifying the number of neurons per hidden layer. The number of hidden layers increases as a power of 2, starting with 2, followed by 4, and finally 8 hidden layers. For the dropout values that establish the probability that a neuron remains activated, values that vary by 20% were established, starting from 40%, 60% and 80%, to determine how the models increase their generalization and two sizes were used 100 and 200 to identify the relationship between the dropout and batch size.

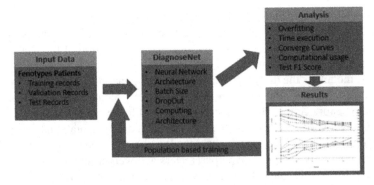

Fig. 2. Diagram of the experimental methodology.

4 Evaluation and Results

Several executions were performed using different hardware architectures, neural network architectures, batch sizes and dropout values, this in order to determine the relationship between these parameters with the execution time and the regularization of the DL model, in order to estimate if an over adjustment occurs, establishing a maximum number of times to stop the training process.

The dataset of input data, which was used consists of 116831 medical records of the patients representing their characteristics, where each record has 10833 patient characteristics and is labeled in 14 classes that represent the purpose of health care of the same. Of these records, 99306 were used as training records, 5841 as validation records, and 11684 as test records.

The testbed architecture that was used for the experiments is shown in Table 1 and Table 2.

Table 1. Testbed architecture (computer)

ID.	Processor	Speed	Cache	Cores	Watts	Memory
PC1	I7 4790 K	4.0 GHz	8 MB	4	88	32 GB DDR3
PC2	I7 4710HQ	2.5 GHz	6 MB	4	47	32 GB DDR3

Table 2. Testbed architecture (GPU)

ID.	Reference	Cores	Speed	Memory	Bus
PC1	GTX 1080 TI	3584	1582 MHz	11264 MB GDDR5	352 Bits
PC2	GTX 980 M	1536	1127 MHz	4096 MB GDDR5	256 Bits

The artificial neural network architectures used were three multi-layer perceptron neural networks, the first NNA1 that has 8 hidden layers of 256 neurons each hidden layer, the second NNA2 with 4 hidden layers of 512 neurons and the third NNA3 with 2 hidden layers each layer with 1024 neurons, that is all the models of neural network architecture maintain the same number of neurons. See Fig. 3.

For the experiments, the batch size, dropout value and neural network architecture were modified.

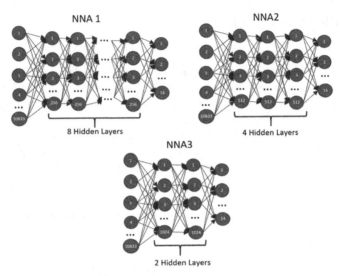

Fig. 3. Neural network architecture

Subsequently, the loss and accuracy graphs were analyzed, both for training and validation. The loss graph measures the uncertainty that our classifier has had with respect to the actual corresponding label, i.e. whether the classification has varied or has deviated a lot or a little from what it should be. This value is intended to be closer to 0. When you have a regularized DL model, the training and validation loss curves are quite close, i.e. the gap between these two curves is as small as possible. The accuracy graph shows the fraction or number of examples that have been correctly classified. If the number of known tags corresponds to the same number of predicted tags, then you have an accuracy of 1.0. In this metric, the better our classifier is, the closer it is to 1.

Table 3 shows the results obtained in the testbed architecture PC1, with the different combinations of parameters with which the tests were executed. The neural network architect, batch size and dropout were varied, and the F1 Score weighted, F1 score micro, loss validation and execution time were obtained. It can be seen that with the different combinations there is not much variation in the execution time for each of the tests, so it is determined that these parameters do not intervene in the training and validation of the DL models. As for the variables F1 score Weighted, F1 Score micro and Loss Validation, the best results are obtained in the combination of NNA2, with batch size of 200 and dropout of 0.6.

Table 3. Testbed table – PC1

Neural network architecture	Batch size	DropOut	F1 score weighted	F1 score micro	Loss validation	Execution time [hours]
NNA1	100	0,4	0,31	0,33	1,62	1,98
NNA1	100	0,6	0,66	0,68	0,94	1,94
NNA1	100	0,8	0,69	0,69	0,90	1,98
NNA1	200	0,4	0,21	0,23	1,63	1,95
NNA1	200	0,6	0,63	0,66	1,03	1,93
NNA1	200	0,8	0,48	0,53	1,38	1,95
NNA2	100	0,4	0,68	0,69	0,95	1,93
NNA2	100	0,6	0,71	0,71	0,90	1,94
NNA2	100	0,8	0,69	0,70	0,88	1,96
NNA2	200	0,4	0,64	0,66	0,95	1,93
NNA2	200	0,6	0,71	0,71	0,77	1,93
NNA2	200	0,8	0,58	0,61	1,09	1,94
NNA3	100	0,4	0,72	0,72	0,86	1,93
NNA3	100	0,6	0,71	0,71	0,87	1,93
NNA3	100	0,8	0,70	0,70	0,91	1,95
NNA3	200	0,4	0,71	0,71	0,79	1,93
NNA3	200	0,6	0,69	0,70	0,81	1,94
NNA3	200	0,8	0,66	0,67	0,90	1,96

Analyzing the loss curves using the NNA1 neural network architecture that contains the 8 hidden layers, see Fig. 4; it is identified that the best combination of parameters that allow to have a regularization of the DL model is the one that uses a batch size of 200 and a dropout of 0.6, this is evidenced because the training and validation loss curves are the ones that present less difference.

When the neural network architecture NNA2 is used, which consists of 4 hidden layers, it is visualized that it diminishes the loss curve a lot, and it improves the accuracy curve reaching almost 80%, as it is visualized in Fig. 5, with the combination of batch size 200 and a dropout of 0.6. As it happened with the NNA1 a better regularization is presented with this combination, since the gap between the training and validation loss curves is quite small.

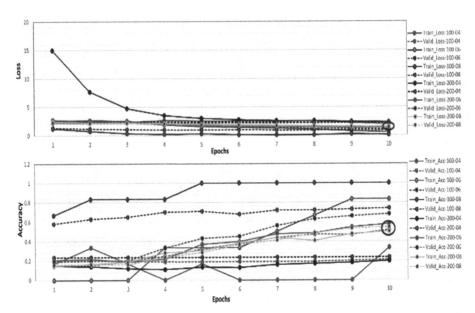

Fig. 4. Loss & accuracy curves PC1 – NNA1

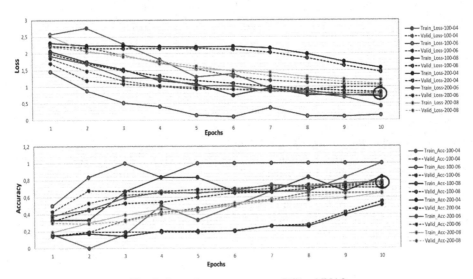

Fig. 5. Loss & accuracy curves PC1 – NNA2

As can be seen in Fig. 6, where the loss and accuracy curves are displayed, for the NNA3 neural network architecture, that is to say, the one that presents only two hidden layers, it is obtained that the best combination is the batch size and the drop-out of 0.4, because the difference between the two curves presents the least varia-tion, besides in the accuracy curve values close to 80% are achieved.

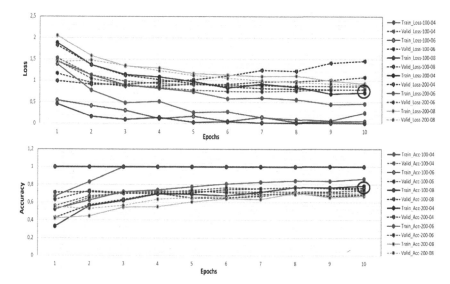

Fig. 6. Loss & accuracy curves PC1 – NNA3

Table 4 shows the results for the testbed architecture PC2. As the PC2 displays the same behavior, the runtime increases because the GPU has fewer cores than the PC1.

Table 4. Testbed table – PC2

Neural network architecture	Batch size	DropOut	F1 score weighted	F1 score micro	Loss validation	Execution time [hours]
NNA1	100	0,4	0,32	0,38	1,65	2,43
NNA1	100	0,6	0,65	0,68	1,02	2,54
NNA1	100	0,8	0,69	0,69	0,91	2,44
NNA1	200	0,4	0,19	0,27	2,25	2,62
NNA1	200	0,6	0,65	0,67	1,28	2,43
NNA1	200	0,8	0,66	0,65	0,94	2,63
NNA2	100	0,4	0,67	0,69	0,95	2,45
NNA2	100	0,6	0,70	0,70	0,89	2,44
NNA2	100	0,8	0,69	0,70	0,89	2,43
NNA2	200	0,4	0,65	0,67	1,26	2,59
NNA2	200	0,6	0,70	0,71	0,97	2,44
NNA2	200	0,8	0,59	0,61	1,12	2,46
NNA3	100	0,4	0,71	0,72	0,84	2,46
NNA3	100	0,6	0,71	0,71	0,86	2,45
NNA3	100	0,8	0,70	0,70	0,93	2,47
NNA3	200	0,4	0,72	0,72	1,08	2,58
NNA3	200	0,6	0,72	0,72	1,06	2,52
NNA3	200	0,8	0,66	0,67	0,91	2,44

As for the convergence curves these present the same behavior which we can see in the Figs. 7, 8 and 9. The loss and accuracy curves for each one of the neural net-work architectures, NNA1, NNA2 and NNA3, are shown.

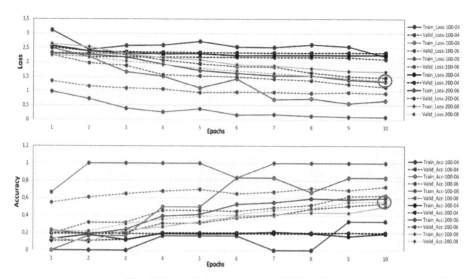

Fig. 7. Loss & Accuracy curves PC2 – NNA1

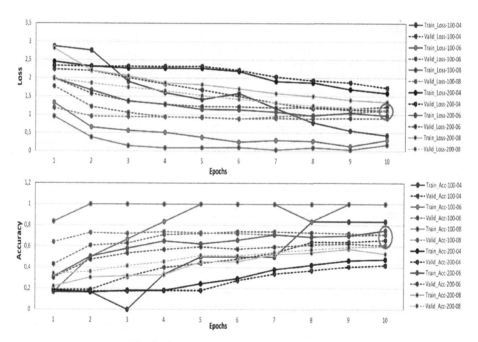

Fig. 8. Loss & accuracy curves PC2 – NNA2

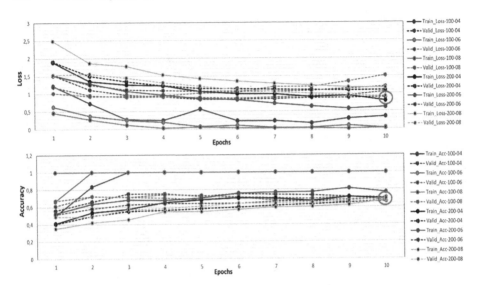

Fig. 9. Loss & accuracy curves PC2 – NNA3

5 Discussion

The dropout is a technique that allows to improve neural networks by reducing the overfitting, however it has limitations when it comes to changing the scale.

There is a close relationship between dropout and the number of hidden layers, the higher the number of hidden layers, the higher the dropout value is needed so that the accuracy of the DL model is not affected.

DL models with many parameters benefit from distributed computational architectures where there is more computing capacity and memory, precisely affects performance and therefore execution time.

6 Conclusions

The dropout improves neural networks by reducing overfitting and in turn improves the accuracy without affecting neural network performance in a wide variety of ap-plication areas.

Regarding the number of hidden layers, it is evident that having a deeper neural network causes a decrease in accuracy for the DL models.

Using very low dropout values in neural network architectures with many hidden layers affects the model's ability to generalize values not seen in the training.

7 Further Work

To analyze the behavior of DL algorithms, the volume of input data will be drastically increased, using HPC computing architectures, in turn, better performance monitors that have an impact on the efficiency of the implementation of DL algorithms for determine the scalability, efficiency, portability and precision of the results using a variety of components both at the hardware/software level and thus determine if these DL algorithms can be implemented with different mechanisms.

This scalability will be measured using the MPI [27] distributed model on HPC machines both synchronously and asynchronously and thus determine the efficiency in terms of runtime.

References

1. Xiong, H.Y., et al.: The human splicing code reveals new insights into the genetic determinants of disease (2015)
2. Esteva, A., et al.: Dermatologist-level classification of skin cancer with deep neural networks (2017)
3. Rajpurkar, P., Hannun, A.Y., Haghpanahi, M., Bourn, C., Ng, A.Y.: Cardiologist level arrhythmia detection with convolutional neural networks (2017)
4. Futoma, J., et al.: An improved multi-output gaussian process RNN with real-time validation for early sepsis detection (2017)
5. Reynaga, R., Mayta, W.: Introduction the pattern recognition. Reconocer Inc. Fides Et Ratio V.3 (2009)
6. Gentimis, T., Ala'J, A., Durante, A., Cook, K., Steele, R.: APredicting hospital length of stay using neural networks on MIMIC III data (2017)
7. Sardanelli, F.: Trends in radiology and experimental research. European Radiology Experimental. Department of Biomedical Sciences (2017)
8. Gal, Y., Ghahramani, Z.: Dropout as a Bayesian approximation: Representing model uncertainty in deep learning. In: Proceedings of the 33nd International Conference on Machine Learning, ICML, New York City, pp. 1050–1059 (2016)
9. Bengio, Y.: Learning deep architectures for AI. In: Foundations and Trends in Machine Learning, pp. 1–127 (2009)
10. Wager, S., Wang, S., Liang, P.: Dropout training as adaptive regularization. In: Advances in Neural Information Processing Systems, pp. 351–359 (2013)
11. Erhan, D., Bengio, Y., Courville, A., Manzagol, P.A., Vincent, P., Bengio, S.: Why does unsupervised pre-training help deep learning? J. Mach. Learn. Res. **11**, 625–660 (2010)
12. Moody, J., Hanson, S., Krogh, A., Hertz, J.A.: A simple weight decay can improve generalization. In: Advances in Neural Information Processing Systems, pp. 950–957 (1995)
13. Prechelt, L.: Automatic early stopping using cross validation: quantifying the criteria. Neural Netw. **11**, 761–767 (1998)
14. Srivastava, N., Hinton, G., Krizhevsky, A., Sutskever, I., Salakhutdinov, R.: Dropout: a simple way to prevent neural networks from overfitting. J. Mach. Learn. Res. **15**, 1929–1958 (2014)
15. Warde Farley, D., Goodfellow, I.J., Courville, A., Bengio, Y.: An empirical analysis of dropout in piecewise linear networks (2013)
16. Keras: Backend utilities Homepage. https://keras.io/backend/. Accessed 23 Feb 2018
17. Keras: Why choose Keras Homepage. https://keras.io/why-use-keras/. Accessed 22 Mar 2018
18. Keras Studio Homepage. https://keras.rstudio.com/. Accessed 22 Mar 2020
19. Keras Simple: Flexible. Powerful Homepage. https://keras.io/#why-this-name-keras. Accessed 18 Sept 2016
20. Chollet, F.: Xception: deep learning with depthwise separable convolutions (2016)
21. Sergeev, A., Del Balso, M.: Horovod: fast and easy distributed deep learning in Tensorflow (2018)

22. Shazeer, N., et al.: Mesh-tensorflow: deep learning for supercomputers (2018)
23. García Henao, J.A., Precioso, F., Staccini, P., Riveill, M.: DiagnoseNET: automatic framework to scale neural networks on heterogeneous systems applied to medical diagnosis (2020)
24. García Henao, J.A., Precioso, F., Staccini, P., Riveill, M.: Parallel and distributed processing for unsupervised patient phenotype representation (2016)
25. Jaderberg, M., et al.: Population based training of neural networks. DeepMind. London, UK (2017)
26. García Henao, J.A., Hernandez, B.E., Montenegro, C.E., Navaux, P.O., Barrios, H.C.J.: enerGyPU and enerGyPhi monitor for power consumption and performance evaluation on Nvidia Tesla GPU and Intel Xeon Phi (2016)
27. Open Source High Performance Computing Homepage. https://www.open-mpi.org/. Accessed 24 May 2020

Computer Application for the Detection of Skin Diseases in Photographic Images Using Convolutional Neural Networks

Alejandro Reátegui Pezo[1]([⊠]) [ID], Isaac Ocampo Yahuarcani[2]([⊠]) [ID],
Angela Milagros Nuñez Satalaya[2]([⊠]) [ID], Lelis Antony Saravia Llaja[2]([⊠]) [ID],
Carlos Alberto García Cortegano[1]([⊠]) [ID], and Astrid Fariza Panduro Ahuanari[2]([⊠]) [ID]

[1] Faculty of Systems and Informatics Engineering, National University of the Peruvian Amazon, Iquitos, Peru
alejandroreategui_pezo@hotmail.com, cagaco177@gmail.com
[2] Group Invéntalo, Iquitos, Peru
isaacocampoy16@gmail.com, mily_angela@hotmail.com,
saravia.lelis95@gmail.com, farizapanduro@gmail.com

Abstract. The present work was to generate an efficient computer application for the detection of skin diseases from photographic images, using convolutional neural network algorithms. This tool is aimed at supporting diagnostic processes. For this research, priority has been given to the diseases "Impetigo" and "Psoriasis", which are common diseases in cities of the Peruvian Amazon. The city of Iquitos will be taken as a case study. An image bank of 1640 images has been generated, and 3 algorithms have been experimented with: Inception V3, VGG 16 and ResNet 50. Finally, excellent results have been achieved in the detection of skin diseases with the Inception V3 algorithm.

Keywords: Computer application · Skin · CNN · Impetigo · Psoriasis

1 Introduction

Skin diseases stand out among the chronic health problems present in the population of most countries in the world. However, they are more prevalent in countries and cities with low economic levels and tropical regions such as the Peruvian Amazon [1]. There are a series of factors that influence or favour the expansion of skin diseases, among which the most important are elements associated with the environment such as temperature, humidity, winds, which facilitate the expansion or growth of other factors such as bacteria, viruses, parasites, etc. Also, in several towns and cities of the Amazon there is little access to health services (reduced number of doctors and health centers), while the quality of services are poor which reduces the chances of identifying, controlling and eradicating skin diseases. Currently, through sciences such as computers, various technological solutions are being generated to support access to public health (TELE-SALUD), as well as the detection or diagnosis of diseases using computer tools [2–5]. In this way, the use of computer solutions based on Artificial Intelligence is proposed

© Springer Nature Switzerland AG 2021
S. Nesmachnow et al. (Eds.): CARLA 2020, CCIS 1327, pp. 193–204, 2021.
https://doi.org/10.1007/978-3-030-68035-0_14

as alternative and complementary tools to support the reduction of gaps in public health services.

Among the most widespread skin diseases in the world are atopic dermatitis, measles, infections, hives, and the best known in a chronic state is skin cancer. Also according to the University of Colorado Cancer Center [6], which indicates that skin diseases are the fourth most common cause of disability that develops throughout a person's life. In the case of Peru, according to data from the Ministry of Health [7] at least 1,200 new cases of skin cancer are detected nationwide, not counting the number of cases of other skin diseases that affect both children and adults. Within the group of diseases that stand out mainly in the child and adult population of Peru, we have impetigo, chickenpox and psoriasis, however, there are others like scabies, hives, among others.

On the other hand, according to the report made by the National Institute of Radio and Television [8], in Peru approximately 400,000 people suffer from psoriasis disease, and worldwide the same disease affects more than 125 million people. It is important to note that psoriasis is considered by the World Health Organization [9], to be a very painful, disfiguring and disabling condition. It is also worth mentioning that the Peruvian Ministry of Health [10], has been implementing a warning plan for the increase of chickenpox in Peru since 2016. Cases have been reported in the regions of Lima, Arequipa, Amazonas, Loreto and Piura, with up to 10,000 cases reported in 2016 and 6,000 more by the end of 2017.

In the Peruvian Amazon, specifically in the Loreto region, there have been alarming reports for several years of cases of skin diseases or injuries, as indicated by the website of the newspaper La Región [11], while health campaigns have been promoted for skin care by EsSalud [12], mainly in the city of Iquitos.

Among the determining factors that favour the expansion of skin diseases in Loreto are the low accessibility to health services, determined by the limited number of specialist doctors, the low number of health centres in rural and indigenous communities far from the cities, as well as a weak culture of visiting health centres by a large part of the population (the population probably stays away for fear of invasive procedures, which can cause some degree of pain and discomfort to the patient affected by a dermatological disease or injury), and even limited economic conditions. Likewise, according to the Peruvian Institute of Economics, in the results of the Regional Competitiveness Index - INCORE [13], the Loreto region has been in the last places with respect to the competitiveness index of its health services for more than a decade, which considerably affects the quality of life of the population. Among the most affected groups are children.

Among the more complex problems associated with health service quality are the following:

- Prolonged time in traditional medical care processes for diagnosis of skin diseases in the city of Iquitos.
- Absence of reliable methodological alternatives for diagnosis of skin diseases.
- Difficulties of the population in accessing health care services
- Scarce number of patients diagnosed due to lack of health centers and doctors.

On the other hand, there are a series of limitations typical of the health sector in the Amazon, which could not be solved by the project:

- The Peruvian Amazon, has high rates of skin diseases caused by various factors such as bacteria and insects exposed in the environment, use of contaminated water (contaminated rivers).
- Insufficient number of doctors in hospitals and accessible health centers in the cities and rural communities.
- Insufficient number of hospitals and health centers in the Amazonian cities and rural communities of Loreto
- Poorly equipped hospitals and health centers.
- Relatively high costs for access to health care in the Amazon
- Health centers in rural areas do not have basic conditions for attention (lack of electricity, water, sanitation, and telecommunications).
- Factors such as the intensity of the solar waves, together with the humidity of the Peruvian Amazon, increase the problems of skin diseases.
- All over Peru, due to climate change issues, cases of cancer and other skin diseases are increasing.

Thus, it is necessary the existence of an alternative mechanism that supports the processes of diagnosis of skin diseases that is easily accessible to families without socioeconomic distinction in the urban and rural environment.

Therefore, the development of a computer application that generates relevant information for the diagnosis of skin diseases is proposed (the result could be considered a previous diagnosis verifiable by doctors). The idea of using mobile devices arises due to the high rates of penetration of the use of mobile devices both in the cities and in the indigenous communities of the Peruvian Amazon.

2 Methodology

The development of the software comprised the following steps:

2.1 Disease Prioritization and Requirement Identification

In order to understand the context and processes related to health services in Loreto, officials, medical nurses, and other collaborators associated with the Regional Health Directorate of the Regional Government of Loreto and private entities were contacted and interviewed. The central idea was to identify the main and most common skin diseases, in addition to obtaining important information related to the procedures followed to care for patients with skin conditions or problems, such as tools and studies that are conducted in these conditions.

Bibliographic consultations have also been carried out in data sources such as Scopus, IEEE Xplore, Sciencie Direct, Google Scholar, among others, searching for research (scientific articles, postgraduate theses and even publications in the Peruvian and international press) related to neural networks [14–16] that identify patterns of textures, disease detection systems [17–20] and public health services.

Taking into account the information collected in the above sources, it was determined to generate the application aimed at the recognition of the diseases "Psoriasis" and

"Impetigo", these being the most widespread skin diseases in the city of Iquitos, Loreto, on which Datasets could be built or accessed. However, the limited accessibility to hospitals due to the COVID-19 pandemic has been presented as a limitation. Likewise, these interviews served to analyze the processes and limitations of health services in both cities and rural and indigenous communities, the same ones that were used in the generation of the software requirements, which are described below:

- The system should be accessible in web and mobile formats (the latter especially for rural areas where there is no access to electricity).
- The system must work offline for rural communities or areas far from cities, and at the same time it must be able to provide server-connected service in urban areas.
- The system should be intuitive and its graphics should be understandable, while providing ease of use for users from indigenous peoples who do not necessarily speak Spanish.
- The system should provide guidance on its use, emphasizing that these are preliminary results that should be verified with visits to medical offices.
- The system should have facilities to increase the recognition of other skin diseases.
- The system shall provide graphical and sound information oriented to populations with limited ICT capabilities.

2.2 Dataset Construction

A protocol has been defined and validated with specialist criteria for the acquisition of photographic images of the skin, which has considered aspects such as: the distance from the camera to the photo, lighting, colour, focus, and other conditions. At the beginning of the generation of the datasets, visits to hospitals and health centres in the city were determined, to identify cases of patients diagnosed with the prioritised skin diseases. However, due to security measures associated with the COVID-19 pandemic, access to these facilities has been limited, making it difficult to achieve the datasets entirely. As a solution, it has been determined to obtain the dataset from dermatological image databases, which were:

- DermIS-DATABASE [21]
- Image library: DermNet NZ [22]
- Clinical Images of Skin Diseases: Department of Dermatology [23]
- Dermnet: Dermatology photos - Photos of skin diseases [24]

The set of images downloaded from the dermatological databases made a total of 228 images (102 images of "Impetigo" and 126 images of "Psoriasis") (Figs. 1 and 2).

Adversarial Generative Neural Networks are a new way of using deep learning to generate images that appear real. They can also generate other types of data such as music. Generative Adversarial Neural Networks are also called GANs (Generative Adversarial Networks). Generative models use 2 deep neural networks. These two networks are adversarial, where what one network gains, the other loses [25].

For the generation of images with GANs algorithms, a lot of processing time was required, even up to 10 000 epochs to be able to generate 1000 images of a class in an average time of 15 h, obtaining results that do not adapt to the expected dataset.

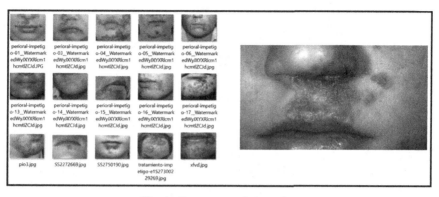

Fig. 1. Dataset sample impetigo

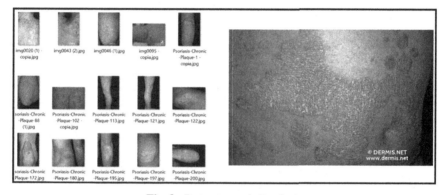

Fig. 2. Dataset sample Psoriasis

The Data Aumentagtion technique is the artificial generation of data by means of disturbances in the original data. This allows us to increase both the size and diversity of our training data set. In artificial vision, this technique became a standard for regularization, and also to improve performance and combat overfitting in CNNs [26].

In this work, offline magnification was used, which is a preferred method for relatively smaller datasets, as it would end up increasing the size of the dataset by a factor equal to the number of transformations it performs, and is applied before pre-processing.

Techniques such as: flipping, rotation and scaling were applied.

On the other hand, experimentation was carried out using the Data Augmentation technique, a technique that occupied less processing time, thus obtaining 1000 images for each class in an average time of thirty minutes per class.

The results of the Data Aumentagtion technique are presented here (Fig. 3):

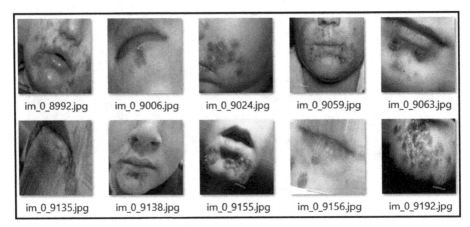

Fig. 3. Dataset with Data aumentagtion

2.3 Algorithm Selection and Experimentation

Taking into account experiences and case studies found in the literature review related to the implementation of texture-oriented convolutional neural networks and computer solutions applied to health, three algorithms were initially identified: Inception V3 [27], VGG 16 [28] and ResNet 50 [29].

We experimented with the 3 algorithms, comparing the results according to the following criteria:

- Algorithm configuration: Number of layers, Number of epochs, Filter size, libraries, among others.
- Processing time based on the collection of similar research with the above mentioned algorithms.
- Significant indicators in training and testing processes: Sensitivity, Accuracy, Specificity, others.

a. Inception V3 Algorithm
    It is the third version in a series of deep-learning convolutional architectures. Inception V3 was trained using a 1,000 class data set from the original ImageNet data set that was trained with over 1 million training images, the Tensorflow version has 1,001 classes due to an additional "background" class not used in the original ImageNet. Inception V3 was trained for the ImageNet Large Visual Recognition Challenge, where it took first place [27, 30].

b. VGG 16 Algorithm
    It was proposed by Karen Simonyan and Andrew Zisserman of the Laboratory of the Visual Geometry Group at Oxford University in 2014 in the article "Very deep convolutional networks for large-scale image recognition". This model won 1st and 2nd place in the above categories in the ILSVRC 2014 challenge. This model achieves 92.7% test accuracy in the top 5 in the ImageNet dataset containing 14 million images belonging to 1000 classes [28, 31].

c. ResNet 50 algorithm

It is a model developed in a residual learning framework to facilitate substantially deeper networking, and has been shown to be easier to optimise and more accurate. This model achieved an error of 3.57% in the ImageNet data set. This result won 1st place in the ILSVRC 2015 classification task. An analysis on CIFAR-10 with 100 and 1000 layers was also presented [29].

These models have the following architecture (Table 1):

Table 1. Architecture of the convolutional neuronal networks

	Inception V3	VGG 16	ResNet 50
Input Image Dimensions	$299 \times 299 \times 3$	$224 \times 224 \times 3$	$224 \times 224 \times 3$
Total number of layers	42 layers	16 layers	50 layers
Error rate	3.46%	6,3%	3.57
Filter size	$1 \times 1, 3 \times 3, 5 \times 5$	3×3	$1 \times 1, 3 \times 3$

The model settings were adjusted for binary classification, as only the classes "Impetigo" and "Psoriasis" are available.

For the execution of the training of the algorithms the Anaconda environment has been implemented with Jupyter's notebook in the version of Python 3.7. Since these algorithms require considerable computing power, the comparative use of a personal computer (laptop), a workstation and a supercomputer was defined at the beginning of the training. The Peruvian Amazon has had a public access Supercomputer since 2017 [32]. Since the execution in the personal computer was quite slow and there was an interruption in the access to the Supercomputer, the experimentation in the Workstation was determined.

2.4   Design and Development of Computer Applications

A series of activities were established to build and develop the application, in order to have an accessible and friendly tool for the end user.

Application Interface Design: To elaborate the design of the web application, the basic and important functions of the application were taken into account, as well as the user experience in the use and handling of technologies in order to obtain a user-friendly software. Within the system is considered the function to attach an image type file from a data source (image gallery, local file folder, etc).

For the development of the web application, the team worked under the XP Methodology (Extreme Programming), considered as an agile methodology that adjusts to the limitations of time and human and financial resources that characterize this development according to the needs identified in the requirements.

Computer Configuration: The web platform was taken into account for the development process of the IT solution, which was developed under the use of tools and free software, the programming language PHP and the programming language Python was used to develop the scripts for the execution of the recognition (Fig. 4).

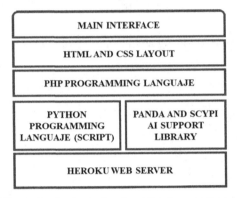

Fig. 4. Design logical web application architecture

3   Results

As a result of the Data Aumentagtion technique, and the training time required by the data set, an average dataset of 1680 images was finally determined for the training of each convolutional neural network model.

At the end of the training and use tests, more favourable results were obtained for the models under the following scheme (Table 2):

Table 2. Results of comparison between CNN models

	Inception v3	VGG 16	ResNet 50
Époch	10	10	10
Time of processing	3 h	1 h	2 h
Batch_size	16	16	16
Data	1680	1680	1680
Time recognition	1 min	31 s	36 s

An average of 12 experiments were performed, 4 for each neural network, with 10, 30, 50 and 100 epochs, with batch_size of 16, 32 and 64, however, better results were obtained at 10 epochs.

Therefore, the comparison of the models to 10 epochs has achieved acceptable results in the Sensitivity, Specificity, Precision and Accuracy indexes detailed in the following table (Table 3):

Table 3. Results of the Metrics

	Inception v3	VGG 16	ResNet 50
Sensibility	94%	92%	92%
Especificity	94%	92%	92%
Precision	94%	92%	92%
Exactitud	94%	92%	92%

Finally, higher indices have been observed in the Inception V3 algorithm, this algorithm was implemented in the computer application in web format (Figs. 5 and 6).

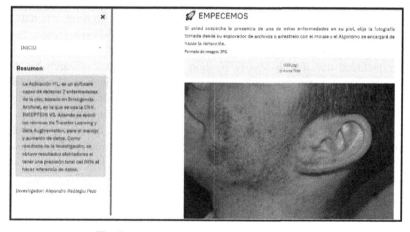

Fig. 5. System image recognizing "Impetigo".

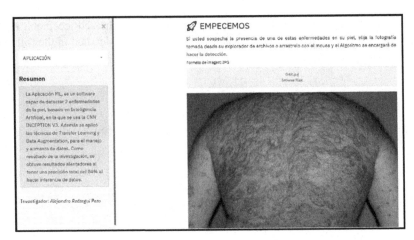

Fig. 6. System image recognizing "Psoriasis"

4 Conclusions

At the end of the experiment, we can conclude that the generation of images from data augmentation techniques is much more favorable with respect to time, whereas GAN images require greater computational capacity, longer times and even greater diversity in the base data set. The Data aumentagtion technique is easier to implement.

It is concluded that the alternative method generated in this research has proven results that indicate that it can be a useful tool in the identification of skin diseases (Impetigo and Psoriasis), and support the processes of recognition with a non-invasive method and with real-time results, from an image taken from a mobile device.

Future work is expected to include more images and diseases, in order to build disease recognition services as a support tool in medical diagnosis in regions with health service constraints.

References

1. Gutierrez, E., et al.: Prevalence of skin diseases in a rural area of Peruvian Amazonia. Dermatología Peruana **19**(2) (2009)
2. Melbin, K., Vetha Raj, Y.J.: An enhanced model for skin disease detection using dragonfly optimization based deep neural network. In: 2019 Third International conference on I-SMAC (IoT in Social, Mobile, Analytics and Cloud) (I-SMAC), pp. 346–351 (2019)
3. Anthal, J., Upadhyay, A., Gupta, A.: Detection of vitiligo skin disease using LVQ neural network. In: International Conference on Current Trends in Computer, Electrical, Electronics and Communication, pp. 922–925 (2017)
4. Rathod, J., Waghmode, V., Sodha, A., Bhavathankar, P.: Diagnosis of skin diseases using Convolutional Neural Networks. In: Second International Conference on Electronics, Communication and Aerospace Technology (ICECA), pp. 1048–1051 (2018)
5. ConSalud.es: Una nueva técnica para detectar rápidamente el cáncer de piel. Redacción ConSalud, 19 Setiembre (2019). [En línea]. https://www.consalud.es/tecnologia/una-nueva-tecnica-para-detectar-rapidamente-el-cancer-de-piel_68526_102.html

6. Todo Dermo. https://www.correofarmaceutico.com/. 4 Marzo 2017. [En línea]. https://www.correofarmaceutico.com/tododermo/enfermedades-de-la-piel/las-enfermedades-de-la-piel-la-cuarta-causa-de-discapacidad-en-el-mundo.html
7. Ministerio de Salud (2016). http://bvs.minsa.gob.pe/. [En línea]. http://bvs.minsa.gob.pe/local/MINSA/3774.pdf
8. Instituto Nacional de Radio y Televisión del Perú. https://www.tvperu.gob.pe/. 6 Mayo 2019. [En línea]. https://www.tvperu.gob.pe/novedades/junta-medica/psoriasis-una-enfermedad-que-debes-conocer-a-profundidad
9. Asociación de Pacientes de Psoriasis, Artritis Psoriásica y Familiares. https://www.accionpsoriasis.org/. [En línea]. https://www.accionpsoriasis.org/recursos/publicaciones.html?catid=0&id=373#:~:text=La%2067%20%C2%AA%20Asamblea%20Mundial,la%20que%20no%20hay%20cura%22
10. Ministerio de Salud (2018). http://www.dge.gob.pe/. [En línea]. http://www.dge.gob.pe/portal/docs/vigilancia/boletines/2018/52.pdf
11. Diario La Región. https://diariolaregion.com/. 26 Noviembre 2012. [En línea]. https://diariolaregion.com/web/enfermedades-a-la-piel-en-loreto-cada-ano-aumentan/
12. EsSalud. http://www.essalud.gob.pe/. 30 Enero 2015. [En línea]. http://www.essalud.gob.pe/essalud-promueve-campana-de-prevencion-de-lesiones-en-la-piel-en-la-ciudad-de-iquitos/
13. Instituto Peruano de Economía (2019). https://www.ipe.org.pe/. [En línea]. https://www.ipe.org.pe/portal/incore-2019-indice-de-competitividad-regional/
14. Venegas, D.: Sistema de Pre-Diagnóstico de Cáncer de Melanomas usando Redes Neuronales Artificiales, Texcoco (2019)
15. Cabezas, E., Galarza, E.: Reconocimiento de patrones de imágenes médicas para establecer diagnósticos previos en trastornos pulmonares, Ambato (2019)
16. Cabezas, E.: Reconocimiento de patrones de imágenes médicas para establecer diagnósticos previos en trastornos pulmonares, Ambato (2019)
17. Kaplan, A., Güldoğan, E., Çolak, C., Arslan, A.K.: Prediction of Melanoma from Dermoscopic Images Using Deep Learning-Based Artificial Intelligence Techniques. IEEE Xplore (2019)
18. Suárez, J., Colín, L., Mejía, A., Ambriz, J., García, J.: Una aproximación al diagnóstico de enfermedades de la piel por medio de aprendizaje profundo. Número Especial de la Revista Aristas: Investigación Básica y Aplicada, vol. 6, nº 12, pp. 13–16 (2018)
19. Coronado, R.: Reconocimiento de patrones en imágenes no dermatoscópicas para la detección de enfermedades malignas en la piel, utilizando redes neuronales convolutivas y autocodificadores (2018)
20. Gavrilov, D., Schelkunov, N., Melerzanov, A., Gorodilov, A.: Artificial intelligence image recognition inhealthcare. IEEE Xplore, pp. 24–26 (2018)
21. Dermis.net: Dermatology Information System. [En línea]. https://www.dermis.net/dermisroot/es/home/index.htm
22. DermNet NZ: Dermatology Image Library. [En línea]. https://www.dermnetnz.org/image-library/
23. University of Iowa: Carver College of Medicine - Clinical Skin Disease Images. [En línea]. https://medicine.uiowa.edu/dermatology/education/clinical-skin-disease-images
24. Dermet: Actinic Keratosis Hand Photos. [En línea]. http://www.dermnet.com/images/Actinic-Keratosis-Hand
25. IArtificial.net (2020). https://www.iartificial.net/. [En línea]. https://www.iartificial.net/redes-neuronales-generativas-adversarias-gans/#:~:text=Las%20Redes%20Neuronales%20Generativas%20Adversarias,generar%20im%C3%A1genes%20que%20parecen%20reales.&text=Las%20Redes%20Neuronales%20Generativas%20Adversarias%20tamb i%C3%A9%

26. NanoNet Technologies Inc. (2018). https://nanonets.com/. [En línea]. https://nanonets.com/blog/data-augmentation-how-to-use-deep-learning-when-you-have-limited-data-part-2/

27. Szegedy, C., Vanhoucke, V., Ioffe, S., Shlens, J., Wojna, Z.: Rethinking the Inception Architecture for Computer Vision (2015)

28. Simonyan, K., Zisserman, A.: Very deep concolutional networks for large-scale image recognition. In: ICLR 2015 (2015)

29. He, K., Zhang, X., Ren, S., Sun, J.: Deep residual learning for image recognition. In: CVPR (2016)

30. Corporación Intel (2019). https://software.intel.com/. [En línea]. https://software.intel.com/content/www/us/en/develop/articles/inception-v3-deep-convolutional-architecture-for-classifying-acute-myeloidlymphoblastic.html

31. Neurohive (2018). https://neurohive.io/. [En línea]. https://neurohive.io/en/popular-networks/vgg16/

32. Diario La región. https://diariolaregion.com/. 28 Enero 2017. [En línea]. https://diariolaregion.com/web/inauguraron-supercomputadora-del-iiap-denominada-manati/

Neocortex and *Bridges-2*: A High Performance AI+HPC Ecosystem for Science, Discovery, and Societal Good

Paola A. Buitrago[✉] and Nicholas A. Nystrom

Pittsburgh Supercomputing Center, Carnegie Mellon University,
Pittsburgh, PA 15213, USA
paola@psc.edu

Abstract. Artificial intelligence (AI) is transforming research through analysis of massive datasets and accelerating simulations by factors of up to a billion. Such acceleration eclipses the speedups that were made possible though improvements in CPU process and design and other kinds of algorithmic advances. It sets the stage for a new era of discovery in which previously intractable challenges will become surmountable, with applications in fields such as discovering the causes of cancer and rare diseases, developing effective, affordable drugs, improving food sustainability, developing detailed understanding of environmental factors to support protection of biodiversity, and developing alternative energy sources as a step toward reversing climate change. To succeed, the research community requires a high-performance computational ecosystem that seamlessly and efficiently brings together scalable AI, general-purpose computing, and large-scale data management. The authors, at the Pittsburgh Supercomputing Center (PSC), launched a second-generation computational ecosystem to enable AI-enabled research, bringing together carefully designed systems and groundbreaking technologies to provide at no cost a uniquely capable platform to the research community. It consists of two major systems: Neocortex and Bridges-2. Neocortex embodies a revolutionary processor architecture to vastly shorten the time required for deep learning training, foster greater integration of artificial deep learning with scientific workflows, and accelerate graph analytics. Bridges-2 integrates additional scalable AI, high-performance computing (HPC), and high-performance parallel file systems for simulation, data pre- and post-processing, visualization, and Big Data as a Service. Neocortex and Bridges-2 are integrated to form a tightly coupled and highly flexible ecosystem for AI- and data-driven research.

Keywords: Computer architecture · Artificial intelligence · AI for Good · Deep learning · Big data · High-performance computing

© Springer Nature Switzerland AG 2021
S. Nesmachnow et al. (Eds.): CARLA 2020, CCIS 1327, pp. 205–219, 2021.
https://doi.org/10.1007/978-3-030-68035-0_15

1 Introduction

Scalable artificial intelligence (AI) is of vital importance for enabling research, yet computational resources to support developing accurate models have largely been based on processor technologies developed for other kinds of applications, and infrastructure to support scaling has been implemented mostly in software, limiting its effectiveness and ease of use. This paper describes a new, ambitious computer architecture for supporting AI-enabled research that balances the most powerful processors ever built with high-performance computing and data infrastructure. The two systems—*Neocortex*, which vastly shortens the time required for deep learning training, and *Bridges-2*, which provides great capacity for the many facets of rapidly evolving research—are integrated into a computational ecosystem to enable research in AI and its applications across all fields of study. They are being deployed at the Pittsburgh Supercomputing Center (PSC), a joint research center of Carnegie Mellon University and the University of Pittsburgh.

In 2012, the artificial neural network AlexNet [11] demonstrated the power of deep neural networks (DNNs) by dramatically decreasing the error rate in image classification and surpassing other machine learning (ML) approaches by 10.8% in the 2012 ImageNet competition. AlexNet achieved a top-5 error rate of 15.3%, with human-level accuracy being 5.1%. AlexNet consists of 8 network layers and 62,378,344 parameters, and it requires 7.25×10^8 flops. It took over five days to train on two NVIDIA GTX 580 GPUs.

The AlexNet result was significant because it convincingly demonstrated the ability of deep neural networks to automatically learn representations. AlexNet surpassed decades of traditional machine learning based on explicit feature engineering and other statistics. Inspired by AlexNet, researchers began developing more deeper, more sophisticated networks with progressively better results. Concurrently, domain scientists started applying the networks being created – and creating their own – to challenging problems in medical imaging, weather, cosmology, and many other fields.

In 2015, a new network, ResNet-152 [8], achieved top-5 error rate of only 4.49%, surpassing human-level accuracy. What changed were that ResNet-152 is an example of a residual network, and it is extremely deep: 152 layers. It has 60,192,872 parameters and requires 1.13×10^{10} flops, over 15 times that for AlexNet. This pattern is repeated across image classification and segmentation, time series analysis, natural language processing, and other fields to which deep learning is applied with great degrees of success: deeper, more complex networks better learn representations and result in higher accuracy. Neural networks for time series analysis and natural language processing (NLP) require recurrence and are much larger, for example, 330 million parameters for BERT [6] and 8.3 billion parameters for Megatron-LM [16]. In 2020, the GPT-3 language model presented another example of larger models yielding more accurate inferences. GPT-3 has 175 billion parameters and required 3.14×10^{23} flops (10 petaflop-years) to train [1]. *Training time is the primary bottleneck in applying AI to research, and the increasing complexity of deep learning models amplifies exacerbates the time required for training.*

Concurrently, researchers have begun to apply deep learning to a wide range of fields in science and engineering with remarkable results. For example, Kasim et al. demonstrated speedups of 100,000 to 2,000,000,000 for a variety of applications including inertial confinement fusion (ICF), a global ocean biogeochemical model (MOPS), and a global aerosol-climate model (GCM) using Deep Emulator Network SEarch (DENSE) to develop and train neural network models [9]. The models are then used as emulators, i.e., as surrogates that replace computationally demanding calculations with much faster inferencing. Using a different approach, Smith et al. demonstrated billion-fold speedup in quantum chemistry with neural network potentials and transfer learning while approaching gold-standard accuracy of CCSD(T)/CBS calculations [17]. In large-scale data analytics, Khan et al. developed a neural network classifier for galaxies in the Dark Energy Survey (DES) that achieves state-of-the-art accuracy of 99.6% and also showed how it can be combined with unsupervised recursive training to prepare for extremely large sky surveys such as will be obtained from the Large Synoptic Survey Telescope (LSST) project [10].

The benefits of high-accuracy models are great. Such models can be applied to analyze and extract information from large datasets and to create surrogate models that substitute for expensive calculations in simulation codes to decrease time-to-solution by orders of magnitude without loss of accuracy. But first, the models must be trained.

Training deep neural networks often takes days, weeks, or even months. For some applications such as image segmentation in radiology, there already exist deep neural networks that are known to work reasonably well. For many other applications, developing a model first requires building and optimizing a neural network architecture. Different types of networks better suited to different types of applications, and the field is evolving rapidly, with new network types frequently emerging. Once a network architecture is selected, and also to choose between network architectures, hyperparameters must be optimized, requiring additional sets of runs. The time requirement can be prohibitive. *It is this challenge that Neocortex is designed to overcome.*

The following sections describe a unique, heterogeneous system architecture for scalable AI, data pre- and post-processing, and simulation. Section 2 summarizes related work. For context, Sect. 3 provides an overview of the integrated system. Sections 4 and 5 then describe the Neocortex and Bridges-2 architectures, respectively. Section 6 concludes with a summary of the ecosystem's novel capabilities and expected opportunities.

2   Related Work

The heterogeneous architecture of Bridges-2 is an evolution of the *Bridges* system [13,14], which pioneered the convergence of HPC, AI, and Big Data. Bridges, which was designed in early 2014 and entered production in April 2016, tightly integrated dual-socket CPU nodes, large-memory four- and sixteen-socket CPU nodes, GPU nodes, and a parallel, disk-based file system with an overarching interconnect fabric. Bridges enabled complex workflows running concurrently on different kinds of compute nodes for which individual components were best-suited. Dedicated nodes containing solid-state disks (SSDs) for high IOPs and hard disk drives (HDDs) for large capacity supported persistent databases and web portals for different kinds of research ("science gateways"). Bridges was the world's first deployment of the Intel Omni-Path Architecture (OPA) fabric.

In November 2018, the authors developed and deployed Bridges-AI [4] as an expansion to Bridges. Bridges-AI consists of two types of AI-optimized nodes: an NVIDIA DGX-2 enterprise AI research system and nine Hewlett Packard Enterprise (HPE) Apollo 6000 Gen10 servers. The DGX-2 contains sixteen NVIDIA Tesla V100 GPUs with 32 GB of HBM2 memory (aggregate 512 GB HBM2), interconnected by the NVSwitch at 2.4 TB/s bisection bandwidth, 30TB NVMe of SSD, two Intel Xeon Platinum 8168 CPUs, and 1.5 TB of CPU memory. Its 10,240 tensor cores deliver 2 Pf/s of performance. Until recently, the DGX-2 was the world's most powerful AI system. The nine Apollo 6000 servers each have eight V100 GPUs with 16 GB of HBM2 memory, 7.68 TB NVMe SSD, two Intel Xeon Gold 6148 CPUs, and 192 GB of CPU memory. They provide additional substantial capacity for deep learning training for models and data that don't require the DGX-2. When Bridges-AI entered production in January 2019, it expanded the aggregate AI capacity of the NSF XSEDE ecosystem by 300%.

The optimization of advanced cyberinfrastructure for AI research is highly complex due to the rapid advance of hardware and software technologies and the differences between models that are important for social networks and business versus models that address the very large images, volumes, time series, and multimodal data of research applications. The Open Compass [2] project aims to evaluate the potential of new AI technologies for research, going beyond standard benchmarks such as MLPerf to also evaluate representative research applications, and developing and sharing best practices.

As more is learned, there exists the potential to apply AI to improve the design of large-scale computer systems and specific workloads. Concurrently, AI can be applied to increase supercomputers' performance, reliability, and usability and to improve user experience. This is the subject of one of the authors' (Buitrago's) *Calima* project, and it is addressed in the report of the NSF Workshop on Smart Cyberinfrastructure [3].

3   Integrated Neocortex + Bridges-2 AI+HPC Ecosystem

Neocortex and Bridges-2, which are detailed in the following sections, are being integrated with each other, Bridges-AI [4], and wide-area networks to national and international cyberinfrastructure, instruments, campuses, and clouds. Figure 1 illustrates the computational and data components and bandwidths of the combined system.

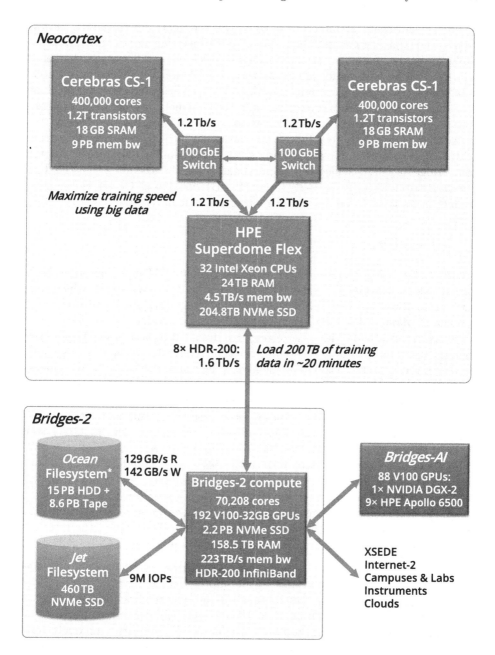

Fig. 1. High-level architecture of the Neocortex and Bridges-2 ecosystem for AI, HPC, and data. Bandwidths are balanced to enable efficient access to data and rapidly staging large-scale data from Bridges-2's Ocean file system to Neocortex's local NVMe flash file system. This facilitates training on Neocortex and doing pre- and post-processing on Bridges-2, as well as equitable access to Neocortex for a large number of users and research projects.

From a hardware architecture perspective, the goals are *capability, performance*, and *efficiency*. Capability arises from processing nodes that are separately specialized for different components of research workflows and that have unified access to high-performance data storage. Performance arises from node architectures that are individually optimized for deep learning and other machine learning, high performance computing, and large-memory tasks. Efficiency arises from balanced bandwidth across the various data paths within the system.

A key metric for the combined system is efficiently transferring data from Bridges-2 to Neocortex, for which loading 200 TB of training data into Neocortex from Bridges-2 can be achieved in approximately 20 min, assuming that the data is well-distributed in Bridges-2's large (15 PB) disk-based Ocean file system, resident in its flash-based Jet file system, or resident in RAM.

4   Neocortex

In early summer 2020, an innovative and unprecedented AI supercomputer, Neocortex, was awarded by the National Science Foundation. Neocortex, which captures groundbreaking new hardware technologies, is designed to accelerate AI research in pursuit of science, discovery, and societal good.

Neocortex is a highly innovative resource designed to accelerate AI-powered scientific discovery by vastly shortening the time required for deep learning training, foster greater integration of artificial deep learning with scientific workflows, and provide revolutionary new hardware for the development of more efficient algorithms for artificial intelligence and graph analytics. Its scale democratizes access to game-changing compute power otherwise only available to tech giants, allowing students, postdocs, faculty, and other researchers who require faster turnaround on training to analyze data and integrate AI with simulations. A primary goal of Neocortex is to inspire the research community to tackle big ideas, no longer constrained by computational resources, and scale their AI-based research and integrate AI advances into their research workflows. Neocortex allows users to apply more accurate models and train on larger data. It also allows scaling model parallelism to unprecedented levels, avoiding the need for expensive and time-consuming hyperparameter optimization.

Neocortex is Designed to Enable Three Exciting Areas of Research. First, the WSE takes processor architecture to an unprecedented scale. Providing the research community with access to that unique and remarkable capability is vital to understand the potential of the WSE approach. Second, as powerful as the WSE is, there are models too large for one WSE. Neocortex uniquely couples two CS-1 systems using a large-memory "front end" to enable research into scaling across multiple WSEs. Third, Neocortex is designed to enable important research for societal good. Examples include discovering the fundamental causes of rare diseases and providing insights into treatments, revealing the low-level mechanisms of cancer to improve understanding of its causes and progression despite its complexity, and improving crops' resistance to climate change to alleviate world hunger.

4.1   Neocortex Overview

Neocortex couples two Cerebras CS-1 AI servers with a large shared memory HPE Superdome Flex HPC server to achieve unprecedented AI scalability with excellent system balance. Each Cerebras CS-1 is powered by one Cerebras Wafer Scale Engine (WSE) processor, a revolutionary high-performance processor designed specifically to accelerate deep learning training and inferencing [12]. The Cerebras WSE is the largest chip ever built, containing 400,000 AI-optimized cores implemented on a 46,225 mm^2 wafer with 1.2 trillion transistors. An on-chip fabric provides 100 Pb/s of bandwidth through a fully configurable 2D mesh with no software overhead. The Cerebras WSE includes 18 GB of SRAM accessible within a single clock cycle at 9 PB/s bandwidth. The Cerebras WSE is uniquely engineered to enable efficient sparse computation, wasting neither time nor power multiplying the many zeroes that occur in deep networks. The Cerebras CS-1 software can be programmed with common machine learning frameworks such as TensorFlow and PyTorch, which for computational efficiency are mapped onto an optimized graph representation and a set of model-specific computation kernels. The CS-1 also supports native code development. Support for the most popular deep learning frameworks and automatic, transparent acceleration will researchers with ease of use. Table 1 summarizes the architectural characteristics of the subsystems of Neocortex.

Table 1. Neocortex architectural characteristics. Each of the two Cerebras CS-1 systems features a Cerebras Wafer Scale Engine (WSE) processor.

Cerebras CS-1

AI Processor	Cerebras Wafer Scale Engine (WSE)
	400,000 Sparse Linear Algebra Compute (SLAC) cores
	1.2 trillion transistors
	46,225 mm^2
	18 GB SRAM on-chip memory
	9.6 PB/s memory bandwidth
	100 Pb/s interconnect bandwidth
System I/O	1.2 Tb/s (12 × 100 GbE interfaces)

HPE Superdome Flex

CPUs	32 × Intel Xeon Platinum 8280
Memory	24 TiB RAM, aggregate bandwidth 4.5 TB/s
Data storage	32 × 6.4 TB NVMe SSDs
	204.6 TB aggregate
	150 GB/s read bandwidth
Network to CS-1 systems	24 × 100 GbE interfaces
	1.2 Tb/s (150 GB/s) to each CS-1
	2.4 Tb/s aggregate
Network to Bridges-2	16 × HDR-100 InfiniBand
	1.6 Tb/s aggregate

The two Cerebras CS-1 systems and the HPE Superdome Flex are balanced to allow running the CS-1 systems concurrently on different models or together on a single model. This includes the bandwidth of the NVMe SSD file system in Neocortex, the bandwidth to each CS-1, and the even higher RAM bandwidth of Superdome Flex.

4.2 Cerebras CS-1 and Wafer Scale Engine

The Cerebras CS-1 is first available system featuring the Cerebras Wafer Scale Engine (WSE) processor, which is the largest chip ever built. Fabricated using a whole silicon wafer, the Cerebras WSE measures $46,225^2$ and contains 400,000 AI-optimized cores and 1.2 trillion transistors. It includes an on-chip 100 Pb/s fabric as a fully configurable 2D mesh with no software overhead. 18 GB of SRAM provides memory latency of only one clock and memory bandwidth of 9.6 PB/s. The Cerebras CS-1 contains one WSE processor, twelve 100 GbE ports, twelve 3 kW power supplies, and self-contained water cooling in a 15U enclosure.

The matrix and vector values of deep neural networks are mostly zeros, which arises from operations such as ReLU (rectified linear unit; 90% natural sparsity) and dropout (30% natural sparsity). For example, Transformer has 50–98% zeros [7]. The inherent sparsity of deep neural networks is not aligned with GPUs and CPUs, the memory subsystems of which have been designed to maximize the efficiency of dense operations. For networks with high sparsity, there is little to no cache reuse. This mismatch manifests as low performance resulting from the high latency incurred when fetching non-sequential data from memory or other processors, potentially across a PCI Express bus. The latency for remote fetches, i.e., at least a microsecond, is at least three orders of magnitude greater than accessing data that is already in cache, only a few clocks away, i.e., on the order of a nanosecond.

The Cerebras WSE overcomes the latency barrier through mutually reinforcing architectural advances in on-chip memory, in-processor communications, optimized compute cores, and software. These synergistic advances overcome the latency barrier by making memory accesses local and explicitly addressing sparsity.

The 400,000 Sparse Linear Algebra (SLA) cores of the WSE are optimized for deep learning. They contain no caches or other unnecessary features that would introduce overhead. The SLA cores are fully programmable, supporting arithmetic, logical operations, load/store, and branching, and they implement optimized tensor operations specific to deep learning. The SLA cores are engineered to exploit sparsity, containing fine-grained dataflow scheduling through which compute is triggered by data. Multiples are performed only for non-zero operands. Both fine- and coarse-grained sparsity are supported to accommodate activations and weights being zero at both the individual and block levels [5].

The WSE includes 18 GB of on-chip SRAM (static RAM), yielding 9 PB/s of memory bandwidth and a latency of only one clock cycle. The distribution of SRAM across the wafer supports sparsity to run all SLA cores at full speed [12].

The Cerebras Swarm communication fabric interconnects the 400,000 cores on the WSE. It is a flexible, all-hardware, 2D mesh that delivers 100 Pb/s of bandwidth, hardware routing, and single-word active messages. Link latency and energy cost are extremely low. The Swarm fabric is fully reconfigurable, allowing optimized communication paths to be implemented for each model, avoiding overheads and improving power efficiency [12].

The Cerebras software stack abstracts the WSE's sophisticated features to allow translation from models expressed in TensorFlow and PyTorch to highly efficient implementations on the WSE. The Cerebras Graph Compiler builds a dataflow representation from the user's model, mapping it onto an intermediate representation and optimized low-level kernels. A place-and-route step maps the model onto the WSE, creating a datapath that is optimized for locality and communications [18].

This hardware and software co-design enables great efficiency and new approaches to model parallelism. For example, by placing an entire network on the WSE at once, data can be streamed through a multi-stage pipeline, effectively running all layers simultaneously.

4.3   HPE Superdome Flex

The HPE Superdome Flex system is a high-end, modular, shared-memory server engineered for mission-critical AI and HPC workloads. For Neocortex, a large Superdome Flex was selected as the most powerful, user-friendly front-end for the two Cerebras CS-1 systems. The scalability of the Superdome Flex allows it to be robustly provisioned to drive the CS-1 systems independently or together. The Superdome Flex builds on experience with large shared-memory servers, which have been observed to support scaling with high ease of use (e.g., Blacklight [15]).

The Superdome Flex in Neocortex consists of 8 chassis connected by an internal interconnect to create a single-system image (SSI) spanning 32 high-end CPUs, 24 TB of hardware cache-coherent shared memory, 204.8 TB (raw) of high-bandwidth NVMe PCIe flash storage, 24 100 GbE ports, and 16 HDR-100 InfiniBand ports. The full 24 TB of RAM is cache-coherent across all 32 CPUs, supported by HPE Superdome Flex ASICs with coherency unit of one cache line (64 bytes). The internal Superdome crossbar interconnect, supported by two HPE Superdome Flex ASICs in each chassis, supports 850 GB/s of bisection bandwidth. The single-system image lets users quickly and conveniently train on their data without having manually to distribute it across a cluster of servers, saving them time and avoiding load imbalance to maximize efficiency.

The Superdome Flex is fully populated with 32 Intel Xeon Platinum 8280 CPUs, which have 28 cores, 56 hardware threads, base and maximum turbo frequencies of 2.70 GHz and 4.00 GHz, respectively, 38.5 MB of cache, and 3 UPI links. The 24 TB memory is comprised of of 192 × 128 GiB DDR4-2933 RDIMMs, with aggregate memory bandwidth of 4.5 TB/s.

Local storage consists of 32 NVMe 6.4 TB PCIe flash cards, for 204.6 TB raw capacity and 150 GB/s read bandwidth, matching the 150 GB/s network connection to a Cerebras CS-1. The local storage is managed by HPE Data

Management Framework (DMF) for user-friendly, efficient data transfer from Bridges-2 over InfiniBand at up to 1.6 Tb/s.

Twenty-four 100 GbE network interface cards (NICs) provide 2.4 Tb/s of Ethernet connectivity, with 1.2 Tb/s (150 Gb/s) to each of the two Cerebras CS-1 systems in Neocortex. Sixteen HDR InfiniBand host channel adapters (HCAs), mounted on sixteen PCI Express Gen 3 ×16 ports, connect to Bridges-2's HDR InfiniBand fabric at 1.6 Tb/s.

The HPE Superdome Flex ASIC differentiates the Superdome Flex from other servers by providing cache-coherent shared memory spanning 32 CPUs. For Neocortex, the SD Flex's 24 TB of cache-coherent shared memory backed by over 200 TB of high-bandwidth NVMe flash storage ease training on very large datasets, avoiding the laborious task of splitting datasets across worker nodes and possibly generating load imbalances.

4.4   Neocortex Interconnect

Each Cerebras CS-1 is connected to the HPE Superdome Flex by twelve 100 Gb/s Ethernet ports, for aggregate 1.2 Tb/s (150 GB/s) from the Superdome Flex to each CS-1 and 2.4 Tb/s (300 GB/s) combined. Each of the Mellanox SN3700cM 32-port switches has eight ports remaining, which are interconnected between the switches to enable research involving communications directly between the two Cerebras CS-1 systems.

4.5   Neocortex Software

The Cerebras Software Stack [18] translates models from widely used frameworks such as TensorFlow and PyTorch to executables for the Cerebras CS-1, as summarized above. Neocortex's Superdome Flex runs the CentOS 8 operating system and is configured with containers, frameworks, libraries, and tools to support the Cerebras CS-1.

5   Bridges-2

Bridges-2 builds on, improves, and extends concepts proven in Bridges [13] to take the next step in pioneering converged, scalable HPC, AI, and data; prioritize researcher productivity and ease of use; and provide an extensible architecture for interoperation with complementary data-intensive projects, campus resources, and clouds. Funded by the National Science Foundation, Bridges-2 is a "capacity" resource, designed to enable rapidly evolving research and an extremely wide range of applications.

Bridges-2 contains 566 nodes, 70,208 CPU cores, and 192 GPUs. Its peak floating-point rates are 5.175 Pf/s fp64 and 24 Pf/s mixed-precision/tensor. It contains 158.5 TiB of memory with 223.4 TiB/s of memory bandwidth, 2.2 PB of node-local NVMe SSD, 15 PB (usable) disk in a high-performance Lustre file system, and 8.6 PB tape (estimated, assuming 20% compression). High bandwidth for efficient data movement was prioritized over raw flops. Figure 2 illustrates the high-level architecture of Bridges-2.

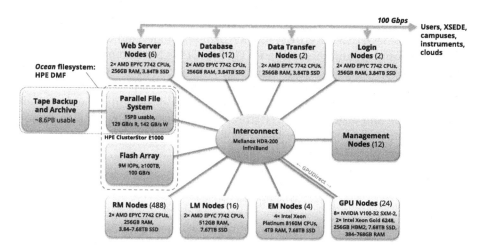

Fig. 2. Bridges-2 consists of four types of compute nodes—Regular Memory (RM), Large Memory (LM), Extreme Memory (EM), and Graphics Processing Unit (GPU)—interconnected with each other, file systems, and utility and management nodes by a high-performance fabric. Persistent data is maintained in the hierarchical Ocean file system. Data requiring high IOPs, such as for deep learning training, is cached to the Jet flash file system. Utility nodes serve persistent databases and distributed (web) services, data transfer (100 Gbps), and logins. Management nodes serve system configuration management, scheduling, logging, and other administrative functions.

5.1 Innovations

Bridges-2 introduces six important innovations beyond Bridges, in addition to greatly improving all aspects of system performance. These innovations, which reflect the evolution of research applications, are as follows:

- **An all-flash filesystem**, *Jet*, provides 9 IOPs (measured on 4 kB reads) of random-access I/O performance to support deep learning training on data that is much larger than node-local storage capacity. Jet has 460.8 TB of capacity (raw) and supports at least 100 GB/s of read/write bandwidth.
- **Enhanced GPU nodes** amplify scalable deep learning. GPU nodes each have eight NVIDIA Tesla V100-32GB SXM2 GPUs (aggregate 256 GB HBM2 memory per node), up to 768 GB of CPU memory, and dual-rail Mellanox HDR-200 InfiniBand (IB) between GPU nodes.
- **Full-system HDR-200 InfiniBand** doubles link bandwidth relative to Bridges and provides 200M messages/s injection rate, and $<1\mu s$ latency, and numerous advanced features for performance, flexibility, and to scale GPU applications, including GPUDirect RDMA communications between GPUs on different nodes.
- **AMD EPYC 7742 ("Rome") CPUs** support PCI Express Gen 4 (31.5 GB/s for 16 lanes), enabling full use of HDR-200 InfiniBand. They also yield excellent performance with 64 cores each.

- **Bridges-2 supports full-system AI.** Its 24 GPU nodes (192 NVIDIA Tesla V100-32GB SXM2 GPUs) provide high scalability and capacity for deep learning training, and its AMD EPYC 7742 CPUs have ample cores (64) for high-performance inferencing, including coupling of surrogate models with simulations. The unified architecture also allows for online training.
- **A hierarchical storage system** provides project storage (disk) and expandable archive and disaster recovery storage (tape), using HPE DMF to expose a single name space with rule-based replication and migration.

5.2 Compute and Utility Nodes

Bridges-2 contains four types of compute nodes:

- **488 Regular Memory (RM) nodes** each have 2 AMD EPYC 7742 ("Rome") CPUs, 256 GB of DDR4-3200 memory, 3.84–7.68 TB NVMe SSD local storage, and 1 HDR-200 IB adapter. RM nodes are HPE Apollo Gen10 plus chassis containing HPE ProLiant XL225n Gen10 plus Servers. RM nodes are used for HPC, data analytics and pre- and post-processing, and other general-purpose computing ranging from 1 core to 61k cores. HPC jobs can be run across all 62,464 (61k) cores of RM nodes.
- **16 Large Memory (LM) nodes** are similar to RM nodes, differing only in containing twice the memory (512 GB) and 7.68 TB NVME SSD. LM nodes are used for genomics and tasks similar to those for RM nodes but that need more memory. Large-memory HPC jobs can be run across all 2,048 (2k) cores of EM nodes, and especially demanding HPC jobs can be run across all 64,512 (63k) cores of combined RM and EM nodes.
- **4 Extreme Memory (EM) nodes** each have 2 Intel Xeon Platinum 8260M ("Cascade Lake") CPUs, 4 TB of DDR4-2933 memory, 7.68 TB NVMe SSD, and 1 HDR-200 IB adapter. EM nodes are HPE ProLiant DL560 Gen10 servers. EM nodes are used for genome sequence assembly and other tasks that require large shared memory.
- **24 Graphics Processing Unit (GPU) nodes** each have 8 NVIDIA Tesla V100-32GB SXM-2 GPUs (aggregate 256 GB HBM2 memory), 2 Intel Xeon Gold 6248 ("Cascade Lake") CPUs, 384–768 GB of DDR4-2933 memory, 7.68 TB NVMe SSD, and 2 HDR-200 IB adapters. GPU nodes are HPE Apollo 6500 Gen10 servers. GPU nodes are used for deep learning, other machine learning, visualization, and accelerated simulation. Preference is given to the 768 GB GPU nodes for deep learning training.

Bridges-2 utility nodes are identical to RM nodes but dedicated to specific purposes (i.e., not available for routine scheduling via Slurm). Of the 22 utility nodes, 6 are dedicated to serving web portals (for example, domain-specific "Science Gateways") that provide HPC, Big Data, and Software as a Service, 12 are dedicated to serving persistent databases to power workflows and web portals, 2 are Data Transfer Nodes for high-bandwidth transfers from and to wide-area networks, and 2 are login nodes. Services and databases running on web server and database nodes are typically isolated in virtual machines and potentially also containerized. If additional web or database nodes come to be needed, RM nodes can be repurposed accordingly.

5.3 File Systems

Bridges-2 supports four file systems: *Ocean*, *Jet*, local, and memory.

The **Ocean** file system is hierarchical, providing user-friendly, seamless management of disk and tape subsystems in a single name space using the HPE Data Management Framework (DMF). The disk component of Ocean is an HPE ClusterStor E1000 storage system, with 15 PB of usable capacity (21 PB raw) and 129 GB/s and 142 GB/s read and write bandwidth, respectively. It runs Lustre, for which 10 data server pairs each serve 2.1 PB (raw) capacity. The tape component of Ocean is an HPE StoreEver MSL6480 Tape Library, initially populated with 5 modules (scalable to 7), where each module holds 80 LTO-8 Type M tape cartridges. Its raw capacity is 7.2 PB. Based on historical data, approximately 20% compression is expected, which occurs at line speed, increasing effective capacity to approximately 8.6 PB. Bandwidth is 50 TB/hour. The tape subsystem is expected to be used for archiving and disaster recovery (DR), and it is expandable, should the need and external support arise, to serve specific projects requiring great amounts of archive/DR capacity.

The **Jet** file system uses NVMe flash storage devices to provide 9M IOPs, at least 100 GB/s of read/write bandwidth, and 460.8 TB of raw capacity. The Jet file system is used to cache moderately large data for which high bandwidth is needed, for example, deep learning training.

Local and memory filesystems exploit NVMe SSD and RAM, respectively, on each compute node, which can substantially increase bandwidth for deep learning training, scratch files, and other ephemeral storage requirements.

5.4 Interconnect

A Mellanox HDR-200 InfiniBand fabric provides high communications performance both between compute nodes (for HPC jobs) and to and from Bridges-2's file systems. It is configured in a leaf-spine topology with 12 spine switches and 26 leaf switches, which cost-effectively supplies ample bandwidth for Bridges-2 diverse workload. The oversubscription is 2.3:1. Dual-rail HDR-200 (400 Gb/s) is used to interconnect Bridges-2's GPU nodes, doubling the inter-node bandwidth to more effectively scale deep learning training across nodes.

5.5 User Environment

The Bridges-2 user environment supports an extremely wide range of applications, libraries, and frameworks. Bridges-2 supports Singularity for containerized applications, including NVIDIA GPU Cloud containers. Conversion from Docker containers is typically straightforward. Both batch and interactive access are supported. System resources are managed by Slurm, and a user-friendly *interact* command is implemented to obtain immediate access to resources ranging from a single core to multiple nodes. Interactivity has proven invaluable on Bridges for analytics, development, debugging, and visualization, and it has been possible to provision resources for interactive use with very low impact on overall utilization.

6 Summary

Neocortex and Bridges-2 form a unique computational ecosystem for scalable AI, data processing, analytics, and management, and high-performance simulation. Their design was strongly influenced by consideration of applications across diverse fields of research, especially for societal good. The innovations that differentiate this ecosystem are great innovation hardware architecture, fully integrated heterogeneous node types to optimally support components of research workflows, and a unified data management system consisting of in-processor memory, conventional memory, flash, disk, and tape layers. Specifically, Neocortex introduces the Cerebras Wafer Scale Engine, the largest processor ever built, to the open research community to accelerate deep learning training by orders of magnitude, potentially to interactive rates, and it couples two Cerebras CS-1 systems through a very large memory HPE Superdome Flex "front end" to explore scaling models to multiple CS-1 systems. Bridges-2 provides high capacity for data pre- and post-processing, other types of machine learning, simulation, and large-scale data management, and archiving through integration of multiple nodes types and hierarchical data storage using a high-performance 200 Gb/s fabric, with 400 Gb/s between its GPU-accelerated AI nodes, also to support scalable deep learning. Both systems are available at no cost for open research.

Acknowledgments. Thanks to Natalia Vassilieva for collaboration on the Cerebras CS-1. The Bridges system, including Bridges-AI, is supported by NSF award number 1445606. The Bridges-2 system is supported by NSF award number 1928147. The Neocortex system is supported by NSF award number 2005597. The Open Compass project is supported by NSF award number 1833317.

References

1. Brown, T.B., et al.: Language models are few-shot learners (2020)
2. Buitrago, P.A., Nystrom, N.A.: Open compass: accelerating the adoption of AI in open research. In: Proceedings of the Practice and Experience in Advanced Research Computing on Rise of the Machines (Learning), PEARC 2019. Association for Computing Machinery, New York (2019). https://doi.org/10.1145/3332186.3332253
3. Buitrago, P.A., Nystrom, N.A.: Strengthening the adoption of AI in research and cyberinfrastructure. In: Pascucci, V., et al. (eds.) Report from the NSF Workshop on Smart Cyberinfrastructure 2020, Alexandria, Virginia (2020)

4. Buitrago, P.A., Nystrom, N.A., Gupta, R., Saltz, J.: Delivering scalable deep learning to research with bridges-AI. In: Crespo-Mariño, J.L., Meneses-Rojas, E. (eds.) CARLA 2019. CCIS, vol. 1087, pp. 200–214. Springer, Cham (2020). https://doi.org/10.1007/978-3-030-41005-6_14
5. Cerebras Systems: Cerebras wafer scale engine: an introduction (2019)
6. Devlin, J., Chang, M.W., Lee, K., Toutanova, K.: BERT: pre-training of deep bidirectional transformers for language understanding (2018)
7. Gale, T., Elsen, E., Hooker, S.: The state of sparsity in deep neural networks (2019)
8. He, K., Zhang, X., Ren, S., Sun, J.: Deep residual learning for image recognition. In: 2016 IEEE Conference on Computer Vision and Pattern Recognition (CVPR), pp. 770–778 (2016)
9. Kasim, M.F., et al.: Up to two billion times acceleration of scientific simulations with deep neural architecture search (2020)
10. Khan, A., Huerta, E.A., Wang, S., Gruendl, R., Jennings, E., Zheng, H.: Deep learning at scale for the construction of galaxy catalogs in the Dark Energy Survey. Phys. Lett. B **795**, 248–258 (2019). https://doi.org/10.1016/j.physletb.2019.06.009
11. Krizhevsky, A., Sutskever, I., Hinton, G.E.: ImageNet classification with deep convolutional neural networks. In: Pereira, F., Burges, C.J.C., Bottou, L., Weinberger, K.Q. (eds.) Advances in Neural Information Processing Systems, vol. 25, pp. 1097–1105. Curran Associates, Inc. (2012)
12. Lie, S.: Wafer scale deep learning. In: Hot Chips 31 (2019)
13. Nystrom, N.A., Buitrago, P.A., Blood, P.D.: Bridges: converging HPC, AI, and big data for enabling discovery. In: Vetter, J.S. (ed.) Contemporary High Performance Computing: From Petascale toward Exascale. Contemporary High Performance Computing, vol. 3. CRC Press, Boca Raton (2019)
14. Nystrom, N.A., Levine, M.J., Roskies, R.Z., Scott, J.R.: Bridges: a uniquely flexible HPC resource for new communities and data analytics. In: Proceedings of the 2015 XSEDE Conference: Scientific Advancements Enabled by Enhanced Cyberinfrastructure, XSEDE 2015. Association for Computing Machinery, New York (2015). https://doi.org/10.1145/2792745.2792775
15. Nystrom, N.A., Welling, J., Blood, P.D., Goh, E.L.G.: BlackLight: coherent shared memory for enabling science. In: Vetter, J.S. (ed.) Contemporary High Performance Computing: From Petascale toward Exascale. Contemporary High Performance Computing. Taylor & Francis Group, Boca Raton (2013)
16. Shoeybi, M., et al.: Megatron-LM: training multi-billion parameter language models using model parallelism (2019)
17. Smith, J.S., et al.: Approaching coupled cluster accuracy with a general-purpose neural network potential through transfer learning. Nat. Commun. **10**(1), 2903 (2019). https://doi.org/10.1038/s41467-019-10827-4
18. Vassilieva, N., Buitrago, P.A., Nystrom, N.A., Sanielevici, S.E.: Technical overview of the Cerebras CS-1, the AI compute engine for Neocortex (webinar) (2020). https://www.cmu.edu/psc/aibd/neocortex/technical-overview-webinar.html

Author Index

Printed in the United States
By Bookmasters